A History of the

British Virgin Islands

1672 to 1970

To
Helen and Marlene
and their
future educational success

A History of the
British Virgin Islands
1672 to 1970

by

Isaac Dookhan

Associate Professor of History
and Historian-Writer in Residence,
College of the Virgin Islands

CARIBBEAN UNIVERSITIES PRESS
in Association with
BOWKER PUBLISHING COMPANY
1975

First published in 1975 by the Caribbean Universities Press in association with the Bowker Publishing Company, Epping, Essex, England.

ISBN 0 85935 026 6

Printed and bound in Great Britain by
Redwood Burn Limited
Trowbridge & Esher

Contents

Chapter   Page

    Preface ix
1. Right of Sovereignty 1
2. The Establishment of a Legislature 18
3. Era of Prosperity and Decline 43
4. Slavery and Emancipation 71
5. The Liberated Africans 97
6. The Aftermath of Slavery 120
7. Problems of Financial Adjustment 147
8. The Social Services 169
9. The Disintegration of the Legislature 194
10. Twentieth Century Considerations 218
    Index..238

List of Illustrations

Pleasant Valley, Tortola 45
The Virgin Islands from English and Danish Surveys 45
Tortola, 1798 76
Birthplace of Dr. John Lettsom 87
Ancient Burial Ground of Friends, Tortola 87
Kingstown 106
The Agricultural Experiment Station 227
The Beef Island Runway 232
Wickham's Cay Development Project 232

KEY TO ABBREVIATIONS

Adm.   = Admiralty Papers
A.O.   = Audit Office
B.T.   = Board of Trade
C.O.   = Colonial Office
Cmd.   = Command Papers
C.S.P.   = Calendar of State Papers, America and
              the West Indies
C.T.P.   = Council of Trade and Plantations
enc.   = enclosure or enclosures
F.O.   = Foreign Office
O.A.G.   = Officer Administering the Government
P.C.   = Privy Council
P.P.   = Parliamentary Papers
P.R.O.   = Public Records Office
S.M.   = Stipendiary Magistrate
S.P.   = State Papers (Spanish)
W.M.M.S.   = Wesleyan Methodist Missionary Society

Preface

The British Virgin Islands are an archipelago of islands with a total area of roughly fifty-nine square miles. They are situated to the east of Puerto Rico and the Virgin Islands of the United States and about one hundred and forty miles north-west of the nearest important British island of St. Kitts, in the latitude 18°.25' north and longitude 64°.30' west. The group is divided by the three to four mile wide Sir Francis Drake Channel. The essential features of the historical geography of the islands are their relatively isolated position as a British possession and, except in the case of the outlying island of Anegada which is completely flat, their steep hilly nature. There is an absence of rivers and streams and this has underlined the importance of rainfall to the islands' economy. The islands consist of shallow, friable and permeable brown loams with frequent outcrops of bare rock. The exception is, again, Anegada which is formed chiefly of coral lime-stone.[1] The islands lie in the track of hurricanes blowing westward from the Lesser to the Greater Antilles, and periodic hurricanes have caused considerable damage and have influenced the course of the islands' history.

The British Virgin Islands were 'discovered' by Christopher Columbus in November, 1493, on his second voyage to the New World. On November 14, the Spanish explorers reached St. Croix and landed at Salt River Bay where they had their first recorded fight with the natives of the New World. From there, taking advantage of a detour caused by a south-westerly or westerly wind which carried the fleet to a point east or south-east of Virgin Gorda, the expedition sailed throughout the entire extent of the Virgin Islands in two divisions, reaching St. Thomas on November 17.[2] Henceforth, except for isolated visits by passing

Europeans, most notably Sir Francis Drake in 1595, the islands remained unsettled until around the middle of the seventeenth century. It was not until the British conquest of Tortola from the Dutch in 1672, that the history of the Virgin Islands began in a real sense.

The purpose of this study has been to examine the changes which occurred in the British Virgin Islands from the time of their conquest by the British, and to trace the interaction of their social, economic and political components. Wherever possible an attempt has been made to show the persisting effects of a particular period, aspect or phase of the history. Though the aim was not to show the rise to prominence and the eventual collapse of the British Virgin Islands, this feature has emerged as the dominant trait of the study.

The history of the British Virgin Islands can be traced by an arc of progress and decline. Initially the period was one of virtual standstill largely attributable to settlers' uncertainty over rights of sovereignty and to discouragement by the British authorities. Thereafter progress was gradual and dependent upon the influx of planter-settlers. After 1750, and coincidental with the period of almost continuous war, the Virgin Islands enjoyed a period of unprecedented prosperity based upon extensive plantation agriculture accomplished by negro slave labour, and wider trading activities, legitimate and illegitimate. The period coincided too with the division of the population into classes according to wealth, colour and education, and its embodiment in discriminatory legislation. The period was climaxed by the institution of legislative government in 1773.

Prosperity was largely dependent upon the incidence of war; peace after 1815 negated most of the factors of progress. Decline was underlined by British neglect. The consequent decrease in the white proprietary population together with the abolition of the slave trade, however, resulted in fairer treatment of slaves and the promotion of the activities of religious bodies. Emancipation was a turning point since it facilitated the rise of peasant farming after the collapse of plantation agriculture. It was followed also by financial decadence due to the failure to promote economic development, and to widespread tax evasion. The result was reflected in the failure of the legislature to institute general and adequate social services, and in considerable reduction of the civil establishment. Together with persisting notions of class and privilege pertaining during slavery, poverty led to the disintegration and eventual abrogation of the legislature in 1902.

Much controversy existed among historians over the origin of the designation of the Virgin Islands. There were those, loyal to Spain and to the memory of Columbus, who ascribed the name to the great discoverer who, they said, named the islands for St. Ursula and her eleven thousand virgins, since he had been influenced by the plurality of the islands in the group. On the other side, there were those, loyal to Britain and to Queen Elizabeth, who ascribed the name to Sir Francis Drake, who, they asserted, named the islands for the virgin queen. The two rival claims need not be irreconcilable; both could be equally correct — both men could have been motivated by the common ideal of allegiance to an idea. As Reverend Thomas Coke explained, 'Columbus might have acted from motives of respect to the Romish ritual, and Drake from those of regard to his Virgin Sovereign.'[3] Undoubtedly the Virgin Islands were so named by Columbus. Assuming Drake's ignorance of the earlier appellation, placed against his overpowering sense of nationalism, and his hatred for Spain, there is nothing inconsistent in his naming the islands in honour of his sovereign benefactress.

Whichever version is accepted, it does not fully explain the variety of names given to the islands. Among them names of Spanish, Dutch, French and British derivation now exist. Though at first applied to the entire group of Danish and British islands, the name 'Virgin Islands' was applied almost exclusively to the British section from around 1735 when the claim to the last disputed island was established by Denmark. When in 1917 the United States of America purchased the Danish islands, and for historic reasons adopted for them the name 'Virgin Islands of the United States' it became necessary to distinguish the British possessions as the British Virgin Islands.

The historical study of an individual colony possesses a number of distinct advantages over a similar study embracing a group of separate colonies. It is easier to focus attention on issues that have a greater significance for a single unit of government than for a more complex grouping. In such a study, also, generalisations assume a greater measure of validity in so far as they are more defensible than if applied to a broader region treated as a whole. As such, history acquires a greater degree of accuracy, and what is 'right' becomes distinguishable from what is merely just probably so. Even where, as in the British West Indies, the patterns of development and change were fundamentally the same, in points of detail their history was undoubtedly different. Both similarities and differences need to be mentioned to a greater or less extent.

The history of the British Virgin Islands could not be written without constant reference to the history of the region of which it forms a part. Their individuality allows for comparisons and contrasts to a greater extent than is permitted in a study dealing with a larger fraction of the whole. Again, the intensive study of a shorter period than here attempted, undoubtedly facilitates the more thorough use of available evidence; nevertheless, it is possible to lose the sense of proper perspective usually acquired by foreknowledge, which should instruct such studies.

This history is the product of extensive research both in the West Indies and in London. In the West Indies full use was made of the libraries of the University of the West Indies and of the Institute of Jamaica. A considerable volume of material dealing especially with the history of the twentieth century was consulted in the archives attached to the Office of the Administrator of the British Virgin Islands. The library in St. Thomas, United States Virgin Islands, in which some original material is stored, was also investigated for information pertinent to the history of the British Virgin Islands and to the inter-relationship between the two groups of Virgin Islands. In London, the repositories of greatest benefit were the archives and libraries of the Public Records Office, the British Museum, the Wesleyan Methodist Missionary Society, the West India Committee, Lambeth Palace, the Commonwealth Institute and the Commonwealth Office.

Books dealing exclusively with the British Virgin Islands and their history are few, and information relating to the British Virgin Islands contained in general works on the West Indies is not always reliable. Accordingly, the history had to be written from such first-hand accounts and information contained in the despatches and reports which passed between the Secretary of State for the Colonies and Governors and Lieutenant-Governors of the Leeward Islands, Presidents of the British Virgin Islands and other individuals interested in the British West Indian colonies.

For assistance in the preparation of this history, I owe a debt of gratitude to several individuals and institutions. I wish to thank the British Ministry of Overseas Development for the generous financial assistance which made this study possible. For his hospitality and keen interest in the production of the history, I am indebted to Mr. Martin S. Staveley who was Administrator of the British Virgin Islands when I began. I gratefully acknowledge the invaluable assistance offered me by the librarians and staff of the various archives and libraries which I consulted. If at times I taxed their patience to unprecedented limits, I can only excuse it in the interest of scholarship. To those who assisted me in the translation of material in foreign print, I give my especial thanks. To the several lecturers of the University of the West Indies and particularly of the Department of History, who have assisted with gentle encouragement and advice, and who provided me with useful incidental information, I express my sincerest gratitude. Lastly, but most importantly, I wish to express my greatest appreciation for the guidance given me by Professor Douglas Hall who supervised this study throughout all its stages, and without whose wise counsel it could never have been completed.

[1] P. H. A. Martin-Kaye: Reports on the Geology of the Leeward and British Virgin Islands. (St. Lucia, Voice Publishing Co., 1953) pp. 95-113.
[2] Samuel Eliot Morison: Admiral of the Ocean Sea: A Life of Christopher Columbus. (Little, Brown and Company, Boston, 1942) pp. 412 ff.
[3] Rev. Thomas Coke: A History of the West Indies, containing the natural, civil, and ecclesiastical history of each island: with an account of the missions instituted in those islands, from the commencement of their civilisation; but more especially of the missions which have been established in that archipelago by the society late in connexion with the Rev. John Wesley. (Liverpool, 1808; London, 1810, 1811; 3 Vols.) Vol. III, p. 91.

Chapter 1

Right of Sovereignty

By the middle of the seventeenth century when the Virgin Islands first began to attract the attention of Europeans, three basic principles underlay the discussions among the colonising nations on the right of sovereignty over newly discovered territories. These principles were prior discovery of the territory concerned, outright conquest by force of arms which might or might not be followed by international treaty agreements, and lastly, that of effective occupation.

These principles were variously used by European nations in contesting a right to the trade and territory of the West Indies. Spain, for instance, used the argument of prior discovery which involved, by implication, the labour and expense of fitting out voyages of discovery. It could resort to this argument because the islands had been discovered by Christopher Columbus in the name of the King and Queen of Spain towards the end of the fifteenth century. Against the Spanish assertion, other European nations contended that only effective occupation, involving the establishment of settlements, could qualify a nation to exercise exclusive proprietary right over a territory, though what constituted sufficient occupation after discovery was never clarified.

In the contest for possession over the West Indian Islands, it was natural that Spain should have resorted to arguments of papal authority and of prior discovery, and that England, France and Holland should have required not only discovery but also effective occupation by settlement. But, as Westlake has pointed out, 'there is no state which has not insisted in its turn on that part of the doctrine which best suited its convenience at the moment, or which has maintained a perfectly uniform attitude on the questions of detail into which the general doctrine resolves itself.'[1] This appeal to arguments to suit the exigencies of the moment had characterised past European negotiations and they were to continue to fill diplomatic exchanges relative to the right of sovereignty over the Virgin Islands.

In general it can be said that in the sixteenth century, the West Indies were regarded by non-Hispanic nations as a valuable sphere for illegal trade in negro slaves, European manufactures and indigenous American products, and also as a rich area for privateering activities. The idea of establishing colonies was not actually pursued until about the beginning of the seventeenth century when the decline of Spain's capacity for maritime defence increasingly demonstrated the possibilities of successful permanent settlement. By that time also the notion that colonies were particularly valuable as outlets for surplus population, as markets for manufactured goods, as sources of raw materials, and as a means of building a large efficient navy, had gained ascendancy over the previous notion of colonies as mere targets of privateering raids and centres of illicit trade.

The assumption by the West Indies of the role of plantation colonies was to introduce new elements into the conflict for possession. As first the tobacco and then the extensive sugar plantations revealed both the actual and the potential value of the islands to the rivalry with Spain was added the contest among the British, French and Dutch for their possession. To the conflict of ideas which had characterised the earlier assertions of right to sovereignty was now added the conflict of arms as the various European nations sought to dislodge each other from the islands and to secure them for themselves. The chaos of conflicting claims was clearly reflected in the case of the Virgin Islands which, though standing on the periphery of the mainstream of West Indian developments, and though not valued as plantation colonies, invited the attention of the several European nations for reasons of protection and of trade.

By the middle of the seventeenth century the Virgin Islands were generally regarded as comprising the whole group of islands which later became distinguishable as the Danish West Indies and as the British Virgin Islands. The principal islands were St. Thomas, St. John and St. Croix (or Santa Cruz) of the former group, and Tortola and Virgin Gorda (then popularly referred to as Spanish Town) of the latter. A large number of tiny islets called cays, and rocks added to the general mass. Neither these cays, nor the islands of Jost Van Dyke and Anegada which were later classed among the more important islands in the

British Virgin Islands, were significantly involved in the ensuing conflict for sovereignty. Their fate was dependent upon that of the larger islands.

Diplomacy concerning the right of sovereignty over Tortola revolved around two major but related questions, namely, whether the island was captured by Colonel William Stapleton (the recently appointed Governor of the newly created English colony of the Leeward Islands) in 1672 shortly after the outbreak of the Third Dutch War, or whether it was simply entrusted to his safekeeping by the Dutch colonists inhabiting the islands, for the duration of the hostilities. An abundance of evidence was presented to the Council of Trade relating to the conquest of Tortola. On July 13, 1672 it was reported that Stapleton had reduced Tortola to the King's subjection.[2] Four days later Stapleton himself reported the event to the Council of Trade and Foreign Plantations together with the information that he had given orders for the demolition of the fort which the Dutch had constructed there, and for the transportation of the guns, and of the several British subjects who were living on the island, to St. Christopher.[3] In December of the same year, he again wrote whether they would 'have the Dutch Commissions which were on . . . Tortola sent home.'[4]

By the Treaty of Westminster between the Dutch and English in 1674, provision was made for the mutual restoration of all territorial conquests during the war.[5] This Treaty provided the Dutch with the right to resume possession of Tortola but fear of French attack prevented such action, and Tortola remained under British control. Nor were the English anxious to part with the island despite its lack of immediate value; its transfer to the Dutch was regarded as pernicious to British trading interests, while its possession by the French would endanger the safety of the neighbouring British islands.[6] After several and prolonged discussions, instructions were issued to Stapleton in June, 1677 to retain possession of the island until further orders.[7]

The cessation of hostilities between the Dutch and the French in 1678 and the conclusion of the Treaty of Nymwegen the next year[8] enabled the Dutch to direct their attention once more towards Tortola, though it was not until 1684 that Arnout Van Citters the Dutch ambassador to Britain requested the return of the island.[9] He did not do so on the basis of the Treaty of Westminster, but rather on behalf of the widow of William Hunthum and companions, proprietors of Tortola, who, he declared, had found it necessary during the war to place the island under Stapleton's protection, and who wished to resume possession. In his opinion Tortola was a charge, not a conquest. Stapleton's earlier promise to restore the island, if directed from the proper quarter,[10] was conveniently interpreted as a tacit acknowledgement that Tortola was merely a temporary charge under British safekeeping for the duration of the war.[11] No action was taken on the ambassador's letter, but a copy was sent to Stapleton for his comments.[12]

Further action was made dependent upon Stapleton's return to England,[13] and when this occurred in 1686, Van Citters no doubt believing that matters could be finally settled, urgently requested 'that without further search for information from other sources, the island may be restored.'[14] Before anything formative could be accomplished news arrived of Stapleton's death in France where he had gone to recover his health.

Conflicting evidence had been presented as to the British right to Tortola, and it was difficult to decide between Stapleton's report of his capture of Tortola and his subsequent seeming acknowledgement that the island was handed over to him for safekeeping. Nor could British claim to the island be made on the basis of effective occupation. English settlers had inhabited the island but it was also settled by the Dutch. In forming a decision cognizance was taken of the case of Saba and St. Eustatius which had been captured simultaneously with Tortola in 1672 but had been restored at the request of the Dutch ambassador in 1679.[15] In August, 1686, the Earl of Middleton informed the Dutch ambassador that orders would be given for the restoration of Tortola,[16] and a few months later the necessary instructions were despatched to Sir Nathaniel Johnson, the newly appointed Governor of the Leeward Islands.[17]

Despite this action, Tortola remained under British control. Several factors accounted for this. In the first place there was some delay in the initial execution of the instructions since the monarchical succession in 1688 diverted attention away from British colonial to domestic affairs. Also, it was some time before Sir Nathaniel Johnson departed from Britain to take up his appointment. Of most immediate importance was the fact that Johnson had been instructed that Tortola should be restored to such person or persons who should have 'sufficient procuration or authority to receive the same . . . in the same state and condition as near as may be, wherein it was heretofore delivered unto our late Governor Sir William Stapleton.'[18] Clearly this would have been impossible: Tortola in 1686 was not in the same condition as it had been in 1672. The most notable difference was that the Dutch colonists had departed, no doubt because they had begun to lose hope of the restoration. Certainly, the neighbouring island of St. Thomas at this time under the control of the notorious Danish Governor Adolph Esmit, offered a more lucrative and attractive livelihood, and it is possible that they grasped at his invitation to settle on the island. Besides, their action was undoubtedly hastened by the growing threat presented to small isolated settlements by the Spaniards from Puerto Rico.

The next phase in the discussion of sovereignty over Tortola took place between Britain and Brandenburg. In November, 1696, a claim was made to the island on behalf of Sir Peter van Bell, the agent of Sir Joseph Shepheard a Rotterdam merchant to whom it was alleged Tortola was sold on June 21, 1695 for 3,500 guilders.[19] Several documents purporting to show the negotiations whereby the islands had become the property of Sir Joseph Shepheard were also submitted.[20] In answer it was shown that though Tortola had little value yet the facilities which it possessed for smuggling and for defrauding the customs made it necessary to discourage any settlement on it. Accordingly, the Brandenburg claim was dismissed on the ground that no evidence existed that Stapleton had taken over the island in trust. The argument of conquest was supported,[21] and the usual delaying tactics were resorted to by forwarding the correspondence to the Governor for his report.[22]

Governor Codrington, as might be expected, supported the British official attitude. He could find no one in his government to substantiate the rival claim, but he clearly elucidated the economic disadvantages of Brandenburger occupation of Tortola. Illegal trade with foreigners on Tortola, which he would not be able to prevent, would reduce the revenues of the Crown; poorer settlers in the British islands would be tempted to migrate to Tortola where there was room for agricultural expansion; the foreigners would benefit by this inflow of British by providing them with slaves, stores and credit; and finally to the foreigners would go the products of the growing industry. Codrington drew attention to St. Thomas as an example of the kind of competition which might be expected and pointed out that Brandenburgers had already established a trading post there in 1685 by agreement with the Danes. Finally, Codrington concluded, it was undoubtedly van Bell's observation of this great increase of an island whose soil was barren compared with that of Tortola which induced him to claim the latter.[23]

To these arguments in support of the retention of Tortola, the Lords of Trade added the British right by discovery. They pointed out, however in error, that Tortola was first discovered by the English. Actually, Tortola with the other Virgin Islands had been discovered by Columbus in November, 1493. They also drew attention to the grant of all the Leeward Caribbean Islands made to the Earl of Carlisle by Charles I in 1628. They reminded the King of an order to the Governor of the Leeward Islands in 1694 to assert the British right to the Virgin Islands and to hinder their settlement by foreigners. To them the claimant's title was not made out, but as a concession they suggested that 'in view of the small value set upon the island, some compensation might be granted.'[24] This stand was abandoned, however, and further diplomatic pressure successfully resisted;[25] in February, 1698 Codrington was directed to observe the 1694 instructions.[26]

The dialogue between the British on the one hand and the Dutch and the Brandenburgers on the other revolved around the central point of conquest. The failure of the latter to emphasise the obligations which devolved upon Britain to restore Tortola under the provisions of the Treaty of Westminster, the refusal of Britain to acknowledge their claim to the island on the ground of previous occupation and proprietorship, while advancing with somewhat less justification its argument of prior discovery fundamentally affected the outcome of the negotiations. The potential threat which the island held out to British navigation and trade should it pass to another nation figured prominently in the British decision to retain it. The importance of this factor was emphasised by the consideration that the real value of the island as a plantation colony was regarded as being insignificant.[27]

In contrast to the prolonged negotiations over Tortola, the dispute between Britain and Denmark over St. Thomas and St. John was settled within a year after it commenced in 1717. That it occurred about 46 years after the establishment of the first Danish settlement in the islands placed the Danes in an almost unassailable position. On the basis of the Treaty of Alliance and Commerce between Britain and Denmark at Copenhagen on July 11, 1670, the Danish West India Company was founded and given its Charter in March, 1671,[28] which permitted it to occupy and take possession of St. Thomas 'and also such other islands thereabouts or near the mainland of America as might be uninhabited and suitable for plantations.'[29] The first Danish settlers landed and took formal possession of the island on May 25, 1672.[30] According to Westergaard, there was no one there to dispute ownership, the English who had occupied it having left six or seven weeks earlier, after burning off the roof of the storehouse.[31] From the beginning the colony received the active support of the British. To the assistance received from Tortola in the form of sugar-cane plants for cultivation[32] was added the willingness of the British Government to assist in the establishment of a stable government in the island. Their action was not inconsistent with British interests. For example, assistance given in the removal of the inept Danish Governor Adolph Esmit and the installation of Governor Gabriel Milan was prompted by the desire to prevent the seizure and confiscation of British vessels and the harbouring of fugitive slaves, criminals and pirates which the former encouraged.[33]

Despite British efforts to secure the establishment of a stable government in St. Thomas, there was no intention of encouraging the territorial expansion of Denmark in the West Indies. British policy, therefore, was one of containment.[34] In this respect, two points must be noted in the Instructions issued to Stapleton in May, 1683.[35] The first was the stated policy of confinement of Danish activities to St. Thomas which, in other words, forbade the Danes from settling on any other island. The second was related to the first: in the event of Danish refusal to submit to the British right of sovereignty over the other Virgin Islands they should be made to understand 'that the King of Denmark hath no good title to St. Thomas itself.' It meant, therefore, that the Danish presence in St. Thomas was permitted on sufferance and that it would be tolerated there so long as they did nothing detrimental to British interests. The assertion of British sovereignty over St. Thomas in 1717 resulted from the belief that the Danes had forfeited any concessions granted under the 1683 Instructions.

Danish ambition to acquire further territory in the Virgin Islands was shown at a very early date when in the Commission to Gabriel Milan in 1684, the authority of the Governor was not confined to St. Thomas alone but extended to include the neighbouring islands as well.[36] Four years later when Adolph Esmit was reinstated as Governor, he immediately sought to implement the provisions of his similar Commission. Milan himself had exhibited no expansionist tendencies, but Esmit, to the chagrin of the British Leeward Islands Governor Nathaniel Johnson, caused instructions to be issued inviting strangers to settle in the Virgin Islands especially on Crab Island (Vieques) and St. John which he claimed for the King of Denmark.[37]

Several other factors strained the relations between Britain and Denmark. The first was that the Danes continuously resorted to the neighbouring islands to procure their supplies of timber thereby violating British sovereignty.[38] A second factor was their use of St. Thomas as a base for pirates and privateers, and as 'the staple for all sort of indirect and illegal trade and commerce,'[39] to the detriment of British shipping. This was especially so during the period of the War of the Spanish Succession when the Danes also supported the French colonies with naval stores and intelligence, and with food, and allowed them to sell their prizes at St. Thomas. The protection granted to runaway slaves and debtors was a long-standing grievance. Combined with these was the oppression of British subjects by the Danes. For instance, should any British vessel happen to become stranded on St. Thomas not less than one third of its overall value was exacted for salvage. This was regarded as 'unreasonable and unwarrantable.'[40] And in 1717 there occurred the case of John Phillip whose possessions in St. Thomas were seized by the Danish authorities on the pretext that he was in debt.[41] The really significant factor which sparked off the controversy was the beginning of a Danish settlement on the island of St. John in March, 1718, under the aegis of the Danish West India Company.[42]

On March 23, 1718 the Danish Governor, Erik Bredal, published his intention to settle on the island and on the following day set out with one sloop and three two-mast boats with about 20 planters, five soldiers, and 16 negroes. On March 25, he took formal possession of St. John, hoisted the Danish flag, and commenced building a fort. Eight Articles of Agreement were then issued including the provision requiring Englishmen and Spaniards desirous of employment to become naturalised Danish subjects and to swear fealty to the existing commander. This was evidently an attempt to eliminate opposition. Provision was also made for the proper distribution and settlement of land, the granting of assistance by the Company in the form of negroes and essential plantation supplies, exemption from taxation for eight years, and the disposal of produce.[43]

The reaction of Walter Hamilton Governor of the British Leeward Islands was immediate. In April, 1718, he despatched Captain Hume of *HMS Scarborough* with a letter to Bredal forbidding the continuation of the settlement and asserting that the Danish King had no good title to St. Thomas itself. He concluded with the threat that if Bredal insisted on keeping possession of St. John he would be obliged 'to take such other measures as are agreeable to my Instructions in order to obstruct your Settlement and to preserve the sovereignty of that and the other Islands within my Government for my Royal Master.'[44] Bredal's reply was a categorical rejection of Hamilton's demands on the grounds that his action had been authorised by the King of Denmark whose orders he was bound to observe and that 'the legitimate occupation of a deserted island and peaceful possession of it for so many years evidently justify it.'[45]

The exchanges between the two colonial governors highlighted and pin-pointed the essential arguments which could be made in the conflicting claims to St. John. The British could point to the grant made of the Virgins along with the other Leeward Islands to the Earl of Carlisle in 1628,[46] but the essential condition which was the recognised requirement for possession, namely, that of effective occupation, had not been accomplished in the case of St. John.[47] The Danes, on the other hand, could plead British acknowledgement and accession to the Danish presence not only in St. Thomas but also in the other Virgin Islands from their interpretation of the orders given to Stapleton in 1672 'to show and exercise all acts of friendship to the inhabitants of the aforesaid Island of St. Thomas and all other Danish subjects in the West Indies.'[48] To the English this referred to Danes only in St. Thomas,[49] while to the Danes it embraced all their countrymen throughout the West Indies.[50]

Failure to produce evidence, and the unwillingness of the British Government to employ or sanction the use of force despite repeated suggestions to this effect by successive Governors of the Leeward Islands,[51] resulted in the loss and eventual abandonment of the British claim concerning the initial Danish settlement. After 1718 the question of right of sovereignty over either St. Thomas or St. John was not actively pursued. Though in 1783 some attempt was made by the British Government to secure evidence to substantiate persisting notions of right to St. John, it was nevertheless forced to drop this issue when no reliable information was forthcoming.[52] Long before then the question of possessory rights to St. Croix had been raised and settled.

Writing to Lord Carteret in 1722, Governor Hart questioned whether the Danes, if allowed to retain St. Thomas and St. John thereby strengthening their rights of sovereignty over these islands, might not sell them to the Dutch or to the French.[53] In another letter to the Duke of Newcastle in 1724 he asked 'whether the Danes if permitted to possess the Island of St. John . . . will not have the same pretensions to the Island of St. Cruz.'[54] In both instances Hart expressed real fears. His concern over the future of the Virgin Islands materialised in 1729 when claims to St. Croix were raised from an unexpected quarter – the French. To understand the basis of the French claim it is necessary to examine the earliest settlement of the Virgin Islands.[55]

The exact date when St. Croix was first settled cannot be certainly established.[56] By 1645, however, a number of English and Dutch as well as about 100 French who had deserted from the settlement on St. Christopher are reported to have been settled on St. Croix.[57] Relations among the settlers were not very good. This was especially so between the English and the Dutch and several fights broke out between them. In 1645 as a result of the murder of the English governor a quarrel occurred which led in the following year to the expulsion of the Dutch by the English. Their French allies at their own request were transported to Guadeloupe. Thereafter, the English remained in sole possession until 1650 when the Spaniards from Puerto Rico attacked St. Croix and the English in their turn, upon capitulation, were also obliged to quit the island.

The Dutch in St. Eustatius, learning of this attack and believing that the Spaniards would return to Puerto Rico soon after expelling the English, thought the time opportune to endeavour to regain possession of St. Croix. Unfortunately, the Spaniards were still there on their arrival and they were either killed or imprisoned. But the Spaniards had little cause to rejoice over their success. M. de Poincy, then Governor General of the French Islands, at his own expense sent a body of men from Martinique to St. Croix who captured the fort and forced the Spaniards to capitulate and to evacuate the island. For a short time de Poincy exercised sole proprietary rights over the island before surrendering the title to the Grand Master of the Order of Malta in 1653, after the collapse of his effort to colonise it. The transfer was subsequently confirmed by the French King by letter patent.[58]

In 1665, St. Croix reverted through purchase to the Company of America which had been formed by the French Minister Colbert the previous year. However, with the collapse of the Company in 1674, the island was taken over by the King of France as part of his dominions. Thereafter, St. Croix fell into a state of depression. As a result of prolonged maladministration of the government and mis-direction of the island's trade, an Order was issued from the French Court for the abandonment of the island and the removal of the population and their effects to St. Domingue. The date of this event constituted the basis of the contention between Britain and France after the question of sovereignty to St. Croix was raised in 1729.

With the departure of the French, St. Croix was treated as a resort for woodcutting by the poor whites and labouring population of the Leeward Islands of whom there were about 150 in 1727, earning roughly 8/– to 10/– a day.[59] No grants of land were issued and no regular plantation or settlement was established. When in 1717 and 1718 the inhabitants of Tortola, Virgin Gorda and Anguilla, as a result of a severe drought which brought them to the point of famine, petitioned for permission to remove and settle on St. Croix, their application was refused.[60] To the Governor of the Leeward Islands, this would deplete the British forces on the settled islands thus reducing their capacity for defence.[61] And the British Government's refusal stemmed from plans to settle the inhabitants on the previously French occupied part of St. Christopher acquired in 1713, 'where they will be more to their own advantage and be much more useful to the publick.'[62]

The question of right of sovereignty to St. Croix was raised in 1729 when a great number of British subjects from the adjacent islands expressed a desire to settle there if they obtained grants of land. Taking into consideration the French association with the island, Governor Londonderry, to whom the request was directed, was not prepared to make such grants without the prior approval of the Secretary of State. The question was apparently not important enough then to demand action, especially since clear evidence to establish an indisputable title was not likely to be obtained.[63]

In 1730 the question of sovereignty again came up for discussion when Thomas Hodgskins a carpenter of St. Christopher, and Walter Chapman reported the seizure of their sloop *Chance* by the French and their expulsion from St. Croix where they were woodcutting. It became necessary to decide how far the French, by this proceeding, might have been guilty of a breach of international law and of the treaties subsisting between the two Crowns.[64]

If the matter was considered simply in the light of a seizure made by a French man-of-war on a vessel belonging to some British subjects, it was undoubtedly a breach of good friendship between the two nations, in violation of the Treaty of Neutrality in America (1686) and of all the other Treaties of Peace and Commerce since that time. On the other hand, if the merit of the question was to turn upon the right which either Britain or France had to St. Croix, it was conceived that it 'will be early enough to enter upon that disquisition, whenever the French shall avow this action, and attempt to justify it upon a pretence of right to the said island.'[65] The British were quite willing to shelve the issue pending French initiative.

The French, to whom the matter was referred by the British ambassador in France, contended that they had a much more legitimate right to complain against English enterprises and on three counts showed that St. Croix belonged beyond dispute to France: it had been conquered nearly eighty years ago from Spain; no other nation had ever claimed it or disputed the right of France to the island; and there had never been any question of it in any negotiations or treaties of peace.[66] Amidst general complaints of British violation of their rights, the French called for a recognition of their claims to preserve peace between the two nations.[67] Unlike the British they were not prepared for the creation of a state of neutrality in St. Croix. Their demands if conceded would indeed have been tantamount to British renunciation of right to the island.[68]

Despite these exchanges neither the British nor the French were prepared to press the question to any conclusion. However, the subject was once more raised in May, 1733 when it was reported that the French ambassador in Copenhagen had sold, or had contracted to sell, St. Croix to the Danish West India Company.[69] However more attractive it might be for the Danes rather than the French to possess St. Croix,[70] nevertheless British acquisition of the island was considered important because the facility it offered as a neutral port enabled it to be used by enemy privateers and pirates against British shipping, and because it attracted British settlers thereby threatening to jeopardise the safety of settled British colonies.[71]

The Treaty between France and Denmark governing the sale of St. Croix for 750,000 French livres was concluded at Copenhagen, on June 15, 1733.[72] One year afterwards, in June, 1734, a large vessel arrived at St. Thomas from Denmark with a Commission for settling St. Croix, with a minister on board as well as 60 soldiers, several tradesmen and some families. Frederik Moth, a former Governor of St. Thomas, was appointed Governor.[73]

For the British to establish a claim to St. Croix, two points needed to be established. The first was in what year the French had removed to St. Domingue: whether in 1671 as the British believed, or in 1695 as the French maintained. If it were the latter, then any British claim would be over-ruled by the Treaty of Neutrality of 1686. The second was what claims had been put in by the French, and when, to preserve their rights to the island since they removed their last colony from there.[74] In the absence of adequate written records in the Office of the Council of Trade, and in the face of failure to find anyone in the West Indies to give an acceptable account,[75] the British were unable to support a claim to the island. On the other hand the Danes could produce a number of documents to establish the French right to the island before sale, on the basis of continuous possession by settlement and by union to the dominions of the King of France. When called upon the Council of Trade admitted that 'upon the whole we must submit . . . whether it may be proper to advise His Majesty to insist any longer upon a title so weakly supported.'[76] This advice brought an end to British efforts to acquire St. Croix.

Spanish threats to settlements in the Virgin Islands were both potential and real. Not prepared to establish settlements themselves, the Spaniards, by giving official backing to piratical raids, sought to disrupt those planned by others, whenever they could. Thus in 1685 the Spaniards attacked Tortola in their bark *Longue* and captured an English sloop and its crew of eight, one of whom was killed.[77] In April of the following year the Spaniards under the guidance of a renegade English doctor again attacked Tortola with the declared intention of murdering all the English and Dutch inhabitants. They pillaged several plantations and seized all the slaves they could find. Damage estimated at £3,977 was done.[78] At around the same time they plundered the few people who were beginning to make a settlement on Virgin Gorda.[79] A rumoured Spanish attack on St. Thomas in 1718 did not materialise,[80] but in 1727 two Spanish sloops, under the command of Captain Juan de Messa, plundered and carried away to Puerto Rico seven British sloops which had gone to St. Croix to supply the wood-cutters there with provisions and to buy their wood.[81] Such Spanish attacks against the Virgin Islands, however, were too sporadic to discourage foreign settlement.

The right of sovereignty to the individual Virgin Islands was definitely settled by 1735. Britain was left Tortola and the undisputed islands of Virgin Gorda, Anegada and Jost Van Dyke, which have remained British possessions. The history of the non-British islands has not been so uniform. The Danish Islands of St. Thomas, St. John and St. Croix, for instance, were taken by Britain in March, 1801 during the French Wars, for their encouragement to privateers, and though restored by the Treaty of Amiens in March, 1802, were retaken by Britain in December, 1807. They were finally returned by the Treaty of Paris in 1815 and remained in Danish possession until 1917 when they were bought by the United States of America for the sum of $25 million. The sale was influenced by American need to secure a strategic base in the Caribbean, and by the fear that the Danish Islands might become a base for German submarines.

The dilatory attitude of the European nations in establishing an early right of sovereignty over the Virgin Islands stemmed from the basic fact that these islands generally were not regarded as valuable plantation colonies. The contemporary view was that they were 'barren and craggy' and unlikely to prove responsive to productive enterprise. They were prized by the Danes only as entrepots from which trade could be beneficially transacted with the neighbouring Spanish and British colonies. Privateering was looked upon as an incidental adjunct and tolerated or encouraged because of the trade which it facilitated. These factors, together with the ability of the Danes to trade on more favourable terms, partly explain the British policy of containment and the Spanish policy of exclusion. Both were concerned over the safety of their own settled colonies and trade.

The struggle over the right of sovereignty was not without effects on the history of the British Virgin Islands. Economic development was retarded by the uncertainty over the outcome of diplomatic negotiations and the recurring threat of Spanish attack. Until the 1730's the pace of population infiltration was slow; thereafter, the greater threat of war to the larger settled islands forced their inhabitants to flee to the comparative safety of the Virgin Islands. Development then became more pronounced. The failure to achieve early economic viability retarded the institution of a regular system of government; it was not until 1773 that permission was given for the establishment of a legislature. The uncertainty of tenure and the ambivalent British attitude also influenced the social behaviour of the people. For many years only debtors from the larger islands, and pirates, fleeing thither to avoid punishment, were prepared to hazard the settlement of Tortola and Virgin Gorda. This factor contributed to the development of a unique trait in the character of the people. Not content with providing supplies to pirates who called there, the inhabitants soon took to privateering themselves, and this activity was continued so long as the wars of the eighteenth century made it both possible and profitable.

[1] J. Westlake: Collected Papers. International Law. (Cambridge, 1914) p. 161.
[2] C.S.P. 1669-1674. No.891.
[3] C.S.P. 1669-1674. No.896.
[4] C.S.P. 1669-1674. No.983.
[5] F. G. Davenport: European Treaties bearing on the History of the United States and its Dependencies. (Washington D.C., Published by Carnegie Institution of Washington, 1927) Vol. 11, pp. 229-232.
[6] C.S.P. 1675-1676. No.785; C.O. 153/2. An Account of Statia, Sabea and Tortola, 25 April, 1678; C.S.P. 1677-1680. Nos. 299 and 679.
[7] C.S.P. 1677-1680. Nos. 299 and 404.
[8] F. G. Davenport: European Treaties . . . Vol. 11, p. 261.
[9] C.S.P. 1681-1685. No. 1593.
[10] C.S.P. 1681-1685. No. 1527.
[11] C.S.P. 1681-1685. No. 1593.
[12] C.S.P. 1681-1685. No. 1615.
[13] C.S.P. 1685-1688. No. 692.
[14] C.S.P. 1685-1688. No. 813.
[15] C.S.P. 1677-1680. Nos. 1472 and 789.
[16] C.S.P. 1685-1688. No. 830.
[17] C.S.P. 1685-1688. No. 1020; C.O.153/3. f. 226.
[18] Ibid.
[19] C.S.P. 1696-1697. No. 382.
[20] Ibid.
[21] C.S.P. 1696-1697. No. 490.
[22] C.O.153/6 ff. 44-45. C.T.P. to Codrington, 22 Jan., 1697; C.S.P. 1696-1697. No. 722.
[23] C.O.153/6. f. 110. Codrington to the C.T.P., 5 July, 1697; C.S.P. 1696-1697. No. 1347.
[24] C.S.P. 1697-1698. No. 156.
[25] C.S.P. 1697-1698. Nos. 220, 290, 613 and 653.
[26] C.S.P. 1697-1698. No. 258.
[27] C.S.P. 1696-1697. No. 382.
[28] F. G. Davenport: European Treaties . . . Vol. 11, pp. 197-8.
[29] Waldermar Westergaard: The Danish West Indies under Company Rule (1671-1754) with a Supplementary Chapter, 1755-1917. (New York, The Macmillan Company, 1917) pp. 32-33.
[30] Ibid., p. 37.
[31] Ibid., p. 37.
[32] Ibid., p. 38.
[33] C.O.153/3. Stapleton to the C.T.P., 11 Nov., 1682; 30 Aug., 1683; 13 Jan., 13 Feb., and 28 Oct., 1684; Minutes of Meeting of the King in Council at the Court of Whitehall, 14 Nov., 1683; A report concerning St. Thomas by the C.T.P., 13 May, 1684; Order in Council, 15 May, 1684; Westergaard: op.cit., p. 58.
[34] C.O.153/3 Stapleton to the C.T.P., 11 Nov., 1682; Order in Council, 28 Feb., 1683; Sunderland to the Danish Envoy, 3 March, 1683.
[35] C.O.153/3. Powers and Instructions to Sir William Stapleton, 7 May, 1683.
[36] C.O.153/3. Stapleton to the C.T.P., 28 Oct., 1684.

[37] C.S.P. 1685-1688. No. 1773.
[38] C.S.P. 1717-1718 No. 298. Enc. No. 10.
[39] C.S.P. 1702-1703. No. 669.
[40] C.S.P. 1717-1718. No. 298. Enc. No. 10.
[41] Ibid., also, C.S.P. 1717-1718. No. 526.
[42] C.S.P. 1716-1717. No. 562.
[43] C.S.P. 1717-1718. No. 494.
[44] C.S.P. 1717-1718. No. 494.
[45] C.S.P. 1717-1718. No. 526.
[46] J. A. Williamson: The Caribbee Islands under the Proprietary Patents. (Oxford University Press, London: Humphrey Milford, 1926) p. 46. An earlier grant to that of 7 April, 1628, was made on 2 July, 1627. Ibid., p. 40.
[47] C.S.P. 1716-1717. No. 8.
[48] C.S.P. 1716-1717. No. 562.
[49] C.S.P. 1716-1717. No. 8; C.S.P. 1717-1718. No. 628.
[50] C.S.P. 1717-1718. No. 593.
[51] C.S.P. 1717-1718. No. 494; C.S.P. 1719-1720. No.39; C.S.P. 1722-1723. No.150.
[52] C.O.152/63. Enc. in Shirley to Lord North, 28 Oct., 1783. No. 39.
[53] C.S.P. 1722-1723. No. 150.
[54] C.S.P. 1724-1725. No. 255.
[55] J. P. Knox: An Historical Account of St. Thomas . . . and incidental notices of St. Croix and St. Johns. (New York, 1852) pp. 21-41; C.O.153/15. C.T.P. to Mathew, 26 Sept., 1734; C.S.P. 1734-1735. No. 323.
[56] Bryan Edwards: A History, Civil and Commercial of the British West Indies. (London, 1819). Vol.1. pp. 183-4 gives 1625 as the date of the first settlement on St. Croix. Knox disputes this but does not offer an alternative date.
[57] Knox, op.cit., p. 25, gives the total number of settlers as 600.
[58] Knox, op.cit., p. 36.
[59] C.S.P. 1727-1728. No. 464.
[60] C.S.P. 1717-1718. Nos. 40, 298 and 442.
[61] C.S.P. 1717-1718. No. 40.
[62] C.S.P. 1717-1718. No. 487.
[63] C.S.P. 1728-1729. Nos. 664 and 821.
[64] C.S.P. 1730. No. 58 and enc.; also, No. 110.
[65] C.S.P. 1730. No. 62.
[66] C.S.P. 1730. No. 93.
[67] C.S.P. 1730. Nos. 149 and 499.
[68] C.S.P. 1730. Nos. 532 and 561.
[69] C.S.P. 1733. No. 169.
[70] C.S.P. 1733. Nos. 169 and 225.
[71] C.S.P. 1734-1735. No. 83.
[72] Westergaard, op.cit., p. 206; C.S.P. 1734-1735. No. 388 and enc.
[73] C.S.P. 1734-1735. No. 288.
[74] C.S.P. 1734-1735. Nos. 308 and 323.
[75] C.S.P. 1734-1735. No. 396.
[76] C.S.P. 1734-1735. Nos. 489 and 537.

[77] C.S.P. 1685-1688. No. 17.
[78] C.S.P. 1685-1688. Nos. 673 and 678.
[79] C.S.P. 1696-1697. No. 1347.
[80] C.S.P. 1717-1718. No. 818; C.S.P. 1719-1720. No. 39.
[81] C.S.P. 1726-1727. Nos. 464 and 503, and enc.

Chapter 2

The Establishment of a Legislature

The history of the British Virgin Islands can, in a sense, be regarded to date from 1672 at the time of the capture of Tortola from the Dutch by Colonel William Stapleton. But it was not until 1773, a complete century after, that the islands were granted the benefits of a legislature similar to the other Leeward Islands. And it required a further decade for settled constitutional government to be established.

The basic reason for the slow rate of constitutional advancement in the Virgin Islands was that they were slow to develop economically. This was partly due to factors inherent in the contentions among European nations for the right of sovereignty over them, and partly because they failed to attract the attention of planters equipped with the capital and knowledge to establish and operate plantations. The productive capacity of the islands, though made the subject of continuous debate and the pawn of colonial governors arguing for and against the settlement of the islands, was later proved to be worthwhile. The nature of the problem was such that only the influx of population inclined to settle permanently and cultivate could lead to the formation of a colony in the sense that institutions of government could be established.

For approximately the first fifty years after the conquest of the islands they were inadequately settled, in terms of both the quality and quantity of settlers. In 1672, there were on Tortola in addition to the ten or twelve Dutch families probably about eighty English, Irish and Welsh settlers.[1] Productive enterprise could hardly be expected from people whose morale had already been weakened by the virtual slavery under which they had existed under the Dutch.[2] Even under the

British the settlers were not allowed undisturbed freedom to pursue cultivation. Spanish depredation of the islands around 1685 resulted in their practical abandonment; between 1685 and 1690 only two persons, Jonathan Turner and his wife, inhabited Tortola and, for a time, Virgin Gorda, where they bred livestock, planted a little cotton and fished in the surrounding waters.[3]

Very little is otherwise known about the Virgin Islands during the period from 1685 to 1711, but that population was inadequate was shown by further reports. In illustrating the effects of possession of St. Thomas by foreign powers on British trading enterprises, Governor Codrington made some mention of Virgin Gorda.[4] In 1690 there were fourteen men, a few women and a few negroes inhabiting the island and planting cotton which was conveyed in small canoes to St. Thomas where they secured a higher price than in St. Christopher. In return they bought Dutch linen and slaves, the latter being between thirty and forty percent cheaper than in St. Christopher. By 1696 the population of Virgin Gorda had increased, but numbered only about fifty armed men and their families, and from seventy to eighty slaves.

Codrington did not state the origin or the nature of the settlers in Virgin Gorda; this information was given by Governor Parke in 1709. By that time Tortola also was being settled. The settlers on both islands had been driven off the Leeward Islands, 'by the rich men's ingrossing their land.' Except for some increase in their numbers, no substantial changes were noticeable in their condition; they lived very poorly, growing cotton which was sold to the Danes. To Parke, they were 'so many families lost in effect to the Crowne of England,' and to alleviate their condition he suggested their removal to Barbuda where they 'might not only make great advantages by raising horses, cattle and sheep, and all sorts of fowles but also by cotton and Guiney corne.'[5]

The absence of any productive element in the islands accounts for the little official cognizance of them. Indeed, the only attention paid to the islands was due solely to the wood they contained and of which there was a shortage in the other Leeward Islands. Tortola, particularly, was prized for its timber.[6] Woodcutters with the consent and under the authority and orders of the Governor of the Leeward Islands, and of the Council of St. Christopher, often resorted there for their much needed supplies.[7] The importance of the timber from the Virgin Islands partly explains why the British were unwilling to tolerate foreign presence there.[8]

The paucity of inhabitants and the lack of official awareness of the potentialities of the islands as a plantation colony determined the nature of their early administration. No proper system of government existed in the Virgin Islands in the seventeenth century. This was because too few inhabitants made it impossible to have either councillors or representatives.[9] While Britain held Saba and St. Eustatius, Tortola was ranged with them and placed around 1678 under the single command of Captain Peter Batterie by the authority of Governor Stapleton. Even then, however, as there were still too few people on the islands and very little business to be transacted, there was evidently no need to multiply offices, either civil or military.[10]

The restoration of Saba and St. Eustatius to the Dutch in 1679 did not terminate the practice of appointing a deputy-governor, as the person holding the office was designated, for Tortola and the other Virgin Islands. But it was difficult to obtain suitable candidates to fill the office. Thomas Bisse who was deputy-governor of Tortola in 1683 was the last resident to hold the post before the Spanish descent on the island in 1685.[11] Thereafter, the captains of visiting vessels seem to have been appointed, and held their commission as deputy-governors for the period of their stay. One of these was Captain John Henselm who was deputy-governor of Tortola in 1685.[12] With the increase in the population during the last decade of the century, the practice of appointing separate deputy-governors for Tortola and Virgin Gorda was instituted.

The office of deputy-governor did not carry any specific executive, legislative or judicial functions. From one extant copy of a commission it is learned that the deputy-governor was 'to have, hold, exercise and enjoy the office . . . for and during pleasure.' He was subject to the instructions and directions of the Governor of the Leeward Islands who appointed him.[13] Neither did deputy-governors of the Virgin Islands receive any salary or other reward. According to the Instructions given to the Governor of the Leeward Islands, there was a salary of £200 sterling a year payable out of the proceeds of the 4½% duty levied on the Leeward Islands, to Lieutenant-Governors appointed by the Crown.[14] But these Instructions did not apply to the Virgin Islands: they did not pay the 4½% duty, and the deputy-governor was not appointed by the Crown. Lacking constituted powers and a salary, therefore, the office of deputy-governor was merely nominal and a symbol of British authority over the islands.

Whenever possible, the subordinate governor was appointed from among the residents of the Virgin Islands concerned, though it was sometimes difficult 'to gett one that's tolerable fitt amongst them to take the command upon them.'[15] Often the islands were left without a person in control. Without any force at his disposal there was little that the deputy-governor could do to maintain law and order. Lawlessness prevailed in the Virgin Islands; the people had no respect for the deputy-governor, or for the laws of civilised society. Commenting on their behaviour in 1709, Governor Parke observed that 'they live like wild people without order or Government, and have neither Divine nor Lawyer amongst them, they take each others words in marriage; they thinke themselves Christians because they are descended from such.'[16] In order to introduce the rudiments of Christianity among them, the Governor was able to influence someone, 'to go to them lately out of charity.'[17]

The really genuine attempt to secure the institution of a regular system of administration was begun in 1711 by Captain John Walton. His efforts were not successful, but the movement which he started was to result in the establishment of a civil government in the islands. In April, 1706, Walton left England to assume control over a company of foot soldiers in the Leeward Islands, but before he arrived, Governor Daniel Parke, as Commander-in-Chief, had otherwise disposed of the Commission.[18] As compensation, Walton was commissioned as Lieutenant-Governor of the Virgin Islands in September, 1707, and served in that capacity until 1709. During this period he developed notions of becoming proprietor of the entire Virgin Islands, but did not at first suggest this when on his return to England in 1710 he presented his case before the British Government. Rather he pointed to the necessity of a regular system of administration to encourage economic development and prevent clandestine trade and lawlessness.[19] He attributed the backwardness and instability of the islands to the absence of a properly constituted governor.[20]

Walton was not merely concerned with securing the adoption of a more efficient administration. His scheme was more ambitious and embraced the formation of a separate government independent of the control exercised by the Governor of the Leeward Islands.[21] A proprietorship for 30 years in the first instance, renewable at an easy quitrent, was to be the first step in this direction.[22] Asked whether he thought the creation of a separate government in the Virgin Islands would be able to support the offices and dignity of a government,[23] Walton could only reply by pointing to the example of the Leeward Islands which at the time of their separation from Barbados in 1670, were not, he said, with the exception of St. Christopher, in a more promising condition than the Virgin Islands were at the time. He believed that a separate government would succeed given the same encouragement from the British Government as that granted to the Leeward Islands when they separated from Barbados.[24]

The intensity of Walton's efforts together with the somewhat ambitious magnitude of his schemes including as they did the delicate question of proprietorship did not appeal to the British Government. After consideration based on evidence acquired in Britain, Walton's proposals were turned down. Lack of the basic harbour facilities and good soil conditions, the possibility of enemy depredation in the absence of fortifications, and the encouragement given to pirates and illegal trade, were the principal arguments which suggested to the Lords of Trade the inadvisability of creating a government in the Virgin Islands.[25] But in order to avert any suspicion or suggestion that they had not acted in the best interests of all concerned, they recommended that the Governor of the Leeward Islands should submit an account of the soil, production, facilities for trade, and population of the Virgin Islands.[26]

Like the Council of Trade and Plantations, Governor Hamilton was more interested in establishing a firm British footing in the four principal Leeward Islands of St. Christopher, Nevis, Antigua and Montserrat, and to avoid a diffusion of British forces which would weaken their defences against foreign attacks.[27] He favoured the transfer of the settlers already in the Virgin Islands to St. Christopher where they could be provided with land in the French sections of that island. His reports on the physical characteristics and productive capacity of the islands were deliberately designed to create an unfavourable impression. The general picture was that the islands were barren, mountainous and rocky, and could produce nothing else but timber.[28]

The population statistics provided by Hamilton were designed to prove the disastrous effect which the Virgin Islands could have on the other Leeward Islands. Within a few years there had been a relatively large increase of population who had migrated from the other islands. In 1716 there were 247 whites and 125 negroes on Virgin Gorda; 103 whites and 44 negroes on Tortola; and 17 whites and 6 negroes on Beef Island. By November, 1717, there was a substantial, and to the Governor, a disconcerting increase; Virgin Gorda, for instance, had 317 whites and 308 negroes being in terms of population, by far the largest island. There were only two families on Beef Island which was a probable decrease in population, but in Tortola there was an increase to 159 whites and 176 negroes.[29]

The fact that the Virgin Islands were suspected of attracting inhabitants because of the harbour facilities which they afforded for privateering and illicit trade was not one to foster confidence in or to encourage their development. This was the main conclusion drawn by Captain Candler of *HMS Winchelsea* who had been directed in October, 1715, to visit and report on the Virgin Islands.[30]

Though Captain Candler was motivated by less prejudice than Governor Hamilton, nevertheless, his report, in general, presented the same unfavourable picture of the islands.[31] He touched on two points not dealt with by Hamilton: defence and administration. With regard to defence, he found only a small fort in Tortola which the original Dutch settlers had constructed but which was in ruins; at Virgin Gorda, he found only one gun, but no carriage or fort. Administration was equally inadequate: a Captain Hall who had been a privateer during the War of the Spanish Succession (1702-1713) was deputy-governor in Tortola, while in Virgin Gorda the recent death of their deputy-governor, and the lack of suitably qualified candidates, had reduced the inhabitants to the expedient of accepting a poor, ignorant man from among themselves as his successor. Additionally, he reported 400 whites and 210 negroes on Virgin Gorda, 320 whites and 203 negroes on Tortola, and four families on Beef Island, thus giving statistics exceeding Governor Hamilton's.

The reports submitted by Governor Hamilton and Captain Candler were to conclude a crucial phase in the history of the Virgin Islands. It was perhaps unfortunate that both men had visited the islands while they were experiencing one of the most severe droughts in their history, which gave them the appearance of barrenness and non-productivity. The Governor suggested an alternative course of action: the removal of the settlers either to St. Croix or to St. Christopher.[32] Decision for the removal of British subjects to the latter had already been taken with regard to those on Vieques,[33] and in April, 1718, a similar decision was taken with respect to the inhabitants of Tortola and Virgin Gorda.[34] Walton's insistence on a separate, independent government under his control,[35] when offered a Lieutenant-Governorship of Virgin Gorda under the Governor of the Leeward Islands if he could settle 50 families on it,[36] deprived him of whatever chance he had of governing. His ambition outweighed the realities of the situation: he could not meet the population requirement. Accordingly, the Lords of Trade recommended that he should be given just a gratuity in recompense of his past services to the Virgin Islands which he had undertaken without a salary.[37]

Walton had failed to achieve his objectives, but his representations had the effect of focusing attention on the problems and needs of the Virgin Islands. And despite resolutions to the contrary, the islands not only remained inhabited but their population increased. By August, 1720, Virgin Gorda had 371 whites and 364 negroes, while Tortola had 203 whites and 266 negroes.[38] By 1724, after the settlers had refused an invitation by the Governor of Jamaica, Sir N. Lawes, to remove to that island in return for better land and security,[39] the population numbered 340 whites and 650 negroes in Virgin Gorda, and 420 whites and 780 negroes in Tortola.[40] This represented an overall increase of over thirty percent. The heavier concentration of population on Tortola in 1724 should be noted as this was indicative of future trends. Production, however, remained confined to small· quantities of sugar, molasses and cotton, some of which was exchanged with the Dutch at St. Eustatius and the Danes at St. Thomas for essentials. As yet there was no trade with Britain and the people possessed only a few small sloops for inter-island trade.[41]

Except for a faint attempt to put the settlements on Tortola and Virgin Gorda on a more organised basis in 1724, the inhabitants were allowed to shift for themselves until 1735 when a major new effort was made to institute a sound administration in the islands. The population included those who 'had fled from Barbados and the greater islands (of the Leeward Islands) for debt, or to avoid the punishment of their crimes, and have since been increased by pirates, who have come in upon acts of Grace, and are married and settled there, whose posterity not knowing the world, remain there and cultivate the ground for a wretched subsistence.'[42] They probably did not engage in piracy but it was believed that they held 'correspondence with them (pirates), and furnish them with provisions.'[43] A fierce contention existed among the people for property and because they had no medium for the administration of justice Governor Hart in 1724 appointed six Justices of the Peace, a Secretary and a Provost Marshal. He also organised a militia in each island, consisting in Tortola of 100 men, and in Virgin Gorda of 78 men, and put them under the control of commissioned officers.[44] The functions of these separate bodies were not outlined, but it is probable, as was afterwards shown, that the Justices together with the deputy-governors were responsible for making ordinances for the peace and good government of the islands, and to raise money for public utilities by taxation, while the Secretary and Provost Marshal on the one hand and the militia on the other were responsible respectively, for the collection of taxes and the maintenance of internal security.[45]

Events after 1724 demonstrated the need for a better system of government and the administration of justice. Of particular importance was the trial of William White of Virgin Gorda for murder. In May, 1725, White was charged with shooting and killing one Cary for attempted robbery for which he was confined by the deputy-governor of Virgin Gorda. As there was no Court of Justice to try the type of offence for which White was charged, it was decided, at White's suggestion, that he should be carried to St. Christopher to be tried there. The Solicitor-General of the Leeward Islands, however, advised that White could not be tried by the ordinary courts of St. Christopher as the murder was not committed within the judicial district of St. Christopher. Accordingly, the trial was executed under Statute 33 Henry VIII by the Council of St. Christopher and four judges, and White was found guilty of murder. But Statute 33 was enacted before the settlement of the Leeward Islands to which its application was therefore doubtful.

On the recommendation of both the Solicitor-General and the Attorney-General of the Leeward Islands, Governor Hart forwarded the particulars of the case to the Council of Trade and Plantations for their opinion.[46] The ruling of that body that the trial was illegal,[47] opened the whole question of the administration of justice in the Virgin Islands. Two factors were involved: the legality of trying criminal cases outside the Virgin Islands, and if this was impossible, the problems of trying cases there in the absence of Courts of Justice. And even if these were established, there remained the additional difficulties of securing the services of lawyers, and of being able to form juries. The immediate need, however, was for the formation of some court to deal with the 'continuous contentions about their meum and teum poor as tis' which existed among the population, 'where every man may be heard to tell his own story,' and where they could get some remedy against wrongs. In the absence of organised justice, the premium was placed on the use of force for as it was 'the strongest has the best title.'[48]

The evident need of institutions to administer justice and to govern the islands led Governor Mathew in June, 1734, to consider the appointment of a circuit court consisting of three or four justices to visit the islands once or twice a year to try criminal cases,[49] and to establish in early 1735 Councils and Assemblies in Tortola and Virgin Gorda to prepare laws on models furnished by him.[50] Each Council consisted of six members and each Assembly of nine. For the purpose of electing members to the Assembly, Tortola was divided into three divisions: Fat Hog Bay Division, Road Division and Saka Bay Division, each of which returned three members; and Virgin Gorda was divided into two divisions, namely, the Valley Division which returned six members, and the North and South Sound Division which returned three.[51] Members of both Councils were nominated by the Governor while the members of the Assemblies, because of the unsettled nature of land ownership, were elected generally by the inhabitants of the respective divisions, rather than by free-holders only as specified in the Governor's Commission.[52] By the institution of such a system of government which was acceptable to the people as a whole and which could pass requisite legislation, the Governor hoped that in the Virgin Islands 'murthers and the greatest crimes will hereafter not be committed there with impunity for want of proper laws and Courts of Justice for trying offenders, as heretofore.'[53]

Mathew misinterpreted the words of his Commission empowering him with the advice and consent of the Councils to summon General Assemblies within any of the islands under his government;[54] consequently his establishment of legislatures was illegal.[55] No justices had as yet been appointed to conduct courts of law, and following a sharp reprimand from the Lords of Trade for his irregular action, the Assemblies were terminated shortly afterwards.[56] Thus when in May, 1737, Mathew submitted the names of the members of the Councils, no mention was made of the existence of Assemblies.[57]

The Governor's action terminating the Assemblies did not affect the Councils; these continued to exist and their members executed the magisterial and tax-levying functions of the old bodies composed of the six Justices of the Peace which they replaced. The extent to which these duties were performed should not be over-estimated. Single magistrates dealt with trivial cases while the Council as a whole decided disputes over property and actions for debts. There were no juries. For these hearings the Councils met once a month from March 1 to July 31, and appeals from their decisions could be made to the Governor of the Leeward Islands.[58] The cases dealt with were all civil suits; the problem of criminal cases, though fortunately few, still remained.

Besides, injustices over the possession of lands could not always be dealt with by the Councils or Governor, and it was sometimes necessary to appeal to the Secretary of State to secure redress of grievances.

The effect of the irregular and partial mode of administering justice was evident. To one observer who visited the Virgin Islands in 1739, the people lived 'in a most abandoned manner, if in their cupps or passion they commit murder they must remain unpunished, having no regular courts.'[59] The greatest weakness of the system of administering justice, however, lay in the difficulty of getting men sufficiently qualified to adjudicate. In this respect Tortola was more fortunate. In Virgin Gorda the flagrant proofs of mal-administration led a later Governor to dismantle the Council and transfer its functions to the Council in Tortola.[60]

As in the administration of justice, the power of the Councils with regard to taxation was likewise limited. Taxes were only occasionally levied on the inhabitants to cater for cases of emergency and other necessary matters such as the construction of batteries in times of war, and even then their prior consent as to the amount to be collected and its appropriation had to be obtained.[61]

The period after 1735 seems to have been one of rapid economic development in the Virgin Islands. Contemporary reports gave an impressive account of both the actual and potential sugar and cotton output of the islands. Hopes were raised by the beginning of cultivation on Jost Van Dyke. In 1739, for example, Tortola and Virgin Gorda were expected to produce an estimated 750,000 pounds of cotton, and 350 hogsheads of sugar as well as large quantities of provisions.[62] These estimates were exceeded the following year,[63] and by 1751, Lieutenant-Governor James Purcell was reporting the production of one million pounds of cotton and one thousand casks of muscovado sugar each weighing one thousand pounds from the entire Virgin Islands.[64] Even admitting slight exaggeration for propaganda purposes, the increase was reassuring. A copper mine discovered in Virgin Gorda was also believed to be a potential source of great wealth.[65]

In his report of 1751, Purcell was careful to point out that increased production could only result from an increase in the number of slaves. By inference he touched on one of the most serious problems of the Virgin Islands, namely, that of escaping slaves. Slaves were induced to escape to Puerto Rico because of its proximity and because it promised freedom to all those who embraced the Catholic faith by baptism. Repeated requests from the Governor of the Leeward Islands to the

Governor of Puerto Rico for the return of the slaves produced no results.[66] Later, the authorities in the Virgin Islands appealed to the British Government to secure their return by diplomatic action with the Spanish Government, but no positive results were achieved.[67] It was not until the 1780's after the institution of a legislature in the Virgin Islands made it possible, that measures were taken locally to curtail the practice. Meanwhile the islands suffered four ways from the desertion of the slaves: planters were deprived of their services and production was consequently hampered; slaves constituted an investment in capital which was lost when they escaped; slaves effected their escape by stealing small boats and sometimes large vessels belonging to the planters which were normally used to transport produce to market; and lastly, in times of war the fugitive slaves were employed aboard Spanish privateers which preyed upon the shipping of the Virgin Islands, while in peace time they were engaged on commissioned periaguas and other small vessels which raided fishing boats.[68]

The inadequate system of administering justice, increased production, and the problem of runaway slaves, emphasised the need for established government in the Virgin Islands. The need to organise trade was also a significant factor. In 1739, Dinwiddy had found that Virgin Islanders were as unconfined in their trade as in their morals.[69] In addition, the growth of trade between the Virgin Islands and Britain, British North America, and other West Indian colonies after 1740 made it necessary that they should be brought under the laws of trade and navigation.[70] These conditions gave point to Dinwiddy's recommendation relative to smuggling, that the islands should be 'duly reduced to order of Government, by giving them a Legislative power, with a Governor and proper instructions.'[71]

Increased population also contributed to the creation of a favourable attitude towards the need for constitutional government. By 1756 population had increased from an estimated 760 whites and 1,430 negroes in 1724,[72] to 1,184 whites and 6,121 slaves, despite the emigration of some of the former to St. Croix during the intervening wars to avoid enrolment to fight as ordered by the British Government and the escape of some of the latter to Puerto Rico.[73] The increase was due to an influx of settlers from the other British West Indies escaping from the dangers of war to the comparative safety of the Virgin Islands. Two aspects of the migration are noteworthy. The first was the heavier concentration of population on Tortola: in 1756 there were 465 whites and 3,864 slaves on Tortola; 396 whites and 1,204 slaves on Virgin Gorda; and 323 whites and 1,053 slaves on the remaining islands. The quality of the settlers also showed a marked improvement over that of the first settlers, judging from their greater awareness of Christianity, from the large-scale sugar and cotton cultivation indulged in, and from the growing inclination of the more leisurely to spend holidays in neighbouring islands.[74]

It was largely due to the continuous agitation by James Purcell that the question of civil government for the Virgin Islands was kept alive and put before the Lords of Trade after he was appointed Lieutenant-Governor in 1747. Petitions in 1751,[75] and again in 1753,[76] were followed by a personal visit to Britain in 1754 to present his case before the Lords of Trade. Supported by several agents of and the principal merchants trading with the Leeward Islands, in a number of interviews, Purcell was able to persuade the Lords of Trade 'that the establishing of some form of government in (the Virgin Islands) would be of great publik utility and advantage,' subject only to the condition that they should not be 'erected into a government independent of the other Leeward Islands.'[77] The Lords of Trade undoubtedly saw the need to consolidate the administration of the Leeward Islands.

When the question as to the best form of government for the Virgin Islands was raised,[78] as might be expected, Purcell favoured constitutional government, but he believed that legislative power should be vested in a Governor and Council. He was against an Assembly partly because he considered that parliamentary privileges would be grossly abused by such a constituted body, 'and instead of forwarding lay numberless impediments in the way of making laws and of all other public business.' But if an Assembly were decided on, he suggested a single Assembly for the entire Virgin Islands. Both voters and candidates must satisfy property and residential qualifications. He proposed the continuation of the prevailing system of administering justice in civil cases, plus a 'settled yearly or half yearly sessions, or occasional commissions of Oyer and Terminer' from the Governor of the Leeward Islands to determine criminal cases, juries to be drawn from all the Virgin Islands. He also recommended public participation in taxation, such as an elected Assembly of twelve persons, and taxes to be levied on the basis of slaves possessed, the money to be used for general public services by the Governor and Council; a single Treasury for all the islands; and freedom of trade based on a free port. Lastly he suggested a force of about one hundred soldiers posted at several points in Tortola to prevent slaves from escaping and illicit trade, and to reinforce the system of defence by several batteries and a fort recently constructed.[79]

Purcell's enthusiasm was unfortunately not shared by Governor George Thomas who was unsympathetic towards the aspirations of Virgin Islanders in 1755. The Governor considered that 'the inhabitants of those Islands are generally so illiterate that their heads are more likely to be turned by the privileges of a legislative body.'[80] Commenting on Purcell's recommendations, Thomas insinuated that it would undoubtedly be to Purcell's own advantage to have a Commission independent of the Governor of the Leeward Islands, a company of soldiers, and a free port where he was the principal merchant.[81]

The conflicting opinions of Purcell and Thomas, and the outbreak of the Seven Years' War in 1756 resulted in the suspension of any possible decision. Even when peace was established in 1763, the unsettled state of British politics, and the death of Governor Woodley who in 1769 had secured the Secretary of State's agreement to establish some sort of government,[82] left the question once more in abeyance. It was not until 1773 after Sir Ralph Payne assumed the governorship, that positive action was taken. Payne was impressed with the productivity of the islands, especially Tortola, the prospects of augmented trade, and the willingness of the people to be governed. He deplored their neglect, 'half a century having elapsed since the Virgin Islands had been visited by the Chief Governor.' Vexed by the 'most irregular and impolitic constitution and nature of Government' which existed in the Virgin Islands, and prompted by a petition from the inhabitants, which his own encouragement stimulated, Payne recommended the early institution of civil government there.[83] In July, 1773 he was directed to issue writs to convene an Assembly the composition of which was left to his discretion. Together with a Council of twelve members to be appointed by Payne from among the principal planters, it was empowered to pass necessary laws.[84]

The decision to introduce into the Virgin Islands a representative system of government, as it was called, based on a Governor, a nominated Council, and an elected Assembly, was due to a number of considerations. The Secretary of State for the colonies was undoubtedly influenced by conditions in the British West Indies where representative government was being established: it would surely be easier to administer a number of colonies if each had a similar legislative system than it would be if they were different. Virgin Islanders were for the most part people who had migrated from the older British colonies where representative government was already established. It was the system to which they were accustomed and the one which they aspired to obtain for the Virgin Islands. Representative government by Governor, Council and Assembly resembled in structure and in some of its functions the British system of government. If Englishmen in the colonies were deemed entitled to the same rights and privileges as Englishmen at 'home' then the argument was conclusive that their opportunities for political expression should approximate.

Permission for the convention of a legislature climaxed a number of changes which had already been introduced in the Virgin Islands. The death of Purcell in 1771[85] had led to a change in policy with regard to the appointment of Lieutenant-Governors. Henceforth, it was decided, Lieutenant-Governors would be appointed from Britain and receive their commission from the King.[86] This change was not without some significance to the later history of the Virgin Islands. Mention has already been made of the termination of the Council in Virgin Gorda and the transference of its functions to the Council in Tortola. In June, 1773, Payne took further steps towards the creation of a unified system of control. He began unifying the militia into a single regiment which he anticipated would eventually consist of 250 men.[87] Next he abolished the position of deputy-governor of Virgin Gorda because he could find no one to occupy the post to his satisfaction, and because he thought that the nearness of the island to Tortola made this office quite unnecessary. The Lieutenant-Governor of Tortola was left in complete command subject to the authority of the Governor. The civil establishment was placed under the control of the ordinary magistrates who were sufficient for the immediate preservation of the public peace, and the military establishment was organised under the captain of the fort and the commanding officer of the militia.[88] The centre of administration of the Virgin Islands had gradually shifted to Tortola which by this time had outstripped Virgin Gorda in economic prosperity. It was natural that when the new Assembly was formed, it should meet in Tortola.

By 1773, the Virgin Islands from their increased prosperity, their greater population, and their disorganised condition, needed the stimulus of a constitutional government. It is extremely doubtful whether they would have been accorded one then had the inhabitants not agreed to an impost of 4½% on all their produce, similar to that levied in the other Leeward Islands and Barbados.[89] This agreement was embodied in their petition for an Assembly, though not without stiff opposition. In June, 1773, Payne warned the Secretary of State,

Lord Dartmouth, that he might need all possible aid to enable him 'to carry the measure into effectual execution.'[90] Dartmouth's stand was firm and uncompromising. He directed that the first act of the new Assembly should be to enact the 4½% duty, and that it should not be allowed to proceed to any other business until this was done.[91] The same attitude was adopted when in January, 1774, the people showed signs of repenting.[92] Dartmouth's unhesitating reply was that it would 'be very unfortunate, indeed, if after such solemn assurances, there should be any difficulty in the accomplishment of that business.'[93] He did not elaborate on the threat but his attitude was probably indicative of the strength of the anticipation of benefits to be derived from the augmented productivity and trade of the islands.

The proclamation for the institution of a legislature in the Virgin Islands was issued by Governor Payne on November 30, 1773.[94] It provided for a Council of twelve members nominated by the Governor, and for an Assembly of eleven members of whom eight were to represent Tortola, two to represent Virgin Gorda and one Jost Van Dyke. Both electors and elected were to be drawn from among the planters and free-holders of the population. All white men who had attained the age of 21 years and who possessed 40 acres of land or a house worth £40, and all sons of the required age who were heirs apparent of persons possessing 80 acres of land or a house valued at £80, were eligible as candidates for election. Qualification of electors included possession of 10 acres of land, or a building worth £10. For the purpose of elections each island was to be treated as a single constituency and both voters and candidates had to be residents of the particular island for which they sought participation in the elections.

With certain modifications, the provisions of the proclamation of 1773 were embodied in an Act of the local legislature in 1776,[95] which provided for constitutional districts, an increase in the number of representatives, and for the conduct of elections. For the purposes of election, Tortola was divided into three constituencies – Road Division, Eastern Division and Western Division – each to return three members with an additional member for Road Town; Virgin Gorda was divided into two constituencies – Valley Division and South Division – each to return one member with an additional member for Valley Town; and Jost Van Dyke was retained as a single constituency to return two members. The total number of representatives was 15; and new Assemblies were to be elected triennially, 'as a good medium between the shortness of the annual and the length of the Septennial both of which have their disadvantages which this term may meliorate.' Residential qualifications for candidates were eliminated, and in order to ensure the formation of quorums, elected members who refused to serve were subject to a fine of £100.

With the creation of the legislature consisting of a Council and Assembly, the Virgin Islands were given complete control over the regulation of internal matters. Henceforth the islands became a colony of the Leeward Islands. It was in effect an 'auspicious revolution' in government.[96] But the revolution was not complete. For instance, the colony was still under the general administration of the Governor of the Leeward Islands, and in other respects it was subject to imperial legislation. Besides, its laws were subject to the approval of the Governor in the first instance, and then to the power of approval, suspension or veto of the Crown.[97] Though the legislature had the right to make whatever laws it chose these precautions sought to ensure that the laws were not repugnant to the laws of England or unduly restrictive of the royal prerogative.

By 1774, in addition to the legislature, there was in the Virgin Islands, a civil, judicial and military establishment consisting of a Chief Justice appointed by the Governor, a judge of the Vice-Admiralty Court and a Master in Chancery both of whom were also appointed by the Governor, a Collector of the Customs appointed by the Lords of the Treasury in Britain, and a deputy Secretary, a deputy Provost Marshal, and a deputy Naval Officer who were appointed by their principals in Barbados. A Colonel of the Military Regiment was appointed by the Governor in his capacity as Commander-in-Chief of the Leeward Islands.[98] It is of significance for future consideration that though these offices were held by separate individuals there were two exceptions — the office of Collector of Customs held by the Lieutenant-Governor, and that of Colonel of the Military Regiment held by the Chief Justice. Wherever possible, officers were paid in the fees of their respective offices.[99]

In his speech which opened the first legislature on January 31, 1774,[100] Governor Payne stressed the need for immediate action to pass certain laws necessary for the welfare and good government of the Virgin Islands.[101] The legislature's promise of speedy execution of these matters[102] was not, however, matched by a corresponding achievement. The haste with which they proceeded, together with their legislative inexperience, were effective obstacles to successful accomplishment. By April, 1776, only 10 Acts were passed and of these three were rejected, one for being obscure and badly drawn, and two others for not carrying clauses postponing their implementation. Others dealing with the appointment of a colonial agent in Britain, fines and forfeitures, confirmation of marriages, the imposition of a gunpowder tax, the establishment of a militia, and the regulation of the constitution, were provisionally approved by the Governor.[103] These Acts were passed according to models provided by the Governor.[104] Important as these were, they were overshadowed in terms of political significance by three Bills which determined the tone of future developments, and seriously affected the legislative performance of the newly established Assembly.

The first of these Bills was one imposing a 4½% duty on all produce of the Virgin Islands for the benefit of the King. On his arrival in the Virgin Islands to open the new legislature, Governor Payne discovered among all sections of the population great reluctance to pass the Bill.[105] For their part, the Assembly put forward a number of proposals for which they sought prior approval; these included the use of the proceeds of the impost to erect public buildings and cater for other public services, and the postponement of the implementation of the Bill when passed to December 31, 1774.[106] The first was ignored, but as a compromise on the second, Payne agreed to suspend the operation of the Bill to August 20, 1774, when it was finally passed on February 2, 1774.[107]

The other two Bills related to the quieting of possessions, that is, the confirmation of land ownership, and the establishment of Courts of Justice. The need for the better administration of justice in the Virgin Islands had long been recognised. In January, 1774, pending an Act to achieve this, Governor Payne issued an Order for the appointment for six months of a court comprising the members of the Council who were empowered to sit as judges for the recovery of debts and for the removal of impediments to the trade and commerce of the colony.[108] No comparable arrangements could be made to give legal validity to the right of possession to lands held, except those made by the proper legal instruments. In the past, lands in the Virgin Islands had been granted under patents by the Governor of the Leeward Islands.[109] It had become apparent that much of the land thus granted was included in several of the patents, 'by which means and by the loose description and ascertainments of the bounds described in many of the grants' there was great confusion and uncertainty about titles and extent of properties. Consequently there were recurring disputes among title-holders. A new element of conflict was introduced when, with the expansion of cultivation, a few wealthy landowners began to encroach upon the possessions of the poorer inhabitants.[110] The local magistracy had never been able to handle the old problem,[111] and urgent action was needed to deal with the new situation.

The problems relating to the passing of a Court Bill and a Quieting Bill were inter-related. The members of the Council and Assembly who were among the largest landowners were averse to passing a Bill to establish courts prior to a Quieting Bill from fear that these courts would be used to deprive them of their possessions. In 1776, they adopted the expedient of passing a Quieting Bill and a Court Bill and omitting the suspending clauses. By this expedient it was hoped that both would come into operation simultaneously and that thereby possessions would remain secure in so far as the Court Act could not be used to upset titles already confirmed. But both were rejected by the Governor on the additional ground that the Court Act appeared very exceptional in form and that the Quieting Act was 'covered with imperfections.'[112] This seemed to confirm suspicions that an attempt would be made at dispossession, and fears assumed greater proportions by the subsequent insistence that a Court Bill should be passed before a Quieting Bill.[113] The Secretary of State's concurrence in the Governor's opinion that the Quieting Bill was inadequate and improper[114] was regarded as a betrayal of an earlier assurance that the Bill would be given the Royal assent when passed.[115] The situation was further aggravated when a Chief Justice was appointed from Britain to assume jurisdiction of the Virgin Islands, at a salary of £200 a year to be paid from the money received from the 4½% duty,[116] and when the Governor was authorised to establish Courts of Justice without the sanction of an Act of the colonial legislature.[117]

The Council and Assembly were split over the issue involved, but opposition was nevertheless intense. Members of the Assembly refused to take the oaths of allegiance, supremacy and abjuration, or to subscribe to the religious test.[118] The opposition had strong public support. When in 1777 the Governor issued writs for new elections and declared five opposition members of the Assembly ineligible, Dr. James Dawson, a prominent member, refused a seat in the Council to lead the attack in the Assembly to which he secured election.[119] Permission to publish the Governor's patent to establish courts was refused,[120] authority to pay the salary of the Chief Justice was temporarily withheld,[121] and members of the legislature abstained from attending meetings.[122] The legislature's lack of confidence in the Governor found expression in a petition to the Lords of Trade protesting against his withholding assent to the Court and Quieting Bills, and resulted in a delayed contribution to his salary.[123]

Visiting the Virgin Islands in mid-1777, the Governor reported that he had 'never met with such chaos, such a mass of confusion and disorder as in the Virgin Islands.' He found that there was 'a bare shadow of subordination and Government.'[124] By 1778 the situation had worsened. Lawlessness and confusion were reported to dominate inside and outside the legislature, originating according to Governor Burt, 'from an expectation that Lieutenant Governor Nugent will make them a government' independent of the Governor of the Leeward Islands.[125] In this belief he was supported by Chief Justice Suckling.[126] From the absence of intense public discussion of the question of 'secession' beyond a minor resolution to the effect by the Assembly on April 9, 1776,[127] it is apparent that the Governor and Chief Justice exaggerated the seriousness of the desire of Virgin Islanders to be free from central control. Nevertheless even from the limited discussion of the subject it is evident that Virgin Islanders were not averse to using the threat of 'secession' to achieve their ends.

By his too firm attitude and policy of non-appeasement, the Governor had contributed in substantial measure to the state of unrest. His impatience was reflected in his first recommendations to deal with the situation, namely, that the legislative system should be abolished, and that the colony should revert to the system of government by Governor and Council with power to enact laws.[128] His direct interposition to secure political calm and continued legislation was requested by fifteen Virgin Islanders though no method as to how he was to achieve this was suggested.[129] He did not favour the idea of dissolving the Assembly a second time to hold new elections as he believed that not only would the same members in opposition be re-elected,[130] but that the members favourably disposed towards his policy might not be returned.[131] Failing the adoption of his previous solution to the problem, he suggested the annexation of the Virgin Islands to St. Christopher with representatives of both colonies meeting in common session at certain fixed periods to enact legislation for the Virgin Islands, and the adjudication of cases from the Virgin Islands in the courts of St. Christopher until courts were established there.[132]

Instead of accepting these proposals, the British Government sought pacification, and a solution was found to the political impasse by compromise on the Quieting Bill. A slight shift in the British stand was indicated in August, 1778, when Lord Germain, the Secretary of State, issued instructions that the Act for quieting possessions need not be kept back any longer and a draft Bill was prepared and approved by the Board of Trade.[133] The Governor was advised to give his assent to the Bill if it were passed by the Virgin Islands, even if it did not carry a suspending clause.[134] This Bill gave validity to all titles to lands acquired before July 8, 1773, but included several exceptions which could frustrate the intentions of the Act.[135] The effort was at best half-hearted and the legislature responded to this imperfect bill by incorporating the Court Bill and Quieting Bill into one enactment.[136] By so doing it showed its determination not to be coerced into acceptance of an unpopular measure and its unwillingness to compromise. In the end the British Government gave a firm guarantee to waive its right to all lands settled without grant which had been effectively barred by the provision of the draft Quieting Bill.[137] The way was paved for the separate and willing adoption of both the Court Bill and Quieting Bill in 1783 by the legislature of the Virgin Islands.

After a decade of political unrest the Virgin Islands settled down to constitutional rule. In July, 1785, Governor Shirley, who had replaced Burt in April, 1781, could report that the Virgin Islands were beginning 'to feel the beneficial effects of good order' and he had little doubt, 'that in the process of time they will be a very well regulated community.'[138]

Inadequacy of population and of productivity had been the fundamental obstacles to the introduction of constitutional government. To a large extent both were due to the adverse attitude of the British Government and successive Governors of the Leeward Islands. This attitude explains the abortive attempts of John Walton after 1711 and Governor Mathew in 1735 to secure a more regular system of government for the islands, though the former was rebuffed also for over self-ambition and the reactionary nature of his proposals, and the latter because he had insufficiently prepared the British Government for the change. The gradual evolution of government, or rather administration for such it was, by deputy-governors after 1672, to Justices of the Peace and deputy-governors after 1724, to Councils and deputy-governors after 1735, was the natural concomitant to slow economic development. Relatively rapid population increase and, as a consequence, economic prosperity after 1735 made the maintenance of the several offices and expenses of a properly constituted government possible, and pointed the way for the establishment of a legislature consisting of Council and Assembly in 1773, after temporary deferment by war.

The preponderance of the new inhabitants on Tortola rather than on Virgin Gorda which, until around 1720, was the major island, and their concentration on sugar production instead of cotton as in the other islands, shifted the economic and consequently the political balance, and led to the emergence of Tortola as the premier island of the group. The concentration of governmental activity, culminating in the establishment of the legislature there in 1773, was in recognition of the superior status of the island.

The character of the inhabitants was fashioned by the isolated position of the islands, their neglect by the Governor, and their long denial of government. Grown accustomed as they were to almost unlimited freedom unchecked by regulations, their natural inclination rebelled against attempts designed to impose undesirable legislation upon them. This behaviour was exemplified by their reaction to the Quieting and Court Bills. And being accustomed only to an occasional impost to satisfy immediate and urgent public requirements they sought to evade the burden of regular taxation, as shown in their attempt to obstruct the introduction of the 4½% levy on their produce. This opposition to taxation was to remain a persisting characteristic of Virgin Islanders and eventually resulted in fundamental changes in the economic and political structure of the colony.

[1]   C.S.P. 1696-1697. No. 1347.
[2]   C.O. 153/2. An Account of Statia, Sabea and Tortola. (1672)
[3]   C.S.P. 1696-1697. No. 1347.
[4]   Ibid.
[5]   C.S.P. 1708-1709. No. 597.
[6]   C.S.P. 1675-1676. No. 1152.
[7]   C.O. 153/2. Stapleton to the C.T.P., 22 Nov., 1676; C.S.P. 1675-1676. No. 954; C.S.P. 1677-1680. Journal of the Council and Assembly of St. Christopher, 29 April, 1677; and, No. 599.
[8]   C.O. 153/3. Stapleton to the C.T.P., 11 Nov., 1682.
[9]   C.S.P. 1677-1680. Nos. 404 and 741.
[10]   C.S.P. 1677-1680. No. 1418.
[11]   C.S.P. 1696-1697. No. 1347.
[12]   C.S.P. 1685-1688. No. 520.

[13] C.S.P. 1714-1715. No. 668.
[14] C.S.P. 1716-1717. No. 153.
[15] C.S.P. 1716-1717. No. 350.
[16] C.S.P. 1708-1709. No. 597.
[17] Ibid.
[18] C.S.P. 1714-1715. No. 464.
[19] C.S.P. 1710-1711. Nos. 705 and 731.
[20] C.S.P. 1710-1711. Nos. 601 and 731.
[21] C.S.P. 1710-1711. No. 801.
[22] C.S.P. 1710-1711. Nos. 740 and 801.
[23] C.S.P. 1710-1711. No. 731.
[24] Ibid.
[25] C.S.P. 1710-1711. Nos. 601 and 813.
[26] C.S.P. 1710-1711. No. 813.
[27] Cf. C.S.P. 1714-1715. No. 586.
[28] C.S.P. 1714-1715. No. 620, C.S.P. 1716-1718. No. 118; and C.S.P. 1717-1718. No. 298.
[29] C.S.P. 1717-1718. No. 298. Enc. Nos. 4, 6, 8, and 9.
[30] C.S.P. 1714-1715. Nos. 614 and 648.
[31] C.S.P. 1716-1717. No. 639.
[32] C.S.P. 1717-1718. No. 298.
[33] C.S.P. 1717-1718. No. 408.
[34] C.S.P. 1717-1718. No. 487.
[35] C.S.P. 1714-1715. No. 613.
[36] C.S.P. 1714-1715. No. 609.
[37] C.S.P. 1716-1717. No. 118.
[38] C.S.P. 1720-1721. No. 204.
[39] C.S.P. 1720-1721. Nos. 213, 288, 459, 500, 597, and 640.
[40] C.S.P. 1724-1725. No. 260.
[41] Ibid.
[42] Ibid.
[43] Ibid.
[44] Ibid.
[45] C.S.P. 1735-1736. No. 168; C.O. 152/22. No. W. 32. Mathew to the C.T.P., 14 Nov., 1735.
[46] C.S.P. 1724-1725. No. 692.
[47] C.S.P. 1728-1729. No. 24.
[48] Ibid., C.S.P. 1734-1735. No. 216. In this respect a Deputy-Governor suffered similarly: 'if his cudgell happen to be a whit less than a sturdy subject's, Good-night Governour'. The difficulty of securing Deputy-Governors always acceptable to all parties sometimes added to the problems of maintaining law and order in the Virgin Islands where the inhabitants lived 'like so many bandits in open defiance of the laws of God and man.'
[49] C.S.P. 1734-1735. No. 216.
[50] C.S.P. 1737. No. 148. Enc.
[51] Ibid.
[52] C.O. 152/22. No. W. 95. Mathew to the C.T.P. 5 Feb., 1737.

[53] C.S.P. 1735-1736. No. 105.
[54] C.S.P. 1735-1736. No. 168.
[55] C.S.P. 1735-1736. No. 60.
[56] C.S.P. 1735-1736. No. 168.
[57] C.S.P. 1737. No. 148.
[58] C.O. 152/27. No. Aa. 39. Purcell to the C.T.P., 11 July , 1751.
[59] C.O. 152/23. No. 27. Dinwiddy to the C.T.P., 29 April, 1740.
[60] C.O. 152/54. Enc. in Payne to Dartmouth, 26 June, 1774. No. 17.
[61] C.O. 152/27. No. Aa. 39. Purcell to the C.T.P., 11 July, 1751
[62] C.O. 152/23. No. 77. Dinwiddy to the C.T.P., 29 April, 1740.
[63] C.O. 152/23. The Virgin Islands: An Account received from Lieutenant General Fleming, 18 May, 1740.
[64] C.O. 152/27. No. Aa 77. Purcell to the C.T.P., 11 July, 1751.
[65] C.S.P. 1724-1725. No. 260.
[66] C.O. 152/45. Fleming to Bedford, 10 Nov., 1750; C.O. 152/47. Aa. 40. Colon to Mathew, 22 Nov., 1749; C.O. 152/45. Enc. in Fleming to Holderness, 14 Dec., 1751; C.O. 152/28. No. BC.7. and BC.8. Enc. in Thomas to the C.T.P. 6 Feb., 1754.
[67] C.O. 152/47 Enc. in C.T.P. to Halifax, 1 March, 1765; C.O. 152/30. No. Dd. 41. Purcell to the C.T.P., Feb., 1764; C.O. 152/53. Enc. in Payne to Dartmouth, 24 July, 1773. No. 8; C.O. 152/60. Enc. in Burt to Germain, 26 Sept., 1780. No. 93; C.O. 152/60. Germain to Burt, 7 Dec., 1780. No. 43.
[68] C.O. 152/27. No. Aa 39. Purcell to the C.T.P., 11 July, 1751.
[69] C.O. 152/23. No. 77. Dinwiddy to the C.T.P., 29 April, 1740.
[70] C.O. 152/27. No. Aa. 39. Purcell to the C.T.P., 11 July, 1751; C.O. 153/18. Representation to the King, 20 March, 1755; Journal of the Commissioners of Trade and Plantations, Jan., 1749/1750-Dec., 1753. (H.M.S.O., London, 1933.) p. 271.
[71] C.O. 152/23. No. 77. Dinwiddy to the C.T.P., 29 April, 1740.
[72] C.S.P. 1724-1725. No. 260.
[73] C.O. 152/28. No. Bc83, and No. Bc86. A List of the Inhabitants of the Islands of Tortola and Spanish Town. . . . taken on 1 Jan., 1756; also, C.O. 152/44. Mathew to Newcastle, 13 Oct., 1740.
[74] C.O. 152/55. Nugent to Dartmouth, 30 July, 1775.
[75] C.O. 152/27. Purcell to the C.T.P., 11 July, 1751; C.O. 152/27. No. Aa. 41. Extract of a letter from James Purcell, 26 Dec., 1751.
[76] C.O. 152/27. No. Aa. 75. Purcell to Hill, 31 Jan., 1753.
[77] Journal of the Commissioners of Trade and Plantations, Jan., 1754-Dec., 1758. (H.M.S.O., London, 1933.) pp. 102 and 114.
[78] C.O. 153/18. C.T.P. to Thomas, 6 Aug., and 8 Oct., 1755.
[79] C.O. 152/27. No. Aa. 75. Purcell to Hill, 31 Jan., 1753.
[80] C.O. 152/28. No. Bc. 82 Thomas to the C.T.P., 12 Aug., 1755.
[81] Ibid.; also, Letter to George Thomas, 6 Aug., 1755.
[82] C.O. 152/50. Woodley to Hillsborough, 7 Nov., 1769. No. 27; and Hillsborough to Woodley, 23 Feb., 1770. No. 22.
[83] C.O. 152/53. Payne to Dartmouth, 20 Jan., 1773; Payne to Dartmouth, 4 April, 1773, and enc.; Payne to Dartmouth, 24 July, 1773. No. 8; C.O. 152/32. No.

Ff. 48. Payne to Dartmouth, 10 June, 1773. No.6.

[84] C.O. 152/53. Dartmouth to Payne, 5 July, 1773. No. 10.

[85] C.O. 152/51. Losack to Hillsborough, 28 Feb., 1771. No. 10.

[86] C.O. 152/51. Hillsborough to Losack, 4 May, 1771. No. 30.

[87] C.O. 152/32. No. Ff. 48. Payne to Dartmouth, 10 June, 1773. No. 6.

[88] C.O. 152/54. Enc. in Payne to Dartmouth, 26 June, 1774. No. 17.

[89] C.O. 152/53. Enc. in Payne to Dartmouth, 4 April, 1773.

[90] C.O. 152/32. No. Ff. 48. Payne to Dartmouth, 10 June, 1773. No. 6.

[91] C.O. 152/53. Dartmouth to Payne, 5 July, 1773. No. 10; and 6 Oct., 1773.

[92] C.O. 152/54. Payne to Dartmouth, 24 Jan., 1774. No. 14.

[93] C.O. 152/54. Dartmouth to Payne, 6 April, 1774. No. 14.

[94] C.O. 152/40. Enc. in Payne to Dartmouth, 17 Dec., 1773. No. 12; C.O. 152/54. Payne to Dartmouth, 6 Oct., 1773. No. 10.

[95] C.O. 315/1. Act No. 7.

[96] C.O. 152/54. Payne to Dartmouth, 2 March, 1774. No. 15.

[97] C.O. 152/53. Dartmouth to Payne, 5 July, 1773. No. 10.

[98] C.O. 152/54. Enc. in Payne to Dartmouth, 26 June, 1774. No. 17.

[99] Ibid; C.O. 152/28. No. Bc. 82.

[100] C.O. 316/1. Meeting of the Council in Road Town on Monday, 31 Jan., 1774. The first meeting between the Governor, Council and Assembly was on 27 Jan., 1774, when members were sworn in.

[101] C.O. 152/54. Enc. No. 1 in Payne to Dartmouth, 2 March, 1774. No. 15.

[102] C.O. 152/54. Enc. No. 2 and No. 3 in Payne to Dartmouth, 2 March, 1774. No. 15.

[103] C.O. 152/55. Nugent to Germain, 20 April, 1776; and Greathead to Germain, 31 Oct., 1776.

[104] C.O. 152/54. Payne to Dartmouth, 6 Oct., 1773. No. 10; and Payne to Dartmouth, 2 March, 1774. No. 15.

[105] C.O. 152/54. Payne to Dartmouth, 2 March, 1774. No. 15.

[106] Ibid., and enc.

[107] C.O. 152/54. Payne to Dartmouth, 2 March, 1774. No. 15.

[108] Ibid.

[109] C.O. 152/27. No. Aa. 39. Purcell to the C.T.P., 11 July, 1751; C.O. 152/22. No. W. 95. Mathew to the C.T.P., 5 Feb., 1737.

[110] C.O. 152/27. No. Aa. 75. Purcell to Hill, 31 Jan., 1753; C.O. 152/53. Payne to Dartmouth, 23 July, 1773. No. 7.

[111] C.O. 152/27. No. Aa. 75. Purcell to Hill, 31 Jan., 1753.

[112] C.O. 152/55. Greathead to Germain, 27 March, 1776.

[113] C.O. 152/55. Germain to Greathead, 9 Oct., 1776; C.O. 316/1. Minutes of a Meeting of the Council held on 24 Feb., 1775.

[114] C.O. 152/55. Germain to Greathead, 17 May, 1776.

[115] C.O. 152/55. Germain to Nugent, 23 Dec., 1775; Germain to Greathead, 23 Dec., 1775.

[116] George Suckling: An Historical Account of the Virgin Islands in the West Indies. (London, 1780) p. 65; C.O. 152/34. Suckling to Germain, 17 Nov., 1778; C.O. 314/1. Treasury to Customs, 1 June, 1779. George Suckling who had been Attorney General at Quebec, was appointed Chief Justice in Oct., 1777. He arrived

in the Virgin Islands on 22 Jan., 1778, and remained Chief Justice until his death in January, 1783.

[117]   C.O. 152/58. Germain to Burt, 5 Aug., 1778. No. 16.
[118]   C.O. 152/33. No. Gg. 86. Burt to Germain, 30 July, 1777.
[119]   Ibid.
[120]   C.O. 152/59. Burt to Germain, 2 Nov., 1778. No. 21, and 24 May, 1779. No. 39.
[121]   George Suckling: An Historical Account of the Virgin Islands. (London, 1780); C.O. 152/34. Suckling to Germain, 17 Nov., 1778.
[122]   C.O. 316/2. No Meeting of the Council and Assembly was held between 17 July, 1777 and 8 April, 1778, because of lack of a quorum.
[123]   C.O. 152/33. No. Gg. 72. Pownall to C.T.P., 23 Oct., 1776.
[124]   C.O. 152/77. No. Gg. 86. Burt to Germain, 30 July, 1777.
[125]   C.O. 152/33. No. Gg. 86. Burt to Germain, 30 July, 1777; C.O. 152/88. Burt to Germain, 28 April, 1778.
[126]   George Suckling: An Historical Account of the Virgin Islands . . . (London, 1780) pp. 44-47.
[127]   C.O. 316/1. Minutes of the Assembly, 9 April, 1776.
[128]   C.O. 152/33. No. Gg. 86. Burt to Germain, 30 July, 1777.
[129]   C.O. 152/33. No. Gg. 87. Petition: Tortolans to Burt. (1777)
[130]   C.O. 152/34. No. Hh. 8. Burt to Germain, 1 Nov., 1777.
[131]   C.O. 152/58. Burt to Germain, 28 April, 1778.
[132]   C.O. 152/34. No. Hh. 8. Burt to Germain, 1 Nov., 1777.
[133]   C.O. 152/58. Germain to Burt, 5 Aug., 1778. No. 16.
[134]   Ibid.; C.O. 152/59. Germain to Burt, 3 March, 1779. No. 20.
[135]   C.O. 152/34. No. Hh. 32. Jackson to the C.T.P., 1 Dec., 1778.
[136]   C.O. 152/32. Enc. in Townshend to Shirley, 11 Sept., 1782.
[137]   Ibid.
[138]   C.O. 152/64. Shirley to Sydney, 23 July, 1785. No. 115.

Chapter 3

Era of Prosperity and Decline

The decision to institute constitutional government in the Virgin Islands was taken against the general background of their greater economic prosperity. By 1773 the Virgin Islands had advanced considerably economically from the position they occupied before the middle of the eighteenth century, and this prosperity was to continue for some time longer before the blight of depression set in.

In the second half of the eighteenth and the early nineteenth centuries, three major wars occurred – the Seven Years' War (1756-1763), the American War of Independence (1775-1783), and the French Revolutionary and Napoleonic Wars (1793-1815). None of them was West Indian in origin but the West Indies became directly involved as colonies of participating powers. The period covered by these wars was one of unprecedented economic prosperity for the British Virgin Islands since circumstances they created favoured prosperity.

The freedom of the islands from external enemy attack, despite continuous threats, allowed full advantage to be taken of the price boom during the second half of the eighteenth century. Other factors boosted the development of an otherwise sluggish economy, namely, the indulgence by the colonists in privateering and smuggling to provide for the deficiencies created by war, and the institution of a Court of Vice-Admiralty in Tortola for the detention, trial and condemnation of captured enemy vessels. Also important were the extension of trading opportunities through the adoption of free port and other facilities, the introduction of the convoy system to safeguard exports to Britain, and the establishment of a packet station in Road Town to facilitate communication. Even so the islands were never free from the threat of depression and when the wars ended they lapsed into their former insignificance.

Because of the recurring incidence of war in the eighteenth century, Virgin Islanders and those who were associated with them in trade were always fearful of enemy attack.[1] This was especially so since they apparently lacked the means of adequate self-protection. Appeals to the British Government for arms and ammunition failed to produce results since it was considered that similar appeals from other colonies would lead to far too onerous expense.[2] Reliance had to be placed on the British naval force stationed in Antigua for the defence of the Leeward Islands generally and on the promise of the Admiral to take measures to counter possible attacks.[3] The response of the Governor of the Leeward Islands was typical of the general attitude towards requests by Virgin Islanders for military assistance. He believed that the legislature of the Virgin Islands should take measures to muster local resources for self-defence.[4] But local initiative was retarded until 1774 by the absence of a legislature, and thereafter until 1783 by the unsettled political situation. Moreover, the jealousies which existed between the two branches of the legislature on matters of finance and taxation threatened on several occasions to block effective action.[5] Nevertheless Powder Acts and Militia Acts enabled local defences to be strengthened.[6] With the establishment of settled constitutional government after 1785 enabling the adoption of money bills thereafter, the question of finance for fortifications did not pose an unsurmountable obstacle. Increased and heavy expenditure on fortifications was shown in a return in 1801 by which time a sum of almost £36,724 currency had been expended.[7] Such precautions, however, could not remove the fundamental dependence on external naval assistance in case of heavy enemy attack with warships and frigates.

As a result of repeated threats against the Virgin Islands in 1794 and 1795, arrangements were so made in distributing the ships of the Leeward Islands squadron throughout the extended command that the best protection could be given to every colony.[8] These contributed to the better security of the entire region though their effectiveness was greatly reduced by the necessity to use some of the ships to protect convoys to Britain.[9] It was probably only the supremacy of British sea-power in the Caribbean which averted actual invasion of the Virgin Islands. But it is doubtful, considering the proximity of St. Thomas and the facilities it afforded as a base for privateers and enemy vessels,

Pleasant Valley, Tortola, showing the estate of William Isaacs, from a contemporary drawing.

The Virgin Islands from English and Danish Surveys by Thomas Jefferys, Geographer to the King. Published by Robert Sayer, London, 1775.

whether the Virgin Islands could ever have considered themselves altogether free from the possibility of attack. It was not until the Danish Islands were captured by Britain in March, 1801, and again in December, 1807, after being restored by the Treaty of Amiens in March, 1802, and retained under British control for the duration of the war with Napoleon, that the Virgin Islands were safe from invasion organised from St. Thomas.

Under the British mercantilist laws, the staple colonial products were marketed in Britain. Because of the restrictions imposed on trade in staples such as sugar and cotton, with foreign countries, the condition of the British market would naturally determine the prospect of profitable cultivation in the colonies. It would mean, for instance, that if prices were high a stimulus would be given to plantation agriculture; alternatively, if prices were low, the disincentive could lead to depression. British West Indian agriculture was considerably influenced by this fundamental principle.

By the middle of the eighteenth century sugar produced in the British colonies could no longer meet the rising British and American demands. The shortage of supplies, further aggravated by war, resulted in a heavy increase in price compared with the first half of the century, and a consequent increase in production. Between 1733 and 1747, for instance, the price of sugar rose from 16/11¼ to 42/7½ a cwt.[10] Despite fluctuations, the high prices were maintained throughout the century, with higher peaks during the periods of war, culminating under the impetus of the revolution in St. Domingue and civil disturbances in the French West Indian colonies which created a scarcity in the European market, in the highest maximum for the eighteenth century of 83/- a cwt. and 87/- a cwt. in 1798 and 1799 respectively.[11] Cotton, the other major product of the Virgin Islands, was also given the stimulus of higher prices during the second half of the eighteenth century especially after 1770. The rapidly increasing demand for cotton by British cloth manufacturers of the Industrial Revolution could not be met from the traditional markets in the East. The chief beneficiaries were the West Indian colonies, and their sea-island cotton obtained a ready market in Britain until it was gradually driven out by the less expensive green seed cotton of the southern states of America during the early nineteenth century.

In the main, the emphasis in the Virgin Islands was on sugar production, and by 1759, the value of sugar exported to Britain exceeded that of cotton. Because of smuggling, it would be incorrect to attribute the whole increase to local production. Nevertheless, sugar-cane cultivation was expanded, sometimes at the expense of other agricultural products. In Tortola cotton lands were converted into sugar-cane fields, and cotton estates contiguous to sugar estates were absorbed by them. As President Fahie reported in 1784, 'It is here as it is elsewhere the large fish swallow up the small.'[12] Slave grounds were also reduced to accommodate sugar-cane cultivation, and sub-marginal sugar producing lands were allocated to slaves and cotton production. One result was the concentration of cotton on the outlying islands of Virgin Gorda, Peter Island, Salt Island and Cooper Island which were less suited to sugar-cane production. Even Anegada with its porous limestone and patches of cultivable ground, which by 1784 was just beginning to be settled, was devoted to cotton.[13] To facilitate cotton production the legislature in 1783 prohibited slaves from growing the crop hitherto permitted by the planters.[14] It was evidently an attempt by planters to limit the economic activities of slaves in their own behalf; henceforth slave grounds devoted to cotton could be utilised by the planters for their own benefit.

An indication of the increased production of sugar and cotton in the Virgin Islands, can be seen in the exports to Britain. In 1748, 1,475 cwt. of sugar valued at £2,029 were exported; in 1759, 8,799 cwt. valued at £12,540; and in 1770, 23,050 cwt. valued at £31,794. In 1774 just before the outbreak of the American War, and in 1792 following the outbreak of the revolution in St. Domingue, 33,963 cwt. and 51,707 cwt. valued at £46,699 and £70,409 respectively were exported.[15] Increased production of cotton can be seen in the fact that whereas in 1780 cotton exports to Britain amounted to about 212,465 pounds valued at £7,080, in 1792 exports totalled 765,063 pounds valued at £27,061. These quantities included an indefinite amount of smuggled and condemned goods, but these were probably more than offset by amounts exported to North America.[16]

Throughout the American and French wars the over-powering fear among Virgin Islanders was that of offensive action by enemy privateers. But this fear did not prevent them from adopting measures designed to weaken and destroy the enemy's commerce and influence around the Virgin Islands. By so doing, they ensured their own safety to some extent, and gained financially. Their chief instruments were the privateers whom they fitted out to prey upon vessels which plied the sea about the Virgin Islands, primarily those trading with St. Thomas and St. Bartholomew.

It is not known when privateering by Virgin Islanders started, and the first clear incident occurred over the *Nuestra Senora de Guadeloupe*. In August, 1750, the Spanish Frigate *Nuestra Senora* and a number of merchantmen which it was convoying from Havana to Spain were forced to seek shelter from a storm when they were off the coast of North Carolina in America. Here, while awaiting the outcome of efforts by the British Governor of the territory to impose a heavy levy on the cargoes of the vessels, the crew of *Nuestra Senora* mutinied at the instigation of its mate. Part of its cargo was subsequently loaded into two bilanders one of which was manned by Owen Lloyd and some other Englishmen.[17] It was estimated that this vessel contained 55 chests each with about 3,000 dollars in silver coin, two chests of Church and other wrought plate, and other cargo including 120 serons of cochineal, 17 bags of indigo, and 60 bags of tobacco, all to the total value of about 250,000 Spanish dollars. The other vessel perished on reefs but Lloyd and his vessel escaped. After landing at St. Croix where he disposed of some of the money, he proceeded to Norman Island, one of the Virgins situated a few miles south of Tortola, where he buried the loot. Lloyd and some of his confederates then proceeded to St. Eustatius where they were apprehended. Meanwhile, Tortolans who had heard of the treasure buried on Norman Island acquired and divided it among themselves.

As a result of the prompt and energetic but compromising action of Gilbert Fleming, Lieutenant-General of the Leeward Islands, at least a part of the booty was recovered. On being informed of the plunder, Fleming who regarded it as a 'national as well as important concern,' proceeded immediately to Tortola with two companies of soldiers. *En route* he secured William Blackstock one of Lloyd's associates, who had been arrested and detained by Deputy-Governor Gumbs of Anguilla, and who made a full confession of the piracy. Arriving at Tortola on November 25, Fleming by 'a mixture of mildness with resolution,' as he described it, obtained the support of Abraham Chalwill, the acting Lieutenant-Governor (who had led in the search for and shared in the treasure on Norman Island) and of the Council which enabled him to issue a proclamation offering a reward of one-third of all moneys returned by those who had any. In the end a sum of $20,429 together with a quantity of cochineal, indigo and hides was recovered, the people themselves being allowed to retain $7,514.[18]

In the early years of the settlement of the Virgin Islands, the inhabitants had been accustomed to deal with pirates though it is not evident that they indulged in piracy themselves. The incident of the *Nuestra Senora* proved to be a turning point in their attitude towards maritime exploits, and opportunities were provided by the outbreak of war in 1756. Their activities were recognised and given official backing when on the outbreak of the Seven Years' War a Vice-Admiralty Court was established in Tortola,[19] to deal with captures brought into port by the privateers. It does not appear that the Judge of the Court was very discriminating, and even neutral vessels were sometimes condemned.[20]

In contrast with the Seven Years' War, and to a less extent with the French Wars, the period of the American War of Independence was the 'golden age' of privateering for the Virgin Islands. The declaration of independence by the American colonies in 1776 was followed by the seizure by American privateers of several vessels trading with the Virgin Islands. In 1776, for instance, six vessels leaving the Virgin Islands with cargoes including 1,421 hogsheads and 23 barrels sugar, 225 bales cotton, 73 puncheons rum and 186 tons fustic, and two other ships bound for the colony loaded with British manufactures valued at £10,000 and Irish salted provisions were captured.[21] In retaliation, a number of the most wealthy and influential planters, merchants and marines of Tortola, including Richard Hetherington who later became Chief Justice of the Virgin Islands, equipped and armed seven sloops and two schooners to operate against American vessels which traded with the neighbouring islands. As a result of their activities, seizure was made of twenty-nine vessels trading between several American ports and the islands of St. Thomas, St. Croix, St. Eustatius, St. Domingue, Guadeloupe and Martinique, and carrying cargoes chiefly of lumber, textiles, foodstuffs and munitions valued at about £18,000 sterling.[22] These were tried and condemned by the Vice-Admiralty Court in Tortola which awarded half of the prize to the Crown and the other half to the captors.[23]

Prompted by the losses they had suffered, and the efforts they were making for their own protection unaided by the British squadron, Virgin Islanders successfully petitioned the king to be allowed to retain the whole of the net proceeds from captures.[24] After 1777 there was a significant broadening of the privateering policy of the British Government. In June, Governors of the British West Indies were for the first time empowered to grant letters of marque to vessels fitted out in the islands. In addition, privateers were permitted a greater share of the spoils taken. Previously the most that could be expected without special permission was one half. Henceforth, while non-commissioned vessels still had to depend on the benevolence of the Crown for their reward, owners of commissioned vessels were permitted to retain the whole of whatever prizes they made.[25] The advantage taken of these changes was seen in the fact that by 1783, even members of the Council and Assembly were engaged in privateering.[26]

The step between legal capture of American vessels and illicit plunder of neutral ships was not wide, and the middle years of the American War of Independence were filled with reports of Danish vessels being taken by Virgin Islands privateers and condemned. As in the case of action against American vessels, the aggression of Virgin Islanders against the Danes was retaliative. It was sparked off by repeated reports of Danish ill-usage of, and partiality against Britishers in St. Thomas.[27] Evidences of such discrimination, however, were eclipsed in importance by the repeated instances of recognition which the Danes accorded the Americans: constant exchanges of salutes between American vessels and the forts of St. Croix;[28] shelter given to American agents;[29] and permission given to American privateers to operate from St. Thomas against vessels trading with the Virgin Islands.[30] Reports also confirmed the long held suspicion that American factors were residing in the Danish Islands, especially at St. Croix, where they had established trading factories, and were publicly receiving consignments which were sold there or were covered as Danish property and transmitted to Europe.[31]

In an attempt to put an end to these practices Governor Burt brought in the privateers of the Virgin Islands as the instrument of his policy of retaliation.[32] The fact that not all owners of armed vessels applied for commissions made no difference to his intention to countenance their activities. The effect of this policy was soon evident. In March, 1778, Baron Druyer, the Danish ambassador in London, forwarded two memorials to the Earl of Suffolk, the British Foreign Minister, complaining of the capture, detention and condemnation of several vessels engaged in trade with the Danish West Indies. The most important of these were two brigantines *La Dorothea* and *L' Elizabeth Christine,* which in June, 1777, had been seized and taken into Tortola by some non-commissioned armed vessels as they sailed from St. Croix for Dunkirk and Amsterdam respectively with cargoes of tobacco, rice and rum.[33] The result was that strict orders were issued to prevent future irregularities or unfriendly conduct towards the Danes,[34] and for the restoration to the Danish claimants of the produce of the sale of the two vessels.[35]

Expectations that Virgin Islanders would be deterred by instructions issued in London, especially as they had the support of the Governor, were disappointed.[36] The seizure and condemnation of neutral vessels continued, encouraged by the favourable operation of the Vice-Admiralty Court. And because there were no civil courts in the colony, damages could not be sued for and recovered, and no reparation could be obtained by the injured parties against the owners of privateers. The replacement of Burt by Thomas Shirley as Governor of the Leeward Islands, in April, 1781, enabled the British Government to take more effective action to secure compliance with its directions. To curb the action of the privateers which threatened to disrupt the relations between Britain and neutral countries, Shirley was ordered to suspend the operation of the Vice-Admiralty Court, and to require bonds from an acceptable surety resident in another part of the Leeward Islands, before granting letters of marque to any Virgin Islander.[37] These instructions were implemented in December, 1781.[38]

If the aim of the British Government was to teach Virgin Islanders a lesson, it succeeded. Privateering, primarily on American vessels trading with the Danish West Indies, constituted the only means whereby Virgin Islanders could obtain their supplementary supplies of lumber, flour and other foodstuff which had previously been obtained by legal trade with the American colonies. The outbreak of the war had brought a cessation of this legitimate intercourse. With the suspension of the Vice-Admiralty Court, supplies were cut off completely.[39] Their 'extremely hard' condition reported by the Governor,[40] eventually led to the restoration of the Court towards the end of 1782, but this was accompanied by the understanding that 'the late restraint they have been under will have a tendency to check in future such unwarrantable and unprecedented proceedings as have been practised by the privateers belonging to those islands.'[41] The end of the American War shortly after gave very little opportunity to Virgin Islanders to take advantage of the renewed privilege.

During the French Revolutionary and Napoleonic Wars privateering was of less importance to the Virgin Islands than it had been during the American War. Four factors were responsible for this: the firm attitude of John Stanley, acting Governor of the Leeward Islands, in restraining the activities of privateers; the expansion of trading opportunities by the Virgin Islands; the better policing of the surrounding sea by British ships of war; and finally, the capture of the Danish Islands by Britain.

To guard as much as possible against the irregularities that were being daily committed by all privateers in the Leeward Islands, Stanley decided on a strict adherence to the system of bonding those commissioned. Virgin Islanders retaliated by refusing to apply for letters of marque; when the first application without the required security was rejected, no further application was made.[42] Nevertheless, Stanley's action had produced the desired results. Existing registers of official statistics show that between 1793 and 1803 only eight vessels had been captured, while between 1803 and 1815, there were 82 captures. None of these was taken by privateers. Indeed, in 1806 it was reported that Tortola had no privateers.[43]

The absence of heavy privateering activities by Virgin Islanders during the Napoleonic Wars (1803-1815) can be attributed in part to the fact that for the greater part of the period the Danish Islands which had previously acted as ports of convenience for enemy vessels, thus making privateering prospects particularly attractive, were brought under British control. The presence of British naval vessels in and around Tortola made privateering by non-commissioned vessels hazardous. The naval vessels also performed the functions of privateers and made these superfluous. Another influential factor was the diversion from privateering created by the agitation for and the eventual adoption of free port and other wider trading opportunities by the Virgin Islands after 1801.

Under the laws of trade and navigation governing colonial commerce, the import and export trade of the British colonies was confined to Britain to the exclusion of vessels owned and navigated by foreigners. The privilege allowed to foreign colonial vessels to enter certain British West Indian ports under free port acts, and to import and export certain types of goods, was not a departure from the principles laid down in the navigation acts. Goods that could be imported were those which did not compete with British and colonial products, and goods that could be exported were confined to those which Britain wanted to sell to foreigners.

The principle of establishing free ports in selected British West Indian islands had been accepted and implemented by the British Government as early as 1766 when free ports were created in Jamaica and Dominica. Thereafter, the principle had been extended to include Grenada, the Bahamas, Bermuda, Antigua, the Caicos Islands, Tobago and Trinidad. Despite efforts made in 1753 by James Purcell, and in 1776 by the

House of Assembly, to secure free port privileges, it was not until 1802 that any positive result was achieved. St. Thomas, where a free port had been in existence since 1764, had recently been captured by the British.

Free port privileges had made St. Thomas into one of the most important trading centres in the Caribbean. Indeed, considering its size it was second in importance only to St. Eustatius. While it was under British control, its immense trade with the United States was sufficiently disrupted to encourage Virgin Islanders to petition for similar free port privileges. The intention was to seize the trading benefits from St. Thomas before the island was returned to Denmark.

A number of specific advantages was envisaged from the establishment of a free port in Tortola. Because of the colony's strategic geographical position a free port would promote the most valuable and lucrative commercial intercourse with the surrounding non-British colonies, in almost every specie of colonial commodity. The resulting diminution, if not total annihilation, of the trade with St. Thomas would prevent enemy forces from procuring supplies there in future, and that it would eventually encourage the British merchants in St. Thomas and Curacao to transfer their capital and other resources to Tortola. Essential supplies of livestock and mill-timber which Virgin Islanders had previously been forced to import from Puerto Rico illegally would now be obtained by legitimate commerce and on more moderate terms. In addition, they could not fail to experience the vivifying influence of being an emporium for trade, 'for commerce, like the Nile, always leaves some deposit, and thereby fertilizes the country through which it flows,' as it was put.[44]

Representation of the advantages anticipated was accompanied by a number of specific proposals by which it was believed they could be achieved.[45] However, these conflicted with British policy, and so the enabling instruments merely embodied the main provisions of free port acts already in force, and allowed a number of enumerated commodities including sugar, coffee, tobacco, livestock, and all sorts of wood, to be imported into the Virgin Islands in foreign single-decked vessels from foreign European colonies in America. They could later be re-exported to Britain.[46]

The Tortola Free Port Act of 1802 was scheduled to be in force for one year until July 1, 1803, but it was not until October, 1802, that the regulations were brought into effect. In 1803, therefore, attempts were made to secure a renewal of the Act and the inclusion of provisions previously denied, namely, direct exportation in British vessels of all legal imports to friendly European ports, the free importation of foreign goods in British vessels, and free intercourse with America.[47] The extension of free port privileges was refused as being contrary to the principles of the laws of trade and the provisions of all free port acts.[48] Nevertheless, the Tortola Free Port Act was renewed in 1803, and in 1805 the privileges were made perpetual.[49] Finally in 1806, foreign sugar and coffee were allowed to be imported into and exported from Road Harbour free of duty.[50]

As a corollary to the extension and expansion of free port facilities in the Virgin Islands, a licensed trade with St. Domingue was permitted to British colonial vessels in 1806.[51] In order to save time and expense, the Governor of the Leeward Islands was empowered to authorise the President of the Council, the Chief Justice or the Collector of Customs, of the Virgin Islands, to grant the licences. At the same time, the Governor was authorised to grant licences to vessels belonging to non-British subjects to trade between Tortola and foreign colonies.[52]

Illegal trade by Virgin Islanders had existed from the early years of the settlement, but it was given impetus by the ensuing wars, and by the failure of Customs officials to enforce the laws of trade when these had been brought into operation in the Virgin Islands. Smuggling was often given unconcealed support by these officials especially before the institution of civil government in 1773. The Danes in St. Thomas and in St. Croix were permitted to export their sugar to England as British produce by obtaining false clearances from obliging Collectors in Tortola and Virgin Gorda. Part of the explanation lay in the arrangement whereby Collectors were appointed by and were subject to the authority of the Surveyor General in Barbados, rather than immediately to the Governor of the Leeward Islands, and as they received no salaries 'so make what advantages they can and anyhow, and are so indifferent as to the value of their station that keeping it or losing it, is of little or no concern to them.'[53] To correct their malpractices, the appointment was given to the deputy-governors of Tortola and Virgin Gorda who were likely to be more amenable to discipline by having more to lose if dismissed.[54]

With the establishment of a Vice-Admiralty Court in Tortola, a further attempt was made to curtail illegal trade by the seizure of goods which were suspected of being smuggled, as well as of the vessels importing them, and libelling them in the Vice-Admiralty Court where they were condemned and afterwards publicly sold.[55] Such methods could only succeed under normal circumstances. Conditions in the Virgin Islands during the second half of the eighteenth century were not normal. The geographical configuration of the islands with their innumerable bays and convenient landing places made discovery of illegal entries impossible in the absence of the necessary means of detection. This factor was intensified by the diversions created by war. Because the islands gained from the illegal trade and because the principal participants were also the chief planters and traders and likewise the legislators and judges, it was not easy to secure convictions. During the American War of Independence, as Governor Shirley explained, even French produce was taken to Tortola, 'where by some means or other it was converted into British produce, and shipped from thence in British bottoms to the ports of Great Britain or Ireland.'[56]

During the period of peace from 1783 to 1793, illegal trade, like privateering lapsed. Like privateering also, it seemed for very nearly the same reasons, to have been confined to the first phase of the French wars. But it was considerable. In 1801 it was estimated that of a yearly average export of 6,000 hogsheads of sugar from the Virgin Islands, only about 3,500 hogsheads were local produce, the remainder being foreign sugars clandestinely imported.[57] These were later re-exported as British colonial produce.

The free port regulations revealed an attempt, probably successful, to curtail illicit trading. By the Acts of 1802 and 1803, it was required that the main items of foreign import, sugar and coffee, should be re-exported in separate packages clearly marked and numbered by the Officers of Customs, to differentiate the foreign from the local produce.[58] By the Act of 1806, the amount of sugar that could be exported from the Virgin Islands as local produce was limited to 5,880,000 pounds annually, that is, roughly the amount which the islands were reported capable of producing. Any amount beyond that total would be regarded as foreign sugar.[59] According to regulations issued in 1806, trade with Spanish colonies in the commodities enumerated in the Free Port Act was confined to vessels which had received special licences.[60] Similar precautions were adopted to regulate the trade with Haiti.[61] The Governor had reserve powers to determine the form of the licences and to issue them himself when he thought fit. Vessels trading with Haiti were not permitted to carry sugar to or to transport negro slaves from or to that island. To prevent evasion, all licences had to be recorded. Moreover, each licencee had to subscribe to an affidavit to observe the instructions prescribed. The response of traders interested in the commerce with foreign areas was unenthusiastic.[62] By June, 1807, only two applications had been made for licences to trade with Haiti and two with the Spanish colonies.[63] It had become obvious to Virgin Islanders that the freedom of trade, and the benefits from the free ports which they had anticipated were not likely to be obtained.

The regulations governing the extended trading privileges were designed not to stifle direct trade between foreign colonies and Tortola, but to prevent any evasion of the laws of trade to the detriment of revenues which could be obtained from the importation of foreign produce into Britain where these paid higher duties than British colonial produce. The purpose of the free port was merely to give legality to trade which would otherwise have been illegal, while the removal of import and export duties from foreign produce entering and leaving Tortola was designed to boost trade with previously prohibited regions.

The explanation always given for the desire by enemy privateers to attack the Virgin Islands was the 'rich booty' which could be obtained in Road Harbour.[64] On each occasion the allusion was to the importance of the Virgin Islands as a base for shipping. Privateering apart, this importance was created by the establishment of a packet station and a rendezvous for the Leeward Islands convoy in Tortola towards the end of the eighteenth century.

Early attempts to get the monthly packets to call regularly at the Virgin Islands on their way to Jamaica, and to remain there for twenty-four hours failed.[65] And it was not until 1785, that the July packet was ordered to stop at Tortola on its return to Europe.[66] By facilitating communication and correspondence, packets were invaluable in fostering trade and other commercial transactions; and the more frequent and regular the service the better it was for the efficient despatch of business. Encouraged by the action recently taken, the Council and Assembly requested that the monthly packets should call at Tortola and remain in port for forty-eight hours.[67] This facility was accorded in January, 1786.[68] In October, 1802, in expectation of the accession of trade arising from the Free Port Act, and in order to improve the general system of conveyance and communication with the Windward and Leeward Islands, and with Jamaica, in giving them frequency and directness, Virgin Islanders unsuccessfully sought the introduction of a second monthly packet.[69] With the failure to secure this concession the existing arrangement remained until 1819 when the declining economy and the destruction of the harbour facilities by the hurricane of that year made the retention of a packet station in Road Town no longer either economically feasible or possible.

The packet service was designed to facilitate commerce; to give safety to that commerce, the convoy system was adopted. By this method trading vessels were escorted in a body to Britain from the West Indies under the protection of one or more warships. Cargoes were thus guarded against enemy and privateer attacks. The benefit of convoy was extended to the Virgin Islands in 1777 when in response to representations from London merchants,[70] the Lords of the Admiralty ordered Vice-Admiral Young at Antigua to include the vessels of the Virgin Islands in his tri-annual convoys leaving St. Christopher on April 30, June 15, and August 1.[71]

This system, however, was imperfect and partial. It was incumbent upon vessels from the Virgin Islands to attach themselves to the convoy at St. Christopher as best they could. But even when they were there, a convoy could be guaranteed only 'as far as was consistent with the safety of the ships from the other Islands.'[72] Such an arrangement was certain to create considerable inconveniences and in 1781 convoys bound for Britain were ordered to take the course between the Virgin Islands and St. Croix in order to give the vessels from Tortola an opportunity to join them.[73]

During the French Wars the convoy system was extended to include Tortola not only as a regular stop for the convoy leaving the Leeward Islands, but as a rendezvous for the vast fleets of vessels trading with the West Indies.[74] Fleets, though varying in size, were large. For instance, the convoy sailing from Tortola in July, 1796, numbered 42 vessels, while another sailing in May, 1799, numbered 260.[75] The assembly of large numbers of vessels in the Virgin Islands made them the object of particular attention by the enemy and in 1806 the question of greater protection was raised.[76] With the seizure of the Danish Islands in the following year the urgency of improved defences for the Virgin Islands was removed, and the islands themselves acquired greater importance as a rendezvous base.[77]

Until the beginning of the nineteenth century when free port and other wider trading privileges were granted, the prosperity of the Virgin Islands in part depended on and was promoted by the freedom from attack which facilitated extended cultivation. Also important were privateering and the confiscations of the Vice-Admiralty Court, illegal trade, the accommodations offered by the packet service and the convoy system, and the relatively high prices in Britain. The prosperity was reflected in the recorded export trade with Britain. An indication of this trade and its progress from 1748 to 1785, for which records exist, is shown in Table 1 giving official values in £ sterling.[78]

Table 1

Export Trade of the Virgin Islands with Britain, 1748-1785

Year	Value	Year	Value	Year	Value	Year	Value
1748	5,939	1758	32,944	1768	50,444	1778	61,840
1749	7,167	1759	24,170	1769	54,560	1779	44,879
1750	24,838	1760	30,352	1770	43,230	1780	49,023
1751	12,336	1761	44,286	1771	41,466	1781	70,960
1752	12,008	1762	33,265	1772	58,111	1782	161,388
1753	26,107	1763	58,571	1773	48,000	1783	138,707
1754	11,010	1764	41,549	1774	57,890	1784	123,581
1755	18,557	1765	38,973	1775	64,526	1785	85,876
1756	21,844	1766	48,280	1776	44,452		
1757	23,056	1767	48,864	1777	46,946		

The outstanding feature of the increase in exports recorded was its relatively rapid development during the periods of war as compared with the periods of peace. From 1748 to 1755 the average annual exports were valued at £14,745; for the next eight years covering the period of the Seven Years' War, the average was £33,561 a year. Thereafter, while exports continued to increase giving an annual average of £47,384, the pace of increase had slackened noticeably. From 1774, values again improved and for the next ten years until 1783, which covered the American War of Independence, averaged £74,061 a year. During the last two years of the American war exports were valued at £161,388 and £138,707 respectively. With the end of the conflict, however, exports once more slumped, and by 1785 were officially valued at only £85,876. This gives a possible indication of the extent of the proceeds from privateering and illegal trade which flourished more in war than in peace.

These figures do not represent all of the trade of the Virgin Islands. An unrecorded volume was transacted with the neighbouring islands, and as opportunities allowed, with North America. The increase in commerce can be illustrated also by the increase in the shipping of the Virgin Islands. In 1774 it was estimated that about 15 top-sails totalling about 3,000 tons burden and employing about 300 seamen were engaged in the trade between the Virgin Islands and London and Liverpool. About 20 vessels consisting of sloops, schooners and shallops belonging to Virgin Islanders and totalling about 500 tons and navigated by about 100 seamen, principally slaves, were engaged in the trade with neighbouring islands.[79]

During the decade after 1774 the number of vessels involved increased with the expansion of trade. Thus the number of vessels entering and leaving the Virgin Islands between January, 1782 and January, 1785 averaged 385 a year.[80] Traffic continued with the surrounding islands principally St. Thomas and St. Croix, as well as with Antigua, Anguilla, Barbados and Jamaica, and the British ports of London and Liverpool. In addition vessels were reaching Bristol and Glasgow in Britain, and New York, Newfoundland and Halifax in North America.[81]

The increased export trade was matched by a comparable increase in the volume of imports. Part of the increased value was due to the increase in prices especially during periods of war, but it was mostly due to increases in the amounts of goods to provide for the increased number of slaves and to meet the conspicuous consumption of the whites which was characteristic of the period. Until 1763, because the trade was not properly organised and because of the danger to shipping, imports were relatively small. According to official statistics, in the sixteen years after 1748 they amounted to only £10,832 sterling. Thereafter there was a marked and continuous increase: between 1764 and 1773 imports totalled £208,245 or an annual average of £20,825; while from 1774 to 1783 imports were valued at £378,837 or an average of £37,884 a year. Greater prominence was attached to trade with Britain during wartime not only because of the safety to shipping given by the convoy system but because of the greater threat presented by privateers to vessels wishing to trade with foreign colonies. Once this threat was removed, direct trade was again possible. This feature was noticeable in the trade of the Virgin Islands where imports from Britain fell from £49,154 in 1783 to £24,002 in 1784, to £18,406 in 1785. The shift was to the Danish Islands to a greater, and to the United States to a lesser extent.

Except for 1792 when exports valuing £106,162 were sent to Britain, trade statistics for the Virgin Islands from 1786 to 1798 do not seem to exist. Hence no proper study can be made of the effect on Virgin Islands trade of the restrictions on American trade after 1783, of the revolution in St. Domingue in 1791, or of the events of the early years following the outbreak of war between Britain and France in 1793. By the turn of the century, however, the Virgin Islands as a market for British manufactures had substantially increased compared, for instance, with the period before 1785. Imports from Britain, 1799-1805, can be seen from Table 2.[82] The Peace of Amiens accounted for the comparatively low imports of 1802.

Table 2

Imports from Britain, 1799-1805

Year	Official Value (£ sterling)	Year	Official Value (£ sterling)
1799	152,789	1803	86,648
1800	216,756	1804	83, 875
1801	111,645	1805	139,034
1802	65,578		

Imports from Britain consisted primarily of manufactures; most of the colony's food-supply including meat, butter, cheese, ham, fish, beans, corn, flour, bread and potatoes, and almost all of the lumber such as staves, boards and shingles, were brought in from the United States.[83]

Comparable figures of total exports are not available except for 1800 when exports valued only £45,987. One account of exports shows the following amounts of sugar shipped to Britain from 1799 to 1804, namely, 36,510; 11,853; 33,570; 51,020; 21,269; and 39,077 cwt. The account, which comprises the produce of both British and foreign plantations, does not include certain quantities of prize sugar. Neither does it include certain quantities of cotton, coffee, and other products which were exported from the Virgin Islands. The colony produced no coffee but between 1799 and 1804 an average of 657 cwt. of coffee was exported to Britain. Until 1802, according to official returns, all the coffee exported from the Virgin Islands was the produce of British plantations; but in 1803 and 1804 of the total amount of coffee exported, 240 cwt. and 2,064 cwt. respectively were the produce of foreign plantations, presumably brought in through the medium of the free port.[84]

The early nineteenth century was with little exception a period of severe depression in the major industries of the Virgin Islands, namely, sugar and cotton. The decline in the sugar industry stemmed partly from the existence of a general economic depression in Britain caused by the circumstances of war and its aftermath. It was also due to increasing competition from sugar produced in newly developed areas in Cuba, Brazil and the East Indies. Such sugar found a ready market in Europe and blocked British re-exports of colonial sugar there. Besides, it resulted in a fall in sugar prices so that the returns on British West Indian sugar could no longer cover production and marketing costs to leave a comfortable profit. Indeed, in 1831 it was estimated that the average cost of producing one hundred-weight of sugar with the expense of marketing it was 24/2 while the average price was 23/8 a cwt., leaving a deficit of 6d.[85]

The falling profitability of sugar production was matched by a corresponding decline in profits in cotton production, due to the increase of cotton cultivation in the virgin lands of the southern states of the American Union. A ready market was obtained for this cotton in Britain to satisfy the demands of the developing cotton manufacturing industry. Land exhaustion and the difficulty of recruiting labour in the old British West Indian colonies, including the Virgin Islands, resulted in such high costs as to make competition with the mainland impossible. Besides, cotton prices fell from an average maximum of 35d. a pound between 1793 and 1802, to an average maximum of 10d. a pound between 1823 and 1833. In 1829 the price was as low as 9d. a pound.[86]

By the nineteenth century, also, the soil of the Virgin Islands as of the rest of the British colonies had deteriorated considerably. One visitor to the Virgin Islands around 1823 observed that 'the poverty of the soil, even in those parts selected for cultivation, was manifest on every side.'[87] Also the emigration of white planters seeking better opportunities elsewhere contributed further towards lower sugar and cotton production in the colony, adversely affected as they were by marketing conditions in Britain.

The disruption of the marketing opportunities for sugar and cotton was not accompanied by any alternative development whereby the production and trade of the Virgin Islands could be improved. Neither did the benefits expected from the free port materialise. During the agitation for the free port it was confidently believed that it would lead eventually to the supersession of St. Thomas by the Virgin Islands as an emporium of trade and as a recipient of British capital investment which would augment their commercial importance and economic viability. That this did not happen was partly due to the firmly entrenched position of the British merchants in St. Thomas and partly to the British acquisition of the Danish Islands in 1807, which cancelled for the Virgin Islands any expectation of considerable free port benefits. The establishment of a free port in Tortola was based on the assumption that it would be able to take advantage of the trade of the Spanish colonies which had been disrupted when Spain became an ally of France in the war against Britain. The creation of an alliance between Britain and Spain in 1807 thereby facilitating direct trade between the latter and its American colonies without fear of attack from British privateers and men-of-war negated much of the advantage anticipated from the free port in Tortola. The establishment of peace in 1815 confirmed the Spanish association with its colonies.

By 1815 many of the factors which had contributed to the prosperity of the earlier years had become ineffective. Privateering had lost its importance, and although the Vice-Admiralty Court was retained in Tortola its scope became limited to the trial of slaving vessels. With the acquisition of St. Thomas by Britain the surrounding sea ceased to be the happy hunting ground it had previously been. The establishment of a licensed free port there attracted trade that might otherwise have gone to Tortola. The unpopularity among traders of the conditions governing trade with St. Domingue nullified the beneficial effects of that privilege. The convoy system and packet service had been established more in order to facilitate trade than to boost it — they were privileges accorded in recognition of the increasing import- ance of trade without which they were themselves unimportant and ineffectual. Of the long list of effectives only smuggling remained to add its quota to an already declining economy. Its effectiveness was more noticeable after 1815.

From 1809 to 1815 exports from the Virgin Islands to Britain averaged approximately £45,350 a year with totals reaching £62,520 in 1810 at the height of the trade war between France and Britain known as the Continental System, and £62,310 in 1812 at the beginning of the War of 1812 between Britain and the United States.[88] After 1815 the export trade of the Virgin Islands improved and for the next three years reached an annual average of £73,628; in 1819 exports totalled £55,834 due to the hurricane of that year. Thereafter exports showed considerable fluctuation but the decline, according to Table 3, is noticeable.[89]

Table 3

Value of Exports from the British Virgin Islands 1820-1834

Year	Value (£)	Year	Value (£)	Year	Value (£)
1820	27,785	1825	23,846	1830	25,212
1821	37,731	1826	32,626	1831	22,333
1822	36,979	1827	33,359	1832	23,733
1823	36,550	1828	20,934	1833	21,352
1824	33,777	1829	33,244	1834	31,720

The decline in exports to Britain after 1815 was accompanied by a similar decline in direct imports though some British produce reached the colony through the medium of other British West Indian colonies. On the other hand a substantial amount of imports were brought in from the United States and other foreign colonies in the West Indies presumably St. Thomas especially. The pattern of the import trade from 1822 to 1825 is given in Table 4.[90]

Table 4

Recorded Value of Imports into the British Virgin Islands, 1822-1825

Year	Britain	West Indies	United States	Foreign Colonies	Total
1822	£5,917	£3,279	£2,796	£4,548	£13,745
1823	5,917	3,279	2,796	4,548	13,745
1824	4,000	8,754	780	1,794	15,328
1825	1,200	44	1,032	2,806	5,080

The relative proportion of trade transacted with the various territories did not remain uniform. In 1834, imports from Britain were
valued at £1,641, from the British West Indies at £56, and from foreign
states at £2,442.[91] The declining importance of imports from British
sources in favour of imports from foreign countries should be noted as
being indicative of a continuing trend which finally culminated in the
emergence of St. Thomas as practically the sole supplier of the Virgin
Islands.

The increase in exports after 1815 was even larger than recorded
because of large-scale smuggling, both open and secretive. Vessels were
entered and cleared 'in ballast,' others were given 'general clearance'
without ever coming near the port of Road Harbour at all; and yet
others often carried two sets of papers, British and non-British, under
different names, to be used as occasion warranted. Sometimes more
elaborate precautions were taken by the organisers of smuggling who
provided for the changing of ships' masters and crews, or even for the
repainting of the vessels to avoid detection.[92] Smuggling had indeed
been reduced to a fine art, but sometimes cruder though equally
effective methods were adopted. Carthaginean and other armed vessels
operating under the new republics of South America frequently carried
the Spanish vessels which they captured to the North Sound in Virgin
Gorda, and to Jost Van Dyke and Anegada, somewhat remote and
unfrequented parts of the Virgin Islands, where they were stranded
awaiting confiscation.[93]

Smuggling was not confined only to export commodities but
included articles of local consumption designed to alleviate distress. The
dearth of provisions after 1815 consequent upon the continuing
restrictions on trade with America, and the inability of the British North
American Colonies to satisfy the demand as was expected,[94] gave
Virgin Islanders no alternative. The proximity of St. Thomas always
provided the temptation to smuggle goods which could not be imported
legally.[95]

The most shattering blow to the economy of the Virgin Islands was
given by the hurricane of September 21 and 22, 1819. It is sufficient to
note that destruction to public and private dwelling, shipping, livestock
and sugar estates amounted to an estimated £302,669 currency, while
fourteen whites and over eighty negroes were killed.[96] To mitigate
distress, the Governor was induced to open the port on five separate
occasions each of six months duration, sometimes against the wishes of
the Colonial Office, to admit foreign vessels with provisions and

lumber,[97] and to suspend the collection of taxes.[98] Among the long term effects was the heavy accumulation of debt by planters to repair the damages incurred. Many large proprietors who before 1819 had been considered persons of opulence found great difficulty in obtaining sufficient credit to enable them to carry on the cultivation of their estates, little prospect being attached to their ability to repay. Nor was there a possibility of realising the means to satisfy either debt or credit by sale of property the value of which depreciated to almost half of what it had been before 1819. Many planters reacted by emigrating, and leaving their properties in the hands of attorneys or throwing them into chancery.[99] Following the hurricane and its destruction of the harbour facilities of Road Town, the packet station was removed to St. Thomas. This reinforced their increasing isolation already created by the decline of trade and communication. The hardships encountered resulted in the refusal of the local legislature to initiate taxation to defray public expenses with the consequent accumulation of a tremendous public debt.

For the alleviation of their worsening economic situation in the early nineteenth century, Virgin Islanders turned to Britain for assistance, but the negative response to their approaches was indicative of the colony's declining importance. Early requests for allowances out of the proceeds of the 4½% duty[100] were refused on the assumption that a concession of this nature to one colony would inevitably lead to similar requests by other colonies similarly circumstanced. When in 1819, Governor Maxwell supported a request for the total or partial suspension of the payment of the 4½% duty for a limited period,[101] his action was condemned on the ground that the duty had not been granted for local use but only in return for the benefits of a local legislature in 1773.[102] The British Government consistently adhered to this argument until 1838 when it abolished the 4½% duty throughout the West Indies.

Further appeals for financial assistance were refused on the grounds that they 'might be construed into a precedent for claiming Gifts from the Crown.'[103] When in 1823 Virgin Islanders sought a loan of £10,000 to be repaid in ten equal instalments in twelve years at 4% interest on the principal, repayment to commence from the third year, their request went unanswered.[104]

Failing to induce the British Government to concede financial assistance to the Virgin Islands, the colonists tried after 1830 to secure approval for the establishment of unlimited free port privileges in

Tortola by the removal of all existing restrictions on foreigners to trade there,[105] as well as the re-institution of the rendezvous for the mail packet service.[106] With regard to the former, the British Government would not go beyond the creation of a free ware-housing port in Tortola,[107] since the concessions asked for were considered subversive of the laws of trade and navigation, and might, if granted, 'excite murmurs from all the other colonies.'[108] The reception of the latter was even less accommodating. There was no nautical objection to the establishment of a packet station in Road Town,[109] while something could be said in favour of transferring the packet station from St. Thomas to Tortola in order to give preference to a British over a foreign colony.[110] The proposal was rejected, however, on the grounds that the advantages hoped for were trifling and would not compensate for the inconveniences which would result from the change. The Lords of Trade were reluctant to break up establishments founded upon long acquired habits of trade.[111] They feared too that concession of a packet station would inevitably lead to further requests for a free port. The crucial fact was that their lordships recognised and accepted the predominant position of St. Thomas as an established trading centre, and were not desirous of removing the packet station 'from the great seat of business, to a spot described to be deserted by trade.'[112]

Under the colonial system, colonies were valued only to the extent that they contributed to British commercial and industrial prosperity. By the nineteenth century, the Virgin Islands had already declined considerably as a market for British manufactures and as a source of raw material. In 1773, in anticipation of the economic benefits to be derived from the 4½% duty, the British Government had been influenced to grant constitutional government to the Virgin Islands. It was otherwise in the nineteenth century. Its refusal to accord financial assistance and other privileges to the colony was a tacit acknowledgement of the latter's lack of importance. The British Government was not willing that the Virgin Islands should become a 'mill-stone' around its neck. It was immobilised by the obsession that conceding Virgin Islanders' requests for assistance would lead other British West Indian colonies to claim similar advantages. Its refusal to recognise a final responsibility for the welfare of the colony led the Virgin Islands to become a sad case of imperial neglect.

[1] C.O. 314/1. Petition: Virgin Islanders to the King, 4 June, 1740; C.O. 152/28. No. Bc. 71; C.O. 152/29. No. Cc. 17.

[2] Journal of the Commissioners for Trade and Plantations, Jan., 1776 to May, 1782. (London, H.M.S.O., 1938) pp. 78, 107 and 114.

[3] C.O. 316/1. Minutes of Assembly, 21 Oct., 1778; Barrington to Dawson, 30 Sept., 1778.

[4] C.O. 316/1. Minutes of Assembly, 6 Aug., 29 July, and 21 Oct., 1778.

[5] C.O. 316/1. Minutes of Assembly, 25 May, 1778.

[6] C.O. 315/1. Acts Nos. 4, 6, 21, 37, and 38; C.O. 315/3. Act No. 46.

[7] C.O. 316/1. Minutes of Assembly, 21 Sept., 1779; C.O. 152/84. An Account of Sums of Money expended on fortifying the Island of Tortola and the small Islands under the same Government, 12 Dec., 1801.

[8] C.O. 152/75. Enc. in Stanley to Dundas, 18 Feb., 1794; Stanley to Portland, 31 Oct., and 30 Nov., 1794. No. 40, and 10 April, 1795. No. 53.

[9] C.O. 152/79. Thomson to Portland, 24 Jan., 1799. No. 31.

[10] Frank W. Pitman: The Development of the British West Indies, 1700-1763. (New Haven, 1917) pp. 186 and 187.

[11] Noel Deerr: The History of Sugar. (London, 1949-50) Vol. 11, pp. 530-531.

[12] C.O. 152/63. Enc. in Shirley to Sydney, May, 1784. No. 60.

[13] Ibid.; in 1784 there were only three families living on Anegada.

[14] C.O. 152/67. Act No. 6, enc. in Nugent to Sydney, 2 Dec., 1788. No. 16; C.O. 152/63. Enc. in Shirley to Sydney, May, 1784. No. 60.

[15] Customs 3/48 to Customs 3/80; also Customs 5/1A.

[16] C.O. 317/1. Enc. in Shirley to Sydney, 29 Dec., 1785. No. 132.

[17] C.O. 152/45. Bouilla to Ensenada, 15 Dec., 1750; Deposition of Carriedo, 16 Dec., 1750; Valdes to Ensenada, 29 Jan., 1751.

[18] C.O. 152/41 Enc: in C.T.P. to Bedford, 15 March, 1751; C.O. 152/45. Fleming to Bedford, 22 Nov., and 12 Dec., 1750 and enc.

[19] C.O. 152/28. No. Bc. 82.

[20] S.P. 42/42. Volume 2. Enc. in Admiralty to Pitt, 20 May, 1761; C.O. 152/46. Thomas to Pitt, 20 May, 1761; C.O. 152/41. C.T.P. to Holdernesse, 25 June, 1763.

[21] C.O. 152/56. Petition to the King, 1777.

[22] C.O. 152/64. Enc. in Shirley to Sydney, 23 July, 1785. No. 112.

[23] C.O. 152/56. Petition to the King, 1777.

[24] Ibid.; also, C.O. 152/64. Enc. in Shirley to Sydney, 23 July, 1785. No. 112; and 11 Dec., 1785. No. 125; Sydney to Shirley, 6 Oct., 1785.

[25] C.O. 153/32. Germain to Burt, 20 June, 1777. No. 3.

[26] C.O. 152/64. Enc. in Shirley to Sydney, 23 July, 1785. No. 112.

[27] C.O. 152/56. Enc. in Fahie to Germain, 1 May, 1777; and Greathead to Germain, 6 May, 1777.

[28] C.O. 152/56. Enc. in Fahie to Germain, 1 May, 1777; enc. in Burt to Germain, 30 July, 1777; Burt to Germain, 13 June, 1777.

[29] C.O. 156/56. Burt to Germain, 30 July, 1777, and enc.; C.O. 152/58. Burt to Germain, 14 June, 1778. No. 2, and enc.

[30] C.O. 152/57. Burt to Clausen, 27 Dec., 1777; Burt to Dufresner, 5 Jan., 1778.

[31] C.O. 152/58. Burt to Germain, 14 June, 1778. No. 2.

[32]   C.O. 152/56. Burt to Germain, 30 July, 1777.
[33]   C.O. 152/57. Germain to Burt, 10 March, 1778. No. 11; C.O. 152/58. Enc. in Burt to Germain, 14 June, 1778. No. 2.
[34]   C.O. 152/57. Germain to Burt, 1 April, 1778. No. 12.
[35]   C.O. 152/59. Germain to Burt, 4 Dec., 1779. No. 32.
[36]   C.O. 152/59. Germain to Burt, 8 Oct., 1779. No. 29; C.O. 152/60. Burt to Germain, 16 March, 1780. No. 70.
[37]   C.O. 152/61. Germain to Shirley, 1 Sept., 1781. No. 4.
[38]   C.O. 152/62. Shirley to Shelburne, 30 July, 1782. No. 7.
[39]   C.O. 152/62. Enc. in Shirley to Shelburne, 30 July, 1782. No. 7.
[40]   C.O. 152/62. Shirley to Shelburne, 30 July, 1782. No. 7.
[41]   C.O. 152/62. Townsend to Shirley, 27 Oct., 1782.
[42]   C.O. 152/75. Stanley to Dundas, 6 March, 1794. No. 23.
[43]   C.O. 152/88. Lavington to Windham, 3 May, 1806. No. 3; A.O. 3/16. Return of the Vice-Admiralty Court of Tortola; A.O. 3/18. A Register of Crown Droits.
[44]   C.O. 152/84. Colquhoun to Hobart, 9 Feb., 1801; Colquhoun to Sullivan, 15 Feb., 1802; Hetherington to Colquhoun, 30 Dec., 1801.
[45]   C.O. 152/84. Enc. in Vansittart to Sullivan, 19 Feb., 1802.
[46]   27 Geo. 111 c. 27; 32 Geo. 111. c. 43; 33 Geo. 111. c. 50.
[47]   C.O. 152/85. Colquhoun to Sullivan, 20 May and 17 June, 1803, and enc.
[48]   B.T. 5/14. Minutes, 24 June, 1803; B.T. 5/15. Minutes, 14 March, 1803.
[49]   45 Geo. 111. c. 57.
[50]   46 Geo. 111. c. 72.
[51]   B.T. 5/15. Minutes, 17 and 21 Feb., 1806; B.T. 5/16. Minutes 7 and 24 March and 11 Sept., 1806; C.O. 152/88. Fawkener to Shee, 10 Oct., 1806.
[52]   B.T. 5/16. Minutes, 11 Sept, 1806; C.O. 152/88. Fawkener to Shee, 10 Oct., 1806.
[53]   C.O. 152/41. Enc. in C.T.P. to Bedford, 15 March, 1751.
[54]   C.O. 152/28. No. Bc. 82.
[55]   C.O. 152/54. Enc. in Payne to Dartmouth, 26 June, 1774. No. 17.
[56]   C.O. 152/63. Shirley to North, 26 Sept., 1783. No. 36.
[57]   C.O. 152/84. A general view of the national advantages expected to result from an extension and improvement of the Free Port Acts, particularly to the Port of Road Harbour in the Island of Tortola, Nov., 1801. Post Script.
[58]   42 Geo. 111. c. 102; 43 Geo. 111. c. 143; enc. in Cottrell to Sullivan, 17 Aug., 1802.
[59]   46 Geo. 111. c. 72.
[60]   C.O. 152/88. Windham to Lavington, 4 Dec., 1806. No. 10; C.O. 152/89. Lavington to Windham, 21 March, 1807. No. 21.
[61]   Ibid; also, P.C. 2/171. Order in Council, 19 Nov., 1806.
[62]   C.O. 152/89. Lavington to Windham, 21 March, 1807. No. 21.
[63]   C.O. 152/89. Lavington to Castlereagh, 19 June, 1807. No. 1.
[64]   C.O. 152/75. Enc. in Stanley to Dundas, 18 Feb., 1794; enc. in Stanley to Portland, 31 Oct., 1794. No. 38.
[65]   C.O. 316/1. Minutes of Assembly, 9 April, 1776.
[66]   C.O. 152/64. Shirley to Sydney, 16 Nov., 1785. No. 124.
[67]   C.O. 152/64. Enc. in Shirley to Sydney, 16 Nov., 1785. No. 124.

[68] C.O. 152/64. Sydney to Shirley, 5 Jan., 1786.

[69] C.O. 152/84. Colquhoun to Hobart, 28 Oct., 1802.

[70] P.R.O. Index 4808: 1777-1792. Digest. Section 27. Minutes of 6 Feb., 1777. C.

[71] P.R.O. Index 4808: 1777-1792. Digest. Section 27. Minutes of 5 Feb., 1777. S.

[72] Ibid.

[73] P.R.O. Index 4808: 1777-1792. Digest. Section 27. Minutes of 7 Feb., 1781; C.O. 316/1. Minutes of Assembly, 16 Aug., 1780.

[74] C.O. 152/88. Colquhoun to Windham, 17 Feb., 1806.

[75] Adm. 1/2493. Scott to Nepean, 21 Sept., 1796; Adm. 1/2402. Russell to Nepean, 30 May and 30 June, 1799.

[76] C.O. 152/88. Colquhoun to Windham, 17 Feb., 1806; enc. in Crew to Shee, 1 Dec., 1806.

[77] C.O. 152/91. Enc. in Colquhoun to Cooke, 14 Sept., 1808.

[78] Compiled from (a) Customs 3/48: Xmas 1747-Xmas 1748, to Customs 3/80: Xmas 1779-Xmas 1780; (b) David Macpherson: Annals of Commerce, Manufactures, Fisheries and Navigation etc. (London, 1805) Vol. 111; (c) Adam Anderson: An Historical and Chronological Deduction of the Origin of Commerce from the Earliest Accounts (London, 1789) Vol. IV.

[79] C.O. 152/54. Enc. in Payne to Dartmouth, 26 June, 1774. No. 17.

[80] C.O. 152/63. Shirley to North, 26 Sept., 1783. No. 36.

[81] C.O 152/63. Shirley to Sydney, May, 1784. No. 59, and enc.

[82] P.P. 1806. Vol. XII, p. 205.

[83] C.O. 152/89. Enc. in Lavington to Castlereagh, 19 June, 1807. No. 1.

[84] P.P. 1806. Vol. XII, p. 211.

[85] P.P. 1831-1832. Vol. XX, p. 660.

[86] L. J. Ragatz: Statistics for the Study of British Caribbean History 1763-1833. (London, The Bryan Edwards Press) p. 8.

[87] (Trelawney Wentworth): The West India Sketch Book. (London, 1834, 2 Vols.) Vol. 1, p. 167.

[88] Customs 4/5 (1809) to Customs 4/10 (1815).

[89] Customs 5/11 (1816) to Customs 4/29 (1834).

[90] R. Montgomery Martin: History of the British Colonies. (London, 1834.) Vol. IV, p. 494.

[91] C.O. 317/5. Blue Book, 1834.

[92] C.O. 239/7. Enc. in Bridgewater to Bathurst, 8 Nov., 1821.

[93] C.O. 239/7. Dougan to Bathurst, 7 June, 1822.

[94] C.O. 152/92. Enc. in Tyson to Castlereagh, 10 May, 1809. No. 3.

[95] Anonymous: Letters from the Virgin Islands, illustrating life and manners in the West Indies. (London, 1843.) pp. 120-1.

[96] C.O. 239/5. Enc. in Colquhoun to the Treasury, 29 Nov., 1819; C.O. 239/6. Colquhoun to Bathurst, 26 Jan., 1820; Maxwell to Bathurst, 6 Nov., 1820.

[97] C.O. 239/5. Maxwell to Bathurst, 11 Oct., 1819. No. 8; C.O. 239/6. Maxwell to Bathurst, 10 April, 1820. No. 26; Wilson to Bathurst, 20 Oct., 1820; C.O. 239/7. Wilson to Bathurst, 10 March, 1821. No. 14; 26 Oct., 1821, No. 31; C.O. 407/1. Bathurst to Maxwell, 30 Nov., 1820.

[98]   C.O. 239/6. Maxwell to Bathurst, 6 Nov., 1820.

[99]   C.O. 314/15. Longden to Hill, 31 May, 1865.

[100]   C.O. 152/87. Enc. in Colquhoun to Cooke, 19 June and 2 July, 1805 and 14 Sept., 1808.

[101]   C.O. 239/5. Enc. in Colquhoun to the Treasury, 29 Nov., 1819; C.O. 239/6. Maxwell to Bathurst, 6 Nov., 1819.

[102]   C.O. 407/1. Bathurst to Maxwell, 30 Nov., 1820.

[103]   C.O. 239/9. Colquhoun to Bathurst, 22 March, 1823.

[104]   C.O. 239/9. Enc. in Maxwell to Bathurst, 11 March, 1823. No. 46.

[105]   C.O. 239/9. Enc. in Colquhoun to Murray. 17 Oct., 1830; C.O. 239/38. Colquhoun to Stanley, 8 May, 1834; C.O. 239/41. Enc. in Colquhoun to Glenelg, 18 May, 1835.

in Colquhoun to Glenelg, 14 Nov., 1837.

[106]   C.O. 239/41. Colquhoun to Aberdeen, 31 Jan., 1835, and enc.; C.O. 239/36. Enc. in MacGregor to Stanley, 29 March, 1834. No. 63; C.O. 239/38. Colquhoun to Stanley, 8 May, 1834; C.O. 239/41. Enc. in Colquhoun to Glenelg, 18 May, 1835.

[107]   C.O. 239/26. Order in Council, 18 May, 1831.

[108]   C.O. 239/38. Lack to Lefevre, 23 June, 1834; C.O. 239/48. Hume to Grey, 16 Nov., 1837; Grey to Colquhoun, 29 Nov., 1837.

[109]   C.O. 239/38. Lack to Lefevre, 23 June, 1834.

[110]   C.O. 239/38. Colonial Office to Lack, Feb., 1835; Hay to Barrow, Feb., 1835.

[111]   C.O. 239/38. Unsigned Admiralty Note, 20 May, 1834; Lack to Lefevre, 23 June, 1834.

[112]   C.O. 239/41. Lack to Hay, 22 May, 1835.

Chapter 4

Slavery and Emancipation

Cultivation in the Virgin Islands before 1834, as in the rest of the British West Indies, depended on the labour of slaves. As elsewhere in the British West Indies also, importation of slaves in quantum was undertaken to facilitate large scale economic enterprise. In the context of the Virgin Islands, this meant the production of sugar and, to a less extent, of cotton. Without slavery, the production of these commodities for export could not only not be carried on, but as W. L. Burn suggests, could not have been started.[1] As the sugar industry was by far the more important of the two, and demanded a proportionally larger number of slaves to produce the canes necessary to make the costly fixed capital equipment economic, the future of slavery came to be almost exclusively bound up with it.

Existing documents do not give any evidence of the number of slaves in Tortola under the Dutch or in the early years of British occupation. By 1672, slavery was already an established institution in other British West Indian colonies, and the white settlers on Tortola were served by slaves, but these were often seized by raiding Spaniards.[2] When the influx of white population into the Virgin Islands from the settled colonies continued on an increasing scale from around the end of the seventeenth century, many of the settlers were accompanied by their slaves. Others were bought from the Danes in St. Thomas where they could be purchased more cheaply than in the British colonies.[3] This source, however, could only satisfy small demands, and when, after the 1730's, cotton and ground provisions gradually gave way to large scale sugar production for export, planters resorted to direct importation from Africa. Occasionally small shipments of slaves also arrived from other West Indian colonies. Both practices ceased when the Imperial Act for the abolition of the slave trade was brought into effect in 1808. Towards the end of the eighteenth century when sugar production ceased to expand, small quantities of slaves were available for re-export, and these were invariably sent to St. Thomas which, as a trading entrepot, could dispose of such surpluses.[4]

Slavery was not merely an aid to the production of sugar and cotton. It also determined the structure of society and the relationship between the several groups, and it explains the varying attitudes towards the work of the missionaries in religious instruction and in education, and the reaction of planters to amelioration and emancipation.

In common with the rest of the British West Indian colonies, society in the Virgin Islands came to be composed of a number of clearly differentiated categories of people: whites, free negroes and coloureds, and slaves. Until about the end of the eighteenth century, the whites and slaves were increasing groups: the former due to the attraction of the Virgin Islands as a profitable plantation colony; and the latter because of the increasing demand for labour. Thereafter their respective numbers declined; the whites partly because some planters preferred to live in England and to leave the management of their estates to attorneys;[5] and the slaves partly from emigration to accompany their masters to other colonies,[6] partly from manumission by purchase or by gift,[7] and partly from deaths by disease and natural disasters.[8] The abolition of the slave trade made it legally impossible to replenish supplies. In contrast to these two groups, the free blacks and coloureds were an ever increasing group. Many were the manumitted children of masters and slaves, while others had previously been slaves who had been manumitted by their owners. Their numbers were increased by the birth of children to free negro and coloured parents.[9]

Society in the Virgin Islands was not only divided into separate categories, but it was also highly stratified, the basis of stratification being a combination of colour, wealth and education.[10] None of these alone was quite sufficient. The extent to which these properties or attributes were possessed by those who composed the society determined their relative social position. Only if a man had all three qualifications was his acceptance at the top assured. It was natural, therefore, that the white planters, merchants, government officers and professional people who had these qualifications in greatest measure should occupy the apex of the social hierarchy, while the mass of negro slaves who lacked all three should be relegated to a position at the bottom. Intermediate between these two groups were those who possessed the attributes to a greater or less extent, including the white overseers, small shop-keepers and artisans, but dominated numerically by the growing class of free negroes and coloureds.[11] The white missionaries though educated were disqualified by lack of wealth; to preserve their religious freedom and avoid being corrupted they preferred to occupy an independent position on the fringe of the white community.[12]

Generally, among the lower classes both free and slave, the aim of the socially ambitious was to acquire those properties which they lacked, namely, a lighter skin, greater wealth, and higher education, in order to achieve a higher social position. In this respect two observations are particularly relevant; the upward-looking tendencies of the classes tended to make those above unsympathetic with the aspirations of those below;[13] but because 'lower' whites and free negroes and coloureds comprised a single large economic group vis-à-vis the elite whites and the slaves, it was easier, when the time came, for concessions to be granted to the free negroes and coloureds in an attempt by the whites to buttress their declining numbers. By that time social status was becoming increasingly meaningless in the Virgin Islands where it could not be supported by economic resources.

Ownership of lands and slaves constituted a common denominator among the social elite, but the disparity between sugar and cotton planters should be noted, as the difference in their economic position determined their relative political influence. This inequality was founded on wealth and influence measured in terms of slaves and the size of estates. Sugar estates differed from those devoted to cotton by being larger and possessing more slaves. Special privileges accrued to the large sugar planters. For instance, nomination to the Council which was dependent upon wealth and family connections, and as a consequence, influence, was invariably reserved for them.

Differences between sugar cane and cotton planters epitomised differences in the whole class of white population, for example, between the attorneys, overseers, book-keepers, artisans and clerks. But their heterogeneous character should not obliterate the basic cohesiveness of the white group. For those with talent and ambition, society based as it was on the possession of slaves who could be worked or hired out at will, offered opportunities to acquire a higher social status. The small number of whites relative to the size of the other subordinate racial groups made it necessary that they should present a united front.

Despite its heterogeneity, the white community occupied a privileged position in relation to the other groups. Emphasis on status was strong among them as shown in the consideration that only whites possessed the political franchise and the right to become members of the legislature with power to make laws governing the activities and lives of members of other groups. This privilege enabled them to entrench their position legally and created a strong disinclination to change. Even when in 1818 free negroes and coloureds were given the extra privilege of electing a representative to the Assembly, the white legislators firmly safe-guarded their exclusive position by requiring that the representative should be white. Control of the legislature was accompanied by a similar authority over the administration, both civil and judicial, and the military. If the missionaries are included, then the whites also had control over the church.

Social stratification was a feature of society throughout the period of slavery, but it was most rigid during the second half of the eighteenth century.[14] In the face of economic decline in the nineteenth century, it became considerably watered down. The reduction of the planter class by absenteeism and emigration paved the way for the upward mobility respectively of the lower whites and free negroes and coloureds. Not only did the whites become more homogeneous but the line of demarcation separating them from the free negroes and coloureds became less rigid on account of their relative economic position.[15]

While the whites occupied a dominant position in society, their authority could not be abused. Their small and declining numbers forced them at all times to consider the reaction of the other groups. Legislation was confined not only to what was necessary but what was possible to enforce in view of the unwillingness of the whites to maintain a militia throughout slavery. Considerable laxity also existed in the exercise of restrictive legislation. The power of masters over their slaves was also limited by their interdependence. Masters had certain customary and legal obligations towards their slaves in relation to food, clothes, housing and medical care, and were required to show sympathetic attention to individual slave requests. These were all necessary to make the plantation function smoothly and harmoniously.[16] If there had not been some other foundation for the plantation system than fear, it could not have endured for almost a century in the Virgin Islands, but fear was a potent force in curbing precipitate action and it forced the whites to grant concessions which might otherwise have been denied.[17] At the same time, in order to preserve the essential structure of society, free negroes and coloureds and slaves were kept in varying degrees of subordination. This was effected largely by discriminatory legislation.

The economic, social and political rights of the free negroes and coloureds were grossly circumscribed, legal sanction being given to their disabilities.[18] They could own lands in their own right and so could establish themselves as small holders; but the amount of land which they could possess was limited to eight acres, and they could not aspire to become freeholders. Free negroes and coloureds could also own slaves but were limited to fifteen except on the payment of an annual tax of thirty shillings on each extra slave in addition to the yearly poll tax on all slaves. In 1783 when this restriction was imposed the poll tax amounted to 20/− per slave, which meant that they had to pay one-and-a-half times more than a white man for each slave possessed above the ceiling of fifteen.[19] The proportion became correspondingly higher as the poll tax was lowered by subsequent enactments. Socially, the subordination of the free negroes and coloureds to the whites was clearly expressed: every free negro and coloured person was required to choose a patron or protector from among the freeholders, who had to make formal acknowledgement of his charge; legal claim to freedom had to be proved twice yearly, and striking a white person irrespective of social status was a legal offence punishable by whipping, imprisonment and dismemberment. The denial of political liberties was contained in the Constitution Act of 1776 in which the right to participate in elections either as voters or as candidates was reserved for white freeholders, despite the fact that some negroes and coloureds might possess the required property qualifications.[20] The inferior status of the free negroes and coloureds was also distinct in militia service; though permitted to bear arms, they were compelled to serve under white officers, and to receive smaller awards of compensation.

The economic restrictions imposed on the free negroes and coloureds did not prevent them from exerting continuous pressure on the white population, and from indulging in those activities other than plantation agriculture which were likely to give economic benefits. Unhampered by legal restrictions, several of them seized the opportunities presented by the French Revolutionary and Napoleonic Wars to fit out or man privateers which operated around the Virgin Islands. In 1808, Patrick Colquhoun, the agent for the colony in London, condemned 'the most

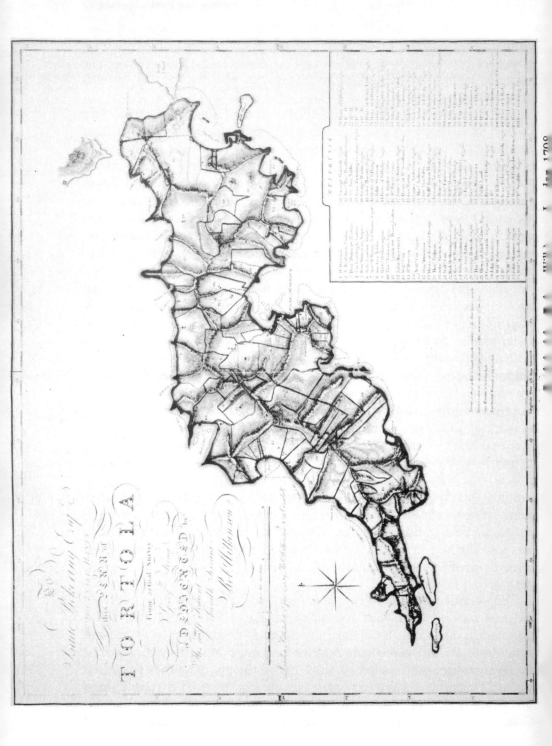

daring outrages which are frequently committed by the people of colour.'[21] From Colquhoun's complaint it appeared that little regard was paid by the free negroes and coloureds even to vessels belonging to Virgin Islanders themselves. Considerable progress was also made in those areas of economic employment from which they were not specifically debarred. The first area of penetration was of course petty trading, especially in hawking and retail selling, despite the high taxation imposed upon them by the legislature. Trade was pursued as an adjunct to other means of livelihood. In the early nineteenth century, the colony was served by five stores but these were inadequate to meet the needs of the entire community. The void was filled by a number of hucksters, generally female coloured persons, who carried about goods in trays for sale. Their enterprise was welcomed rather than resisted by the whites.[22]

While the free negroes and coloureds indulged in trade, agriculture was not neglected. The two activities tended rather to supplement each other though the latter was less attractive on account of the legal restrictions. According to one estimate, in 1815 there were 172 free negroes connected with trade and 67 with agriculture. By 1823 these numbers had risen fairly substantially to 241 and 78 respectively.[23] Numerically and proportionally, the statistics of free negroes and coloureds engaged in trade and agriculture compared favourably with those of the whites, 49 of whom were reported to be connected with trade and 78 with agriculture in 1815, and 64 with trade and 83 with agriculture in 1823.[24]

The relative estimated value of the property possessed by free coloureds, resident whites and non-resident whites was also indicative of the increasingly dominant economic position of the free negroes and coloureds in society. In 1815 and 1823 resident whites owned property worth £510,000 and £161,000 respectively, non-resident whites owned £235,000 and £63,000 respectively, and free-coloureds, £138,000 and £91,000 respectively.[25] In all cases the 1823 value constituted a decline on that of 1815, but in the case of the free-coloureds the decline was proportionally less acute than the others. The progress of the free negroes and coloureds in agriculture was all the more outstanding since they were faced with continuous competition from the slaves for the limited local market. Unlike slaves, free negroes and coloureds always had production costs to consider, a factor which placed them at a competitive disadvantage.

Consciousness of increase in economic status carried with it a corresponding desire for increased civil and political liberties. In 1815 through the medium of Abraham Chalwill Hill a white planter of Tortola, who was then in London on private business, free negroes and coloureds memorialised the British Government protesting against their legal restraints.[26] The response was favourable and after an initial delay which was probably due to lingering planter notions of superiority, and the tensions then existing between the Council and Assembly, an Act was passed in 1818 empowering free negroes and coloureds to acquire, hold and dispose of property in the same manner as the white inhabitants of the colony. In addition, those who qualified for the franchise under the Constitution Act of 1776 were declared legally capable of voting for and electing a qualified white freeholder to represent them in the colonial Assembly.[27]

The concessions granted in 1818, however, were only partial: certain civil disabilities still remained. These were not removed until August, 1831 when another Act was passed repealing all 'restraints or disabilities whatsoever on the free coloured and free-black inhabitants,' and extending to them all the rights, privileges and immunities enjoyed by whites.[28] White action did not stem from sentimentality. In the absence of sufficient white men to present a show of force to the slaves, it was necessary to buttress their position by recruiting support from the body of free negroes and coloureds. Their assistance was considered essential for the preservation of the slave system. The fact that they possessed wealth in lands and slaves made the alliance easier to establish assisted by their desire to dissociate themselves from the slaves and to identify themselves with the whites. Their rapprochement with the whites served to emphasise their dichotomous position in society: while they were rejected as social equals, they were accepted to preserve the inequalities in society.

The basis of plantation agriculture was, of course, the slaves, though not all slaves actually worked on the plantations. Occupational differences were quite evident among them: apart from the field slaves, there were those engaged as domestics, and those employed as artisans, such as carpenters, coopers and masons. Distinctions between these three groups were more clearcut in the eighteenth century when there were more slaves to satisfy demands. In the nineteenth century when domestics were also employed in field work, occupational differences were less distinct; this was to pose one of the major problems of apprenticeship when it was necessary to define and differentiate categories of slaves.

In the field itself a crude system of division of labour pertained. Usually slaves were divided into three gangs: the first was composed of able-bodied men and women who did the heaviest work, digging cane holes, building roads, trashing, cutting, and carting the canes and feeding the mills; the second was made up of the more weakly, elderly men, mothers of suckling children, and youths, whose duties included cleaning the young canes and manuring; the third comprised children between the ages of six and twelve years who did the weeding, less for the sake of the work performed than for the habits of industry which the planters hoped to instil in them.

Because of heavy reliance on slave labour, plantation agriculture remained backward. Instead of adopting such labour-saving device as the plough, where possible, planters stuck to the crude system of hoeing which was wasteful of labour and money. Lands were prepared by a process known as 'holing' whereby slaves equipped with heavy digging hoes dug out holes into which manure was deposited and cane cuttings planted. Professor Douglas Hall attributes the unwillingness of West Indian planters to introduce ploughs and harrows to their preference for slaves as 'multi-purpose capital equipment.'[29]

Commenting on the inefficiency of plantation agriculture in the Leeward Islands, Professor Elsa Goveia ascribes neglect of ploughs to the devotion of insufficient land to pasture making it impossible for an adequate number of ploughing cattle to be reared.[30] Of more relevance to the Virgin Islands, however, was the high percentage of steep hilly land: of the 39,608 acres of land in the Virgin Islands, only about 700 acres, or less than two percent, is flat. In addition, the average slope of the hills ranges from 35° to 50°. Such conditions necessitated terracing and made hoes more convenient agricultural implements. The existence of slaves who could not be paid off was the final disincentive to the use of ploughs on level land.

Milling operations were no more efficient than field labour; the vertical rollers turned by cattle and mules worked very slowly and could extract only between two-fifths and two-thirds of the cane juice.[31] Distrust of innovation was also evident here: as late as the beginning of the twentieth century, cattle mills on the 1790 model were still in operation.[32]

In addition to being wasteful and inefficient, plantation agriculture was harsh based as it was on regimentation, intimidation, dependence and coercion. The slaves' working day began at dawn and continued until night-fall with two breaks for breakfast and lunch. Their gruelling labour was executed under constant and determined supervision and under the discipline of the whip wielded by relentless drivers, themselves privileged slaves, with or without the sanction of overseers, to prevent misapplication of effort. Work was particularly strenuous during harvest-time when the shift system was adopted in a twenty-four hour working day from the necessity to complete grinding early in order to preserve the sucrose content of canes. Even outside croptime the need to procure grass after the normal working day was over added to the slave burden. Whenever necessary, slaves were also required to work building and repairing public roads and fortifications.

The latter part of the eighteenth century was the period of harshest treatment of slaves. Speaking before the Select Committee of the House of Commons in 1790, Thomas Woolrich who had lived in Tortola testified that the treatment of slaves on his arrival there in 1753 was more tolerable than when he quitted it in 1773. During the earlier period when their numbers were small, slaves had been allowed sufficient ground to plant provisions for their subsistence. Years afterwards when numbers had increased, the portion of land 'had a tendency to a scarcity, and want of food for their support.'[33] Several of the negroes' plots were converted into cane-lands, and remaining lands, naturally not the most fertile, divided among a larger number of slaves, consequently provided smaller individual portions. Neither could the deficiency in foodstuff so created always be made good by importation. The disruption of trade consequent upon the wars of the second half of the eighteenth century made it extremely difficult to obtain adequate supplies. During his residence in the Virgin Islands, Woolrich 'never saw a gang of negroes that appeared anything like sufficiently fed; their appearance to the eye fully proves their want and hardships.'[34]

Because slave labour was involuntary and given unenthusiastically, coercion was an essential part of the slave system. According to Woolrich, 'as the quantity of negroes increased . . . punishment of the slaves in general . . . became more and more severe.'[35] The principal form of punishment was whipping not because it was most effective in disciplining slaves, but because, more than any other adequate correc- tive, it ensured planters the services of slaves almost immediately after it was administered. From reports of the effects of some of these floggings, the slaves' backs 'appearing in an undistinguished mass of lumps, holes, and furrows by frequent whippings,'[36] such punish- ments were brutal; equally barbarous were the use of thumb screws and the practice of making slaves stand on one foot on sharply pointed sticks.

Not only were slaves insufficiently protected from ill usage, but there was no way whereby those who offended could be called to account. Until 1798 no legal instrument existed to safeguard slaves against whites, and even when such provision was made, the refusal to acknowledge slave evidence against whites in courts of law reduced the effectiveness of that measure.

In general, the treatment of field slaves was harsher than that of domestic slaves and those engaged as artisans; in addition to having a more certain allowance of provision, domestics and artisans were better provided with food and clothing.[37] Those in Road Town generally had greater independence and freedom of movement.[38] In the main, field slaves depended on the returns from the small plots given to plant provisions. For purposes of cultivation they were usually given Saturday afternoons, except in crop time, and Sundays off. Their clothing was trifling and consisted of a pair of trousers for each man, and a petticoat for each woman; these were made of coarse osnaburg and given once annually.[39] Only after 1798 were planters required to grant two suits a year.[40]

Slave houses were small square huts built with poles and thatched at the top and sides with grass. The interior was devoid of furniture and decorations. Beds were either laid on the bare ground, placed on a board or mat, or raised from the floor on board cabins. A few had blankets and there was generally a small fire more likely used for cooking purposes than for keeping the room warm.[41] The extra amenities undoubtedly distinguished the dwellings of the more privileged slaves.

The working and living conditions of slaves were only two aspects of their inferior social status. In addition, an elaborate system of regulations was adopted to control their lives and activities otherwise, consistent with their position at the bottom of the stratified social structure, in order to preserve the essential characteristics of the slave society.[42] Laws were designed to reinforce the social inferiority of slaves by imposing severe restrictions on their economic opportunities. For example, slaves could not themselves become owners of slaves, or cultivate sugar and cotton.[43] In common with free negroes and coloureds, slaves were subject to severe penalties for striking a white person. In their case the more severe nature of the punishment including execution also was indicative of their more subordinate and inferior social position.[44] Slaves could not leave the plantations, except to go to market, without a pass signed by the owner specifying the time of absence allowed.[45] How far the principle of subordination could be carried was nowhere better illustrated than in the provision regulating the funerals of slaves; no slave could be buried after sunset, or in any other than a plain deal board coffin without any covering or ornament, and no scarves or other favours could be worn at the funeral.[46] At the same time that the person of whites was protected against violation, his right in his slaves as property was guarded against other white persons who might seek the unauthorised employment of those slaves.[47] The question of political rights for slaves did not arise.

Until 1798 the powers of masters over their slaves were left virtually unlimited except in cases of manumission and holidays, and these were regulated in the interest of public finance and public order.[48] Habit and custom were allowed to determine allowances of food, clothing, housing and land which owners should give to slaves. Masters' power of correction was left undefined, and slaves were left without any legal protection against their owners.

Fundamental changes were required in the law governing the responsibilities of masters towards their slaves. These were effected by an Act of the General Legislature of the Leeward Islands in 1798, which provided *inter alia* for compulsory allowances to slaves in clothing, food, medical attention and for the legal protection of the persons and properties of slaves.[49] One aspect of these regulations should be noted as being peculiar to the Virgin Islands. As distinct from the other Leeward Islands where masters were allowed to diminish food allowances by one-fifth during croptime, in the Virgin Islands, masters were permitted to reduce food supplies only out of croptime when slaves could produce their own provision.[50] No reason for this distinction was given but it was probably due to the more limited opportunities which existed in the Virgin Islands to maintain slaves.

Despite the customary and legal disabilities from which slaves suffered they were not always meek and willing instruments of the planters' will. Whenever possible they sought to evade the rigours of the plantation system. Availing themselves of their owners' boats they absconded to Puerto Rico until an Act of 1787 effectively curtailed the practice by making it obligatory to keep a white man on board every fishing boat or cobble not hauled out of the water and secured every night.[51] Malingering in the fields which no amount of supervision could prevent, feigning of illness, suicide by hanging or poisoning especially among the newly-imported negroes, and deliberate destruction of their owners' property, were other ways by which slaves sought to resist their lot. In 1789 and 1790 attempts at arson for the purpose of pillage were so frequent that in the absence of a regular system of police, the young men of Road Town were constrained to form an association to watch by night to prevent them.[52]

Despite the elaborate legal precautions to prevent combinations of slaves, occasional rioting also occurred. Thus in May, 1790, an insurrection broke out among the slaves on the estates of Isaac Pickering from an erroneous belief that their freedom had been granted in England but was being withheld by the local inhabitants. The ringleaders were tried and sentenced, two to death and three to transportation.[53] Self-mutilation was another form of resistance and in 1793 an outstanding case occurred when eight slaves, two of them women, cut off their arms with their bills, as a protest against plantation labour.[54]

Generally, the treatment of slaves in the nineteenth century was milder than in the eighteenth. The abolition of the slave trade meant that there were fewer 'African' slaves likely to resist slavery to achieve a freedom recently lost. The deeper sense of security among the whites was compensated by a decrease in cruelties necessary to make slaves 'toe the line'. The increasing proportion of slaves educated in the plantation system made them more amenable to control, while the accumulated experience of slave management taught less savage and more effective ways of making them work. Faced with the impossibility of replacing lost slaves through purchase, planters had through necessity to adopt more lenient methods. Lastly, the influence of religious teaching and education undertaken by the missionaries became more pronounced and affected both slaves and planters alike for the better. The effective basis of operation was laid by the Melioration Act of 1798 which pointed to the ends to be achieved.

Reports of the improved condition of slaves did not always stem from interested planters' prejudice. For instance, in the 1820's Trelawney Wentworth, a visitor to the Virgin Islands, and Fortunatus Dwarris, a royal agent who examined the operation of criminal justice there, both commented on the better treatment meted out to slaves.[55]

On the principal estates severe or cruel punishment was no longer inflicted. As an indication of this change the use of the cartwhip was abolished as an instrument of punishment or as an incentive to labour. On Hannah's Sea Cow Bay Estate, in order to remove any dread of arbitrary or excessive punishment, slaves were governed by written rules.[56] Allowances of food and clothing were also more generous than they had been previously. Because of the decline of plantation agriculture slaves obtained a greater extent of better quality land for cultivation. They also received extra time, usually the whole of Saturday outside croptime, and Sunday to work their lands. Though slaves employed in works of necessity such as stockkeeping were required to work at all times, they did so by turns. By 1823, the visible property of slaves was estimated as follows:

38 horses at £7. 10s. each	£285.	0s
938 horned cattle at £5. each	4690.	0
2125 goats at 10/– each	1062.	10
1208 pigs at 10/– each	604.	0
33120 poultry at 1/6	2484.	0
23 boats at £5. each	115.	0
Fishpots and Fishing Tackle	123.	10
Property in building chiefly in town	700.	0
Furniture and utensils at 15/– per head	4698.	8
	£14,762.	8s.

These estimates did not include the disposable portion of esculents and fruits, and cotton produced by the slaves on about 1,675 acres of land whose estimated yield annually totalled £5,862. 10.[57]

Amelioration of slavery necessitates an explanation of two apparent contradictions of the new outlook, namely, maltreatment of slaves as evinced in the case of Arthur Hodge, and the several slave disturbances of the nineteenth century.

In 1811, Arthur Hodge, one of the leading inhabitants of Tortola and a member of the Council, who had a reputation for cruelty, was brought to justice for murdering several of his slaves.[58] Many of Hodge's crimes had been committed years before, but partly because of his influence and partly because the new order had not been fully grasped by the white community, he had not been brought to trial. Even in 1811 the ambivalent attitude of the white population still persisted, and the strength of party feeling was such that when the jury brought in a verdict declaring Hodge guilty of the murder of Prosper, his slave, it was accompanied by a majority recommendation of mercy.[59] Governor Elliot, a professed abolitionist,[60] personally supervised the proceedings against Hodge. He was struck by the 'state of irritation ... almost of anarchy' in the Virgin Islands. In order to prevent unpleasant occurrences from taking place 'in a conjuncture so replete with party animosity,' he was compelled to commission a militia, to order *HMS Cygnet* to standby in order to support the civil power if necessary, and to declare martial law between sunset and sunrise every day from the time of Hodge's condemnation on April 30, to the time of his execution on May 8.[61] Sentiment against the execution of a white man for crimes against slaves was still undoubtedly present in 1811, but the fact that Hodge could be brought to trial at all, and on the initiative of the members of the Council and Assembly was indicative of the change in attitude which was taking place among the planters.

None of the disturbances of the nineteenth century was due directly to discontent over bad living and working conditions. Neither can dissatisfaction with the system of slavery in general adequately explain the sporadic outbursts. In 1823 the negroes on Pickering's Josiah Bay Estate were reported to be in a state of rebellion. Investigation showed that the insubordination of the slaves was due to their refusal to be removed to Trinidad on the insistence of their master. The slaves on the Pickering estates, imbued with a greater sense of freedom and independence fostered by absenteeism, had a reputation for disorderly conduct.[62]

The slave disturbances of 1830 on the Lettsome Estates (Cane Garden Bay, Mount Healthy and Lower Estate) also cannot be explained in terms of discontent with slavery. It stemmed rather from the exercise of personal influence by William Payne Georges over the slaves belonging to those estates. The Lettsome estates were held by James MacQueen but claimed by Georges who, in order to enforce recognition of his claim, seized and removed all sugar and rum from the several estates, and committed extensive damage. The slaves were used as the instrument of his design.[63] In cases of disturbances, the fear always existed that an isolated incident would spread and engulf the entire colony, but when Governor Maxwell visited Tortola in response to an appeal for military assistance, he found slaves peaceably at work on several other estates he visited.[64]

It was never possible for ringleaders to muster enough support for a widespread revolt in the Virgin Islands despite the absence of a militia or other law-enforcing body and the comparatively small number of whites. This factor certainly speaks well for the relationship between whites and slaves. It was quite evident in 1831. Like the insurrection of May, 1790, that of 1831 was prompted by a mistaken idea that freedom was being deliberately withheld by the whites. It was due, also, to jealousy by slaves over the concessions granted to the free negroes and coloureds by an Act of that year,[65] and by the intention of the authorities to establish the much despised liberated Africans on a separate settlement with special facilities. The aim of the rebels was to eliminate the white population and then to escape to Haiti.[66] However, the rebellion failed completely. What was intended to be an island wide effort, fizzled out for want of support. Of the 200 men who promised to start the movement on the night of Sunday September 4, only 65 were present at the trysting place called 'Frances' Head' near Road Town.[67] Beyond the burning of the house of Rogers Isaacs, no further damage was done, and peace was soon restored by the prompt response of the Danish Governor of St. Thomas to an urgent appeal for help by the President of the Virgin Islands.[68] When Major Williams, the Governor's Private Secretary, visited thirteen of the supposedly disaffected estates shortly after, he reported the prevalence of quiet and order.[69] By 1831, the complacency of the slaves and their disinclination to disrupt the existing social order can be attributed to the changes which had already occurred in that order making it more tolerable and accommodating.

Despite the restrictions imposed by the Slave Act of 1783, marriages between slaves were never objected to by their masters, though there was a 'general prejudice against the marriage of slaves with free people.'[70] No attempt was made to interfere in the union of slaves or to prevent them. Rather it was an accepted part of estate life that married couples should not be separated by sale or emigration.

The fostering of settled family life among slaves was one of the methods adopted by planters to secure stability on the estates. Encouragement of direct religious instruction and education was another. Religion had never taken a firm hold on the lives of white Virgin Islanders, although they were quite conscious of the benefits which would accrue to them in having the slaves instructed in the Christian faith. So long as religion could be used to further their interest they gave it their active support; when it conflicted with that interest they were not likely to exhibit much enthusiasm. This explains their varying response to the efforts of the Quakers and the Wesleyan Methodist missionaries to introduce religion in the Virgin Islands.

Birthplace of Dr. John Lettsom on Little Lost Van Dyke.

Ancient Burial Ground of Friends, Tortola, showing tomb-stones, foundations of
the meeting house, and Long Look Farm. From a contemporary drawing.

Beginning in 1727 with the activities of Joshua Fielding, attempts had been made to establish Quakerism in the Virgin Islands.[71] Initial response was favourable and sufficient progress was made to encourage Monthly Meetings in 1741, and the initiation of correspondence with Quakers in London and Philadelphia. In 1741 there were about 30 Quakers in the islands but only one Meeting at Fat Hog Bay. A few years later there were four Meetings – The Road Meeting, Fat Hog Bay Meeting, East End Meeting of Jost Van Dyke, and White Bay Meeting. Impetus and encouragement in dedicated devotion were given by the example of visiting ministers beginning with Thomas Chalkley in 1741, and John Cadwallader and John Estaugh in 1742, all of whom died during their ministration and were buried in the Friends' burial ground at Fat Hog Bay.

Quakerism was not destined to run a lengthy course in the Virgin Islands. As early as 1743 in its report to the London Yearly Meeting, the Tortola Monthly Meeting while announcing the admission of several new members envisaged 'great declension' in its numbers. Quakerism was incompatible with the nature of society in the Virgin Islands. Though Quakers themselves held slaves, Quakerism held slavery with a certain moral misgiving. As such, therefore, it threatened to undermine the incipient economic and social structure, and brought upon the Quakers the opposition of those who did not belong to their Society. John Pickering around whom revolved the future prosperity of Quakerism was removed from the influential position as Lieutenant-Governor of Tortola in June, 1742, and replaced by Captain John Hunt who was described as 'a very cruel enemy to Friends, a haughty, proud, austere man whose wife had suffered cruel persecutions on account of her being one.' In explanation of the decrease of numbers in 1743, it was claimed that some members were alarmed at the prospect of persecution, due to the change.

To combat the growth of Quakerism, the first Anglican clergyman, John Latham, was appointed in 1745 by the non-Quaker inhabitants. Latham's activities, including marriage to one of the leading Quaker women, Dorcas Powell, who was consequently disowned by the Women's Monthly Meeting, had some impact: 'his coming made a great noise in the elements, speaking great swelling words.'

Other tenets of Quakerism than disfavour with slave-holding contributed to its decline. Quakers were forbidden to bear arms and were consequently persecuted. In an island which was not particularly noted for its high moral virtues, and where the temptations of illicit trading and the allurements of accumulated wealth had special attraction, Quakerism fought a losing battle. Few could adhere to the strict discipline demanded by their adopted religion. In 1746, was reported 'great declension from the Christian Plainness and humble deportment which our ancient worthies were exemplary in.' Members were admonished or disowned for breaches of discipline and meetings were unattended through indifference. In 1755 it was reported that 'Meetings for business are so much neglected from a supineness among friends that nothing more remains at present than to nominate the date such meetings shall be held on.' By 1762 Meetings for business had ceased though Meetings for worship continued a little longer, and in 1763 the last letter, signed by six Friends, was sent to London. Quakerism was in effect at an end. Those who had not been rejected for breaches of discipline were removed by death culminating with that of John Pickering in 1768. Except for a visit paid by Thomas Gawthrop in 1756 the stimulus of external influence towards the revival and continued growth of Quakerism had disappeared. Internally, it was denied the favourable reception by the whites for whom it catered, and which was so essential to its spread.

Quakerism disappeared from the Virgin Islands but it was not without results. Some of the most influential people had been Friends, and they gave to the islands a dignity which could be used in the agitation for a constitution after 1750.[72] The humane treatment by Quakers of their slaves (some of them like John Coakley Lettsome and Samuel and Mary Nottingham manumitting their slaves), whose greater devotion to their masters and to plantation labour was a direct consequence, revealed to the other planters the value of religion in the control of their slaves.[73] Their frequent petitions to the Governor of the Leeward Islands towards the end of the eighteenth century, for the appointment of clergymen, testify to their belief in the efficacy of religion as a means of making slaves more tractable and consequently more useful and valuable.[74] Their encouragement of the efforts of the Methodist missionaries, and their provisions for an incumbent of the Established Church later on, were motivated by the same idea.

By the middle of 1789 the Methodists had established a station in Tortola and immediately set to work with the zeal which was characteristic of their efforts in the Virgin Islands during slavery. The response was more favourable among negroes than whites: planters were content to see the development of religion among their slaves; and the free negroes and coloureds saw in the activities of the missionaries the means of acquiring the education necessary to the attainment of a higher social status. In 1790 there were 900 negroes in the Methodist Society and no white; in 1791 there were 900 negroes and 18 whites; and in 1793 there were 1,400 negroes but only 6 whites. Between 1796 and 1800 there was an annual average of 2,640 negroes and only 17 whites in the Society. Thereafter, as a result of a number of crises combined with the effects of emigration, deaths, lapses from membership and disciplinary exclusions, there was a substantial fall in membership. From 1802 to 1815 there was an average of 2,185 negroes a year in the Society, while from 1816 to 1823 there was an annual average of 1,819.[75]

The abolition of the slave trade and the reduction of the white population not only resulted in more humane treatment of slaves, but also showed the need for closer co-operation with and support from the missionaries to keep them under effective control. By so doing the remaining whites sought further to maintain their status in society. In 1811, despite the depressed economy, an Act was passed creating the parish of St. George in the Virgin Islands, and providing an annual salary of £550 currency for a clergyman and of £50 currency for a parish clerk.[76] In 1823 the principal planters gave their whole-hearted support to the formation of the 'Wesleyan Methodist Auxiliary Missionary Society for Tortola and the Virgin Islands' which was designed to co-operate generally with other Missionary Societies to evangelise negroes.[77]

The desire of the Methodists to convert as many souls as possible to Christianity dominated every other consideration.[78] It even determined their attitude to education which had a strongly religious flavour. The instruction of the young was viewed 'as an object of supreme importance.'[79] The first schools operated by the Methodists were Sunday Schools in which emphasis was placed on Bible reading and catechism. Later, a day school was opened in Road Town which was taught three mornings a week but there was no significant difference in instruction. In both types of school, rules governing admission and exclusion were those which pertained to the moral behaviour of children. As there were no separate school houses, school was conducted in the chapel or in private houses; and as there existed no fund from which to pay teachers, their services were required gratuitously.[80]

From the early nineteenth century the activities of the Methodist missionaries were assisted by the Anglican clergy who before then had ministered chiefly to the minority of whites. Clergymen were not regularly paid but received fees for officiating at marriages, baptisms and funerals. In the later eighteenth century they held civil and political offices; one clergyman served as a Councillor in the Virgin Islands while another held a seat in the Assembly and acted as Speaker from time to time.

Education, as distinct from religious instruction, was more the undertaking of the Anglican clergyman. Admitting the predominance of the Methodists in spreading the gospel, when he himself had failed to an appreciable extent to attract the negroes, the Rector abandoned his earlier antagonism towards the Methodist missionaries. Co-operation replaced competition. The activities of the two missions became complementary, the Methodists concentrating on religion, and the Anglicans on education.

The first Anglican day school was established in Road Town towards the end of 1827 under the inspiration of the clergyman and the patronage of the Bishop of Barbados.[81] By 1835, four schools were in operation: one at Virgin Gorda, one at Kingstown and two in Road Town. In one of the Road Town schools, instruction was given gratuitously by the Rector; in the others, teachers were paid wholly or in part by the Bishop.[82] Besides religious instruction, the children were taught reading, writing, and arithmetic.[83] Children were admitted irrespective of their status or condition in society: in 1830 the 74 children enrolled in the National School in Road Town included whites, free negroes and coloureds, liberated Africans and slaves.[84] Books were furnished by a donation from the New England Society, but as with the Methodist schools, requirements always exceeded supply. Both Methodist and Anglican schools also suffered from a lack of sufficient or adequately trained teachers.

It was evident from the lack of basic teaching facilities, and from the religious type curricula, that educational standards were very low. Planters' aim to discourage high standards, even if such were possible, was to prevent slaves from contemplating alternatives and to make them more obedient, an objective partly achieved during slavery. The combined effect of religious instructions and education was described as 'less immorality and more genuine religion,' and the creation of a more orderly and stable society.[85]

By the 1820's some progress at least had been achieved in educating the slaves in the norms of Christian ethics, and the treatment of slaves by their masters had greatly improved. These two factors partly

determined planters' reaction towards proposals to ameliorate slavery
and to emancipate slaves. With regard to the former it was believed that
religious instruction was doing for the slaves what was expected of the
British policy of amelioration,[86] and that the actual treatment of
slaves had outstripped opinion, 'the obnoxious parts of the Slave Act
having long been a dead letter.' Amelioration proposals were not
adopted though planters agreed on the need to legalise practice.[87]
With regard to the latter it was asserted that in the semi-barbarous state
of slaves 'Emancipation would prove a Curse instead of a Blessing to the
poor People themselves.'[88]

Planters' reaction to emancipation showed more than a concern for
the welfare of slaves. Self interest was strong as was reflected in their
concern over the future of the sugar industry should slaves be
emancipated. The sugar industry though depressed was the mainstay of
their existence which, they suggested, would be destroyed by emancipation. In 1823 their fears were expressed in terms of their personal
safety,[89] but by 1831 from the failure of the British Government to
grant repeated applications for relief, the collapse of the entire
economy was envisaged, since 'the cultivation of their Estates could not
possibly be carried on by the free labour of those People for any Wage,
or Hire that could be offered them.'[90]

Economic self interest combined with a genuine desire to provide for
the future well-being of the slaves were both explicit and implicit in the
alternative proposals to emancipation suggested by the planters. In
1823 full compensation was demanded if the British Government
interfered 'with their natural and acquired rights' in slave property.[91]
A more constructive and broadly based suggestion was made in 1831
when they proposed the trial prior to emancipation of an experiment in
the Virgin Islands (which from their insular position and small extent
seemed ideal for this) whereby the right in and title to all property, real
and personal, of the inhabitants should be transferred at a fair
valuation, payable immediately or by instalments with interest in three
to five years, presumably to the British Government. After operating
the plantation system for a year or two it could then be ascertained
whether emancipation would benefit either Britain or the slaves.
Success of the experiment in the Virgin Islands might result in its
adoption generally in the British West Indies.[92] Alternatively, if it
failed the insinuation was that the existing system should be resumed
and continued.

When in 1833, the newly reformed British Parliament acting under pressure from the Anti-Slavery Society and other religious and humanitarian organisations in Britain, decided that no other proposal was an acceptable alternative to emancipation which by an Imperial enactment would come into force on August 1, 1834, local reticence and protest were tempered by expressed desire to co-operate. The decline of sugar and cotton, and the migration of most of the planters by then, resigned the others to emancipation. In any event they lacked the power of effective protest, which was further weakened by the promise of compensation.

Overtures made by the Governor of the Leeward Islands in 1833 to ascertain the sentiments of the legislature of the Virgin Islands to the measure for emancipation did not meet with any hostile reaction.[93] The Assembly then probably did not speak out as explicitly as could have been wished, but in March, 1834, resolutions were passed expressing members' detestation of slavery 'as well in the abstract as in the concrete,' and the Emancipation Act was condemned for continuing 'all the evils of slavery in their worst form.'[94] In keeping with the new situation the necessary enactments were passed abolishing slavery in the Virgin Islands and introducing instead a period of apprenticeship ranging from four years for domestic slaves to six years for field slaves while giving full freedom to slaves under six years of age.[95]

[1] W. L. Burn: Emancipation and Apprenticeship in the British West Indies. (Jonathan Cape, London, 1937) p. 33.
[2] C.S.P. 1685-1688. No. 678.
[3] C.O. 153/6. f. 110. Codrington to the C.T.P., 5 July, 1697; C.S.P. 1696-1697. No. 1347; C.S.P. 1716-1717. No. 118; C.S.P. 1724-1725, No. 260.
[4] C.O. 152/79. Enc. in Thomson to Portland, 26 March, 1800. No. 53.
[5] C.O. 152/98. A. M. Belisario to J. M. Belisario, 6 Aug., 1811; C.O. 239/26. Enc. in Colquhoun to Goderich, 20 April, 1831.
[6] C.O. 239/8. Enc. No. 2. in Maxwell to Bathurst, 1 May, 1822. No. 11; C.O. 239/13. Enc. in Maxwell to Bathurst, 10 Feb., 1826. No. 7; C.O. 239/22. Enc. No. 1. in Maxwell to Bathurst, 23 June, 1830. No. 27. These papers reveal that between 1808 and 1822 a total of 95 slaves were exported to several Caribbean territories including St. John, St. Christopher, Nevis, Anguilla, Antigua, Trinidad, and Demerara, and that in 1825, 1,055 slaves consisting of 492 males and 563 females were removed. After 1825, as a result of the Consolidated Slave Trade Abolition Act of that year, removals were reduced, numbering only 11 in 1828. Despite the 1825 Act, planters removed their slaves illicitly by taking advantage of the lax enforcement of the regulations and by having the slaves sentenced to transportation in the law courts.

[7] C.O. 239/8. Enc. No. 3. in Maxwell to Bathurst, 1 May, 1822. No. 11. C.O. 239/22. Enc. No. 3. in Maxwell to Murray, 2 Nov., 1830. No. 53. Between 1808 and 1822, 143 slaves were manumitted by will and 161 by deed; between 1825 and 1830, 147 slaves secured their manumission, 23 by purchase, the others granted for faithful service, and because of 'special love and affection' by their owners. Most of these were individual manumissions; freedom of slaves en bloc was not unknown.

[8] W.M.M.S. West Indies, Box 1803-1813. Coultas to Coke, 26 Nov., 1813; Box 1822-1823. Felvus to Taylor, 15 April, 1822. No. 128; C.O. 239/5. Enc. in Lack to Goulborn, 6 Dec., 1819.

[9] C.O. 152/28. No. Bc 83 and No. Bc 86; C.O. 152/100. Enc. in Elliot to Bathurst, 14 Nov., 1812. No. 13; C.O. 239/8. Maxwell to Bathurst, 1 May, 1822. No. 11; C.O. 239/13. Enc. in Maxwell to Bathurst, 10 Feb., 1826. No. 7; C.O. 317/3. Blue Book for 1828.

[10] M. G. Smith, 'Some aspects of Social Structure in the British Caribbean about 1820'. (Social and Economic Studies, U.C.W.I., 1953, Vol. 1. No. 4.); Douglas Hall, 'Slaves and Slavery in the British West Indies.' (Social and Economic Studies. U.W.I. 1962. Vol. 11. No. 4.) p. 316.

[11] M. G. Smith, op. cit., p. 59.

[12] Elsa V. Goveia: Slave Society in the British Leeward Islands at the end of the Eighteenth Century. (Yale University Press, New Haven and London, 1965), p. 300.

[13] M. G. Smith, op. cit., p. 62.

[14] Cf. Goveia, op. cit., p. 208.

[15] C.O. 152/96. Elliot to Liverpool, 21 Nov., 1810. No. 15.

[16] Smith, op. cit., pp. 73-74.

[17] Burn, op. cit., p. 72, and Goveia, op. cit., p. 202.

[18] C.O. 152/67. Enc. in Nugent to Sydney, 2 Dec., 1788. No. 16. Clauses XXX, XXXI, XXXII, XXXIII, XXXIX, and XL.

[19] C.O. 315/1. Act No. 8.

[20] C.O. 315/1. Act No. 6; C.O. 315/21. Acts Nos. 35 and 37.

[21] C.O. 152/91. Enc. in Colquhoun to Cooke, 14 Sept., 1808.

[22] C.O. 317/3. Blue Book for 1828.

[23] C.O. 239/9. John Stobo: Statistical Table of the British Virgin Islands for two periods.

[24] Ibid.

[25] Ibid.

[26] C.O. 152/105. Hill to the C.T.P., 16 Feb., 1815; Hill to Liverpool, 18 March, 1815.

[27] C.O. 315/4. Act No. 68.

[28] C.O. 315/5. Act No. 77.

[29] Hall, op. cit; p. 308.

[30] Goveia, op. cit., pp. 116-119.

[31] T. Wentworth: The West India Sketch Book (London, 1834) Vol. 1. pp. 161-2.

[32] Report on the Experiment Station, Tortola, Virgin Islands, 1908-9. (Barbados, 1909). p. 8.

[33] Great Britain, Parliament House of Commons: Minutes of the Evidence taken before a Committee of the House of Commons being a Select Committee appointed on 29 Jan., 1790. (Printed in 1790), p. 264.

[34] Ibid., pp. 267-8.
[35] Ibid., p. 265.
[36] Ibid., p. 269.
[37] Wentworth, op. cit., p. 224.
[38] Goveia, op. cit., p. 230.
[39] Great Britain, Parliament House of Commons: Minutes of Evidence . . . p. 268.
[40] Laws of Antigua, Vol. 1. Leeward Islands Act No. 36 of 1798, Clauses VII and VIII.
[41] Great Britain, Parliament House of Commons: Minutes of Evidence . . . p. 268.
[42] C.O. 152/67. Enc. in Nugent to Sydney, 2 Dec., 1788. No. 16. Act. No. 6.
[43] Ibid., Clauses XLII, XXIII.
[44] Ibid., Clause XXIV.
[45] Ibid., Clause XVIII.
[46] Ibid., Clause XLIV.
[47] Ibid., Clause XXVIII.
[48] Clauses XXV, XXXIV, XXXV, XXXVI.
[49] Laws of Antigua, Vol. 1. Leeward Islands Act No. 36 of 1798.
[50] Ibid., Clauses 11, 111, V and VI.
[51] C.O. 315/1. Act No. 19.
[52] C.O. 239/11. Enc. in Colquhoun to Bathurst, 24 March, 1824.
[53] C.O. 152/69. Enc. in Shirley to Grenville, 11 June, 1790. No. 37.
[54] C.O. 239/11. Enc. in Colquhoun to Bathurst, 24 March, 1824.
[55] Wentworth, op. cit., p. 225; Fortunatus Dwarris: The West Indian Question plainly stated, and the only practical remedy briefly considered: in a Letter to the Rt. Hon. Henry Goulburn, Chancellor of the Exchequer. (London, 1828) p. 14.
[56] C.O. 239/26. Enc. in Colquhoun to Goderich, 20 April, 1831.
[57] C.O. 239/11. Enc. in Colquhoun to Bathurst, 25 March, 1824.
[58] P.P. 1810-11. Vol. XI, p. 397.
[59] P.P. 1810-11. Vol. XI, p. 409.
[60] C.O. 152/97. Elliot to Liverpool, 18 May, 1811. No. 44; C.O. 152/101. Elliot to Bathurst, 28 Jan., 1813. No. 29.
[61] P.P. 1810-1811. Vol. XI, p. 410.
[62] P.P. 1825. Vol. XXV, pp. 700-799.
[63] C.O. 239/22. Maxwell to Murray, 4 June, 1830. No. 22., and 3 Aug., 1830. No. 35 and enc.
[64] C.O. 239/22. Maxwell to Murray, 4 June, 1830. No. 22.
[65] C.O. 239/25. Maxwell to Goderich, 5 Oct., 1831. No. 60, and enc.
[66] C.O. 239/25. Enc. in Maxwell to Goderich, 19 Nov., 1831. No. 65.
[67] Ibid.
[68] C.O. 239/25. Maxwell to Goderich, 5 Oct., 1831. No. 60.
[69] Ibid.
[70] W.M.M.S. West Indies, Box 1823-1824. Felvus to Taylor, 23 Oct., 1823.
[71] All information on the Quakers in the Virgin Islands here is derived from Charles F. Jenkins: Tortola: A Quaker Experiment of long ago in the Tropics. (London, Friends Bookshop, 1923.)

[72]   C.O. 152/27. No. Aa. 75. Purcell to Hill, 31 Jan., 1753.

[73]   Fulham Papers. Vol. xx, pp. 105-7.

[74]   Fulham Papers. Vol. xxxi, pp. 229-30, and 241-2.

[75]   Rev. Thomas Coke: A History of the West Indies. (3 Vols. Liverpool, 1808; London 1810, 1811). Vol. 111. p. 124; G. G. Findlay and W. W. Holdsworth: The History of the Wesleyan Methodist Missionary Society. (London, The Epworth Press, 1921) p. 147; C.O. 239/11. Enc. in Colquhoun to Bathurst, 24 March, 1824.

[76]   C.O. 315/4. Act No. 60.

[77]   W.M.M.S. Reports, Vol. 11, 1821-1824. Report for 1824, pp. 73-84.

[78]   W.M.M.S. West Indies. Box 1803-1813. Brownell to Butterworth, 16 July, 1804, f. 122.

[79]   W.M.M.S. West Indies. Box 1816-1818. Raby, Shrewsbury and Hillier to Watson, 11 Oct., 1817.

[80]   C.O. 239/39. Enc. in MacGregor to Aberdeen, 12 March, 1835. No. 73.

[81]   W.M.M.S. West Indies. Box 1827-1828. Manley to the Secretary of the Methodist Society, 13 March, 1828. No. 103.

[82]   C.O. 239/39. MacGregor to Aberdeen, 12 March, 1835, No. 73.

[83]   C.O. 239/22. Enc. No. 7 in Maxwell to Murray, 2 Nov., 1830. No. 53.

[84]   Ibid.

[85]   C.O. 239/11. Enc. in Colquhoun to Bathurst, 24 March, 1824.

[86]   Ibid.

[87]   C.O. 239/9. Enc. in Colquhoun to Bathurst, Nov., 1831.

[88]   C.O. 239/11. Enc. in Colquhoun to Bathurst, 24 March, 1824.

[89]   C.O. 239/9. Enc. in Maxwell to Bathurst, 9 Aug., 1823. No. 71.

[90]   C.O. 239/26. Enc. in Colquhoun to Bathurst, Nov., 1831.

[91]   C.O. 239/9. Enc. in Maxwell to Bathurst, 9 Aug., 1823. No. 71.

[92]   C.O. 239/26. Enc. in Colquhoun to Bathurst, Nov., 1831.

[93]   C.O. 239/34. MacGregor to Stanley, 15 Aug., 1833. No. 107.

[94]   C.O. 239/38. Enc. in Colquhoun to Lefevre, 28 April, 1834.

[95]   C.O. 239/36. MacGregor to Stanley, 17 May, 1834. No. 106.

Chapter 5

The Liberated Africans

Quite distinct from the main body of negroes who comprised the slave population of the Virgin Islands, and also from the class of free negroes and coloureds, was another group of Africans who before 1834 were neither slave nor free. This body consisted of negroes who had been captured on board slaving-vessels and condemned to the Crown by the Vice-Admiralty Court in Tortola under the Act for the Abolition of the Slave Trade of 1807.

From the very beginning the condemned negroes, or liberated Africans as they came to be called, were recognised as the special responsibility of the British Government as specified by the Abolition Act of 1807.[1] Henceforth, direct control from Britain over the welfare of the Africans was a marked feature of their history. The future well-being and prosperity of the liberated Africans was dependent upon the willingness of the British Government to provide overall supervision and to undertake or sanction measures for their proper maintenance.

In order to give effect to the provision contained in the Abolition Act of 1807, with respect to liberated Africans, two Orders in Council were issued on March 16, 1808 for their disposal and governance.[2] Executive authority was vested in the Collector of Customs who was empowered to dispose of the Africans for military and naval service in the Leeward Islands forces, or as apprentices in the Virgin Islands. Close attention was directed towards the latter category especially in relation to fixed employment and the responsibilities of masters and mistresses. The Collector was directed to ensure that husbands and wives or other close relatives were not separated 'except where the employment of either rendered such separation indispensably necessary.'

It was required that apprentices should be bound 'to prudent and humane masters and mistresses,' and not to be employed solely in the fields or as domestics. Rather it was the intention of the British Government that they should 'learn such trades, handicrafts or employment' for which they had some natural aptitude and by which they could gain a comfortable livelihood when their apprenticeship expired. Masters and mistresses were required to provide the apprentices and their dependent children with sufficient food, clothing and other necessary comforts during their term of service. They were forbidden to treat the apprentices with hardship or severity, but to instruct them in a specified craft, trade or employment.

Apprentices were to be instructed as speedily as possible in the Christian religion, and when sufficiently taught were to be baptised. Attendance by apprentices at public worship was to be permitted and encouraged. Their transfer to another island or colony without the prior permission of the Collector of Customs was prohibited, as was the selling of apprentices into slavery. In default of these stipulations the master or mistress was to forfeit his or her right to the further service of the apprentice, and the term of apprenticeship was to cease.

Throughout these regulations the dominant aim of the British Government appeared to be the general welfare of the apprentices and the acquisition of some skill by which they might support themselves after apprenticeship. This claim, however, was weakened by the denial to the Africans of any voice in the manner of their disposal, and by the requirement that the apprenticeship should last for fourteen years. Provisions were even made to lengthen the apprenticeship of women who became mothers, and for reapprenticing those Africans whose master or mistress died, until they had served the entire term.

Accounts of the actual number of Africans captured and liberated under the Abolition Act of 1807 differ.[3] This was partly due to the fact that records were irregularly kept, and differences arose from conflicting oral evidences. All the authorities, however, agree that the bulk of the Africans totalling 1,070 were liberated from the four foreign vessels, the ships *Manuella*, *Venus* and *Atrevido*, and the schooner *Candelaria*, between August, 1814 and February, 1815. By far the largest proportion of the negroes were males over fourteen years of age, with smaller numbers of women, and children.[4]

A striking feature of the circumstance of the liberation was the high proportion of deaths, though again available records are inadequate or conflicting. Thomas Moody who along with John Dougan reported on the numbers and condition of liberated Africans in the Virgin Islands, mentioned that of the 1,318 Africans condemned, 248 died before they could be disposed, leaving a balance of 1,070.[5] Dougan referred to mortality only among the Africans from the *Venus* and *Manuella*; of the 617 Africans condemned 222 died before being apprenticed.[6] The mortality was attributed to an intestinal infection from which they were suffering at the time of capture.[7] Also important was the debilitating effect of the trans-Atlantic crossing.

For the support of the liberated Africans prior to their disposal the Governor of the Leeward Islands was instructed to adjust with the Collector of Customs the expense per head per day at which the negroes were to be maintained and the allowance to be made for essentials and other contingencies. These were to be continued until the Africans were respectively enlisted or apprenticed. As a special remuneration, above all other charges, the Collector was authorised to receive one guinea for each liberated African received and accommodated by him.[8]

Of the whole body of Africans liberated, one estimate placed the number disposed of at 1,070. Of these, 352 were taken into His Majesty's military and naval services, and 647 were indented as apprentices; the fate of the other 71 is uncertain.[9] The Collector of Customs, in his disposal of the Africans as apprentices, appeared to have given preference to the members of the Council and Assembly and the proprietors of sugar and cotton plantations. These received groups of from six to ten Africans who were properly indented to them.[10] But following the death or removal from the Virgin Islands of some masters, the surrender of many apprentices by others, and the diminished white population generally of the colony, the Collector found great difficulty in obtaining suitable masters for the Africans. In consequence many of them were apprenticed to persons who could not support them as they should.[11] Some of these included negroes who had previously been slaves but had subsequently obtained their freedom.[12] But even the well-to-do apparently did not follow either the letter or the spirit of the regulations of 1808.

The treatment of the liberated Africans was marked by negligence, harsh usage and the want of proper support. This stemmed partly from the inability of the masters and mistresses to cater for the wants of the Africans, and moreso, from the ambiguous position which they occupied within the society. They could not be regarded as slaves because of the terms of their indenture, and so were not regarded by their masters and mistresses as their exclusive property. In a slave society this had its corresponding disadvantages since possession carried with it certain recognised and accepted responsibilities.

Since liberated Africans were only valued for their labour, their deaths constituted no financial loss to those responsible for their welfare. Being so much extra labour, their replacement was not considered necessary; hence, no financial burden would result from their demise. Consequently very little attempt was made by most of the masters and mistresses to adopt even those voluntary measures of melioration which they were accustomed to accord their slaves. As the acting Collector of Customs reported in 1821, 'a total inattention to the benevolent views of His Majesty's Government' prevailed in the Virgin Islands.[13] For particular attention he pointed to the state of the Africans apprenticed to the President of the colony as 'such an example on his part must unhappily operate materially in inducing others to follow his example.' The apprentices were depicted as being 'dreadfully clothed, apparently badly fed, and bear strong marks of repeated punishment.'

Rather than being taught a useful trade or skill, the liberated African apprentices were worked in the fields along with the negro slaves. Indeed, very little attention was paid to the terms of the contract requiring the masters and mistresses to instruct their apprentices. In 1823, it was discovered that of 291 apprentices, 200 were indented as domestics and the remaining 91 were classed under the head of trades. Of those in the latter category, 50 were females chiefly employed as laundresses, seamstresses and cooks, while the remainder were recorded as being carpenters, seamen, and fishermen. However, very few of those Africans taken by proprietors of estates and indented to them as domestics were employed in that capacity. For the most part they were engaged in the cultivation of the ground, or as herdsmen.[14] The restriction on the employment of apprentices elsewhere than in the Virgin Islands was also disregarded; large numbers of apprentices were let out on hire in St. Thomas and St. John and obliged to remit weekly earnings to their masters and mistresses.[15]

Africans were not bound to remain with their masters and mistresses for the entire fourteen years. The result was that many of the Africans who were ill-treated, or who were accustomed to being let out on hire, went off in small boats to St. Thomas. From there they were occasionally brought back after application had been made to the Danish Governor, but as no proper masters could be found for them in the Virgin Islands many of them, presumably with the Collector's permission, returned to St. Thomas, where they procured employment for themselves.[16] In explaining the cause of this desertion of the apprentices from the Virgin Islands to St. Thomas, proprietors attributed it to a desire by the apprentices to be their own masters, and a disposition to lead an idle life, working occasionally when so disposed. There were undoubtedly cases of this kind, but there were far more numerous instances to prove that their action was precipitated by ill-treatment or by inadequate attention from indigent masters. The better opportunities offered in St. Thomas provided added incentive for their willingness to desert.[17]

Except for those men and women engaged in trade and as domestics respectively, general pessimism surrounded the notion of liberated Africans being ever able to achieve a decent livelihood by their own efforts. To some the apparent deterioration in the moral and industrious habits of those apprentices who detached themselves from their masters and mistresses to seek their own welfare was due to their preference for a precarious subsistence obtained by casual employment than for regular industry.[18] These accusations are to some extent quite understandable since they were levelled generally against all who were enslaved or apprenticed. However, they could not pertain, for example, to the majority of those Africans who went off to work in St. Thomas. Even in those cases where such criticisms were somewhat more relevant, the peculiar conditions of the Virgin Islands need to be considered.

In the general context of the society in which they lived, the liberated Africans independently stood a poor chance of being able to earn a comfortable living. If they were inclined towards agriculture, it is doubtful whether they could obtain land of their own; and even if they obtained some this could be only so small as to afford nothing more than a bare subsistence. From the contracted state of the trade of the colony, the prospects of obtaining constant employment as porters, boatsmen and sailors sufficient to afford them the common necessities of life, much less comfortable homes and medical care, were dim. From the preference given to negro slaves very few, if any, liberated Africans could hope to be employed as domestics by the richer planters who considered their labour 'as not equivalent to their support in food and clothing.'[19] It was chiefly the poorer class of planters who were more likely to accept their services, probably for no other reason than that the African might be willing to work for the low wages offered.

Meanwhile the presence of the liberated Africans in the colony raised questions touching on their relationship with the other social groups, more particularly with the slaves and free blacks and coloureds. Instances of cordial relations between whites and Africans were not wanting, but the unfavourable attitude of the whites was demonstrated by their reluctance to indenture or gainfully employ the Africans, and in their treatment of those whom they had been prevailed upon to apprentice. The liberated Africans were spurned generally by the slaves and by the free negroes and coloureds whose dislike was directed particularly against those apprentices who were limited to unskilled agricultural labour which was normally the business of slaves. The hatred of the slaves stemmed largely from the fact that the Africans enjoyed the coveted privilege of freedom, while the pride of the free negroes and coloureds was due to their being solely dependent on their initiative for a living which was regarded as being superior to that of the Africans.

Against both of the negro groups the Africans, though in some cases worse off, developed a certain 'hauteur' derived from their privileged position in society, which though not entirely free, was not slavery and made certain demands on those to whom they were attached. The estrangement between the groups, however, did not prevent some Africans from developing intimate relationships with persons from the free and slave groups. However superior the Africans might have regarded themselves vis-à-vis other groups the nature of these relations showed a tacit acknowledgement of their inferior status. As in the slave society proper where status was established and expressed in mating patterns, liberated African males tended to mate 'downwards' with slave women, while the females tended to mate 'upwards' with the whites (primarily their masters) and with free negroes and coloureds. In no case was marriage involved.

Because of the mutual dislike existing between the Africans and the other classes, concern was expressed over public security if the former were allowed to remain after the expiration of their apprenticeship. Not only was it feared that the occasional acts of violence between the apprentices and the other sectors of the negro and coloured population would become more frequent and serious, but that the presence of a body of people claiming to be free was likely to induce the slaves to demand a like concession and attempt to secure it by violent means. The safety of the colony and the lives of the inhabitants were thus endangered, more so in the absence of troops, a militia, or a proper system of police to enforce law and order.

The question was also raised of the financial burden which would be imposed upon the meagre resources of the colony if the Africans were allowed to remain. From the belief that the Africans would be unable to maintain themselves, it was concluded that they and their children would be thrown upon public charity. This was considered contrary to the Abolition Act of 1807 by which the charge for the support of the Africans at the expiration of apprenticeship would accrue to the British Government.[20]

It had become evident by 1823 that the apprenticeship policy of the British Government with regard to the treatment and training of the liberated Africans was not producing the desired results. Instead of being able to earn their independent livelihood after apprenticeship, the Africans promised to become an extra charge on the finances of the British Government. It thus became necessary for further urgent action to be taken for their disposal otherwise. Hitherto the inability of the liberated Africans to secure their own land to cultivate had proved the rock on which British policy had been wrecked.

To teach the Africans industry and thrift it was decided in 1823 to transfer as many of them as possible to Trinidad, where there already were free negroes settled at the Government's expense.[21] There they would be immediately settled as free persons upon allotments of land the extent of which was to depend on individual circumstances but was not to be less than three acres each. Temporary housing would be provided for them until houses could be erected on their respective allotments, where also provisions, clothing, domestic utensils and all necessary implements would be supplied at the expense of the government. Furthermore, the Africans would not be subject to any personal service which was 'incompatible with the principle of freedom, and the uncontrolled enjoyment of the right of whatever property' they immediately obtained or acquired by their own exertions.[22]

The essential precondition for the transfer of the liberated Africans to Trinidad was that it should be voluntarily accepted by the Africans themselves.[23] However, the grant of free choice to them wrecked the effective execution of the plan. Some Africans had formed close attachments to their masters and mistresses, while some others had become attached to slaves and others by whom they had children. Yet others could not envisage better prospects in a new environment especially since no attempt was made to educate them to accept the change. Fear of the unknown though negative proved a powerful factor in creating a disinclination to move. When invited to do so, only one liberated African consented to be removed to Trinidad.[24]

The rejection by the liberated Africans of the offer of settlement in Trinidad left the matter of their future welfare in abeyance until 1828. In 1826, the British Government toyed with the idea of settling the Africans in Sierra Leone but with no great enthusiasm or sense of urgency, the high cost involved being regarded as the dissuasive factor.[25] By 1829, however, the apprenticeship of those Africans who had been captured and liberated in 1814 and 1815 had ended or was about to end. It was necessary that new regulations be adopted with regard to them.

Since under the Abolition Act of 1807 the onus for maintaining the Africans after apprenticeship fell on the British Government, henceforth it became preoccupied with the problem of cost and the methods whereby expenses could be limited or reduced. Only grudgingly was it to yield to requests for money to provide for the welfare of the Africans. Financial considerations were both explicit and implicit in the regulations forwarded by Sir George Murray, the Secretary of State for the Colonies, to the Governor of the Leeward Islands, in October 1828.[26]

The Secretary of State did not think that it was fit that public revenue should be used to maintain persons many of whom, he believed, were perfectly competent to provide for their own maintenance. The Governor was directed that in all cases where the term of apprenticeship had expired or where the apprentices appeared capable of earning their own subsistence, certificates were to be issued entitling them to freedom under the Act for the abolition of the slave trade. Thenceforward, since the Africans had previously shown an unwillingness to leave the colony, they were to be permitted to reside there on the same conditions as the free negroes and coloureds. The British Government's refusal to be unduly burdened financially was implied in the admonition that if within the next seven years any African was convicted of theft, resorted to begging or sought parochial assistance, he would become liable to transportation elsewhere to labour for his own subsistence. No account was taken of the limited possibilities for earning an adequate independent livelihood in the Virgin Islands.

The Secretary of State's circular despatch revealed the general difficulty of applying similar instructions to several territories at the same time. In St. Christopher, Nevis and Anguilla where there were liberated Africans apprenticed also, and to which therefore the circular also applied, the directions could be fully and immediately introduced. But in the Virgin Islands where economic conditions were worse, they could only be partly implemented. In 1828, there were in the colony 297 adult apprentices, 210 children, and 12 motherless orphans. With some exceptions these were granted certificates of freedom; to authenticate the right to freedom of the children born during apprenticeship, their names were endorsed on the parents' certificates.[27] These children remained in the care of their parents, while the orphans were apprenticed to individuals who would have them until they were 18 years of age.[28]

Despite the Secretary of State's instructions, through the initiative of Robert Claxton, the Collector of Customs, who with regard to the African problem revealed remarkable energy and foresight, allowances were given to Africans who from old age, bodily infirmity or extreme youth were incapable of supporting themselves.[29] Funeral expenses of those free persons who might die in absolute poverty, and assistance to others who might in future, through accident or because of advanced age, need help, was also granted. In addition, jail fees and the cost of maintaining Africans imprisoned for misdemeanours, and medical assistance for those in extreme distress, were provided. Even so the Collector of Customs was admonished to exercise great care and precaution to limit the charity to cases of absolute necessity to prevent any abuse of it. Furthermore , he was cautioned to obtain the proposed medical aid at the lowest rate by contract, by accepting the most reasonable tender.[30]

The continuation of the expenses towards the support of the Africans subverted the intention of the British Government to relieve the public revenue from the burden of their maintenance. Nevertheless, in the main, the decision to give the Africans conditional freedom from their apprenticeship was followed by favourable results. It is true that some Africans availed themselves of their freedom to leave the Virgin Islands to seek employment elsewhere, something which could not be prevented.[31] Others moved from the rural areas to Road Town where there was already a large number of Africans. From the depressed state of trade there, they were scarcely able to earn a daily pittance. Of these people it was said that had they devoted 'their strength to agricultural employment, Tortola and its dependencies would furnish them not only a maintenance, but in many cases an independence, and instead of their being a burthen to society, they would by industry prove a blessing.'[32] This criticism, like others of its kind,

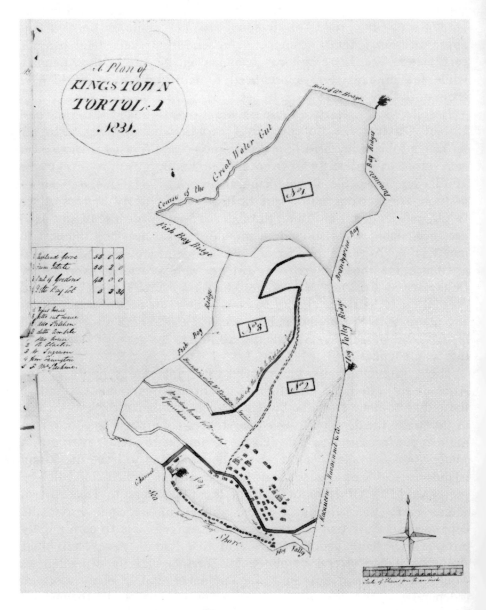

Kingstown

failed to take into consideration the very slim chances which the Africans had of being able to follow such hopeful alternatives.

Despite hardships, a year after the introduction of the free-system some improvement was noticeable among the Africans as shown by the diminution of the expenses in jail fees and warrants, the absence of crime and misdemeanours among them, and if not really an augmentation of their membership in the Methodist church, then at least a greater sympathetic adherence. Greater industry and initiative was shown by them with regard to agriculture, and wherever possible they rented land for cultivation. Progress was relatively pronounced. After a visit to Tortola, the Governor was gratified with the appearance of many of these Africans, and also of the cottages which they had erected on their rented land. He praised their 'industry and quiet demeanour.'[33]

The industry of the liberated Africans, despite the progress made, suffered from a number of adverse conditions. Land rents were high imposing a severe financial strain on their ability to pay; cultivation was destroyed by stray cattle, goats and pigs; and the doubtful tenure of the land by the lessor proved an effective obstacle to the successful procurement of redress by legal action. In cases of such rented land also, the question of whose responsibility it was to erect fences posed problems which were likely to stall their construction. According to Robert Claxton, the Collector of Customs, while the bonus of freedom as an inducement for their own exertions appeared to have been appreciated by the Africans, 'that bonus requires an accompanyment of means whereby to gain a livelihood.'[34] Some measure of assistance was clearly necessary by way of independent holdings so that uninterrupted cultivation could be undertaken.

Economic depression in the Virgin Islands, and the inability of the local government to meet its own financial obligations, made it impossible to look for the desired assistance from that direction. In March, 1831 a grant of £1,025 was secured from the British Government for the purchase of 110 acres of land and the buildings thereon, belonging to Messrs. Crabbe and Isaacs in Baugher's Bay a few miles from Road Town, to defray the law charges for conveyancing, and to erect the labourers' houses.[35] The British Government was undoubtedly induced to make the grant by the firm opinion given by Governor Maxwell that the new settlement would result in considerable savings in the future by enabling the Africans to raise provisions for their own sustenance.[36] Before the settlement was completed, further grants of £300 and £1,000 were made, however reluctantly, in order to purchase more land and to meet increasing costs of material.[37]

Most of the work on the new settlement was undertaken by the Africans themselves by co-operative effort under the supervision of Robert Claxton and the Methodist missionaries. By August, 1831, 152 adults and 145 children were located at Kingstown, as the settlement was named, with about 50 applicants yet unprovided for. Ninety-one dwellings had been completed with fifteen more nearing completion. Several of the cottages had been brought by the Africans from other sites previously rented, and re-erected on the new site at Kingstown, the expense of removal and rebuilding having been defrayed from the fund allocated for that purpose. It was proposed to convert the dwelling house found on the 110 acres into a school room and chapel for use by the Methodist missionaries. Generally, plots about an acre each were distributed by lot and secured to the occupiers by deed, though ownership was retained by the Crown. Sale or transfer by the occupants was altogether forbidden. According to one eye-witness account, Kingstown presented a very attractive appearance, and the hope was expressed that it would not be an ornament only, but by producing provisions be an important asset to the colony.[38]

From the very beginning the liberated Africans in Kingstown were treated as a new and distinct order in society due to the concept concerning the Africans in the community. Their civil existence was regarded as having grown out of the policy of the laws for the abolition of the slave trade and subsequent regulations by which they appeared to be viewed as 'infants in civilisation' and subject to paternal care. They were not considered as labouring under all the disabilities of slavery or entitled to all the advantages of freedom. These attitudes were clearly illustrated by the special treatment they received.

In seeking to put the liberated Africans on an equal footing with the other free negroes by his circular despatch of 1828, the Secretary of State undoubtedly intended to integrate the Africans into the society. The creation of Kingstown, however, was to frustrate the achievement of that design. By the end of 1832 the settlement had taken on the appearance of a distinct community: it was inhabited solely by liberated Africans whose infrequent contacts with the other sections of society reinforced their seclusion outside the town.[39] Indeed, the only regular contact established with the residents of Road Town was through the Collector of Customs and the Methodist missionary.

Though the Africans were subject to the laws of the Virgin Islands, at the insistence of the Collector, proposals were sanctioned for the appointment of a head policeman or supervisor assisted by six other Africans to be chosen weekly by the Collector as petty constables. The appointments were made to maintain order in the settlement since the colony itself lacked a properly constituted police force, and a lock-up was provided to house those arrested. In addition, regulations were made for the encouragement of agriculture — the impounding of livestock found trespassing on provision grounds, and the confiscation and disposal of grounds and houses whose owners had gone off the settlement leaving them to go to ruin.[40] The effect of these regulations further increased the separateness of the settlement. The isolation was made more complete with the establishment of a school and a place of worship in 1833. An allowance of £100 sterling was received from the British Treasury,[41] and £103. 14s sterling from the Society for the Conversion and Religious Instruction and Education of the Negro Slaves in the British West Indian Islands, for remuneration of competent instructors.[42]

Because of the exclusive regulations and the grant of special facilities to Kingstown, the settlement gradually acquired the character of a separate colony within the colony. The transformation would have been complete but for the judicious action of the British Government regarding further suggestions for special privileges for the Africans. The first concerned the importation of all articles and materials for the express use by the liberated Africans free of duty.[43] The second related to the exemption of liberated Africans from the payment of a 2½% house and income tax imposed throughout the Virgin Islands.[44] As the Africans were partly maintained by, and the houses had been built from funds received from the British Government, it was considered anomalous and unreasonable that the King should be taxed in aid of a colonial revenue.[45] The case for discriminatory exemptions was likewise rejected by the law-officers of the Crown, who could adduce no rule or principle of law in its support.[46]

The attempt to secure the exemption of the liberated Africans from the responsibility of paying local taxes was followed by a similar attempt to free them completely from the payment of legal expenses. In cases of complaints among themselves the Collector managed to afford them redress without the intervention of the government officers. It was otherwise in cases involving outsiders; in these instances the Collector felt it incumbent upon him to pay all the expenses involved including court and jail fees.[47] The response of the Secretary of State in 1835 was based on the general principle that all liberated Africans who were in a condition to subsist themselves were to be left to do so like other free inhabitants, and he ordered that they should be left to protect themselves from injury at their own cost.[48]

This conception of the limited liability of the British Government towards the Africans was given further practical expression in the reluctant attitude adopted towards the appeal for assistance made after the hurricane disasters of 1837, and by the initial favourable reaction towards certain proposals by a local planter for the gainful employment of Africans. Finally, it enabled the British Government to adopt appropriate measures for the partial withdrawal of its own financial commitments towards the maintenance of the Africans. On the other hand it had the effect of impressing upon all concerned an awareness of the moral responsibility which the British Government had towards these people, which led to continued British involvement in the support of some Africans.

The number of Africans actually working land on which they had been located in Kingstown and constantly residing there amounted to 282 in 1837. Apart from these people about 70 others sought employment elsewhere, probably in St. Thomas, though they returned occasionally to Kingstown where their families resided.[49] In addition to agriculture, the greater proportion of the people on the settlement were engaged in burning lime for export, and in fishing.[50] The hurricane of 1837 completely devastated the settlement, and all of the Africans' houses were destroyed together with the storehouse and school-master's house. Only the school house and hospital were saved, the former partly, while six lives were lost, and many Africans were severely injured. Vegetation on the settlement was so blasted that it appeared 'to have suffered rather from a raging flame of fire having passed over the country than from the action of the wind.' The destruction of boats, nets and fishpots belonging to the settlement marked the final ruin of the means of livelihood of the majority of the Africans.[51] Their destitute condition evidently demanded assistance. Africans were debarred from parochial relief and as a temporary measure the Collector gave some help in lumber, provisions and other essentials. The British Government, however, refused to grant anything more than a meagre sum of £85 to repair the store-house, school and hospital, and the continuation of customary supplies to the infirm and aged.[52] The Africans were left to rebuild their homes as they best could by their own efforts and resources.[53]

The same reticence towards financial commitment shown by the British Government after the hurricane was evident in the lukewarm support given to the proposals by Robert V. Shew, a local planter, for the general and continuous employment of Africans. Shew was influenced by the noticeable industry of the Africans in Kingstown. He believed that they were retarded by insufficient land and improper direction which his scheme for metairie or share-working would correct. Under this scheme it was proposed to employ a sufficient number of Africans to cultivate half of his 500-acre estate in Sea Cow Bay. About 100 acres would be devoted to sugar-cane and the remaining 150 to provision grounds and pasture. In return for their labour the Africans would get half the sugar crop without production expenses being deducted, and a comfortable two-room cottage with one-third or one-half acre of ground attached, to each adult labourer. Hoes and bills would be provided by the Africans themselves.[54]

Shew's proposals were supported in principle both by the Governor and the Secretary of State primarily because they promised an alternative, though one with apparent advantages, to continued British support. The plan, however, foundered on the question of money with which Shew seemed to have been inadequately equipped. For the successful implementation of the scheme, Shew required a loan of about £500 to £1,000 sterling for the construction of the Africans' houses.[55] Locally the request was rejected on the presumption that no remuneration could induce the Africans to engage in sugarcane cultivation and that they had evinced a strong aversion to Shew's plan.[56] When it was evident that the scheme was not likely to be supported in the Virgin Islands, James Stephen of the Colonial Office minuted that he did not see any 'adequate motive for engaging further in the discussion at present.' He was supported by his colleague Henry Taylor who could not see 'why the system of shares in the produce should be expected to stimulate the negroes more than the system of wages, if the wages offered were of equal value.'[57] So long as the interest of the Africans carried financial involvement, not much enthusiasm was likely to be exhibited.

Reports had made it abundantly clear to British officials that the establishment of the Africans as an independent community was a serious error. After the 1837 hurricane, examples of industrious and prosperous Africans were not lacking. For instance, when it was quite evident that no support would be received for rebuilding their homes, several Africans had erected houses some of which were conspicuously substantial. Although they complained of poverty it was generally believed that they were in 'actual possession of means, or the power of acquiring them, when they chose to apply them.'[58] Some Africans were thus able to attain a position of ascendancy over the less active members of the community. Nevertheless by far the larger number of them never seemed to be able to recover from the effects of the hurricane; these people became categorised as idle and unproductive.

More important than the destruction suffered in 1837, however, was the development of a pernicious attitude among the Africans generally. From the circumstance of their having been supported for so long, they were led not so much to distrust the efficacy of their own exertions, as to look elsewhere for whatever support they might be able to obtain, and to make those exertions for other purposes than for their actual maintenance. Industry became progressively irregular and confined to the burning of lime, portering in St. Thomas, and occasionally farming.[59] Some secured employment with the Virgin Islands Mining Company of Liverpool operating in Virgin Gorda, but this was short-lived. After mining ninety tons of copper in 1841, the Company became bankrupt in 1842 and suspended operations.[60] Taught to regard themselves as the 'King's people' and to look on themselves as a distinct class independent in every way from the rest of the population, they resisted all attempts to deprive them of what they thought were their just rights.

Believing that the uncertain tenure of their holdings had proved unfavourable to the advancement of the Africans as an industrious and thriving community, the Governor in 1838 authorised the sale by public competition of a number of lots in Kingstown which had become vacant by the death of the occupiers without heirs. Other occupiers were also given an opportunity of redeeming theirs at the average value of £50 with appropriate deductions for improvements. Those who delayed in purchasing their allotments were allowed continued occupation until they could acquire the titles by purchase. It was hoped that the realisation that land value was likely to rise would induce speedy purchase by progressive instalments.[61] These expectations were destroyed by the Africans. Some satisfaction was initially shown with the proposed arrangements, but the Governor's intention was soon frustrated by the combined passive resistance of the people against what they deemed an invasion of rights held in quiet possession for some years by gift of the Crown.[62] It was not deemed expedient to procure compliance with the changes by resort to coercive measures and the lands continued to be held by the Africans on the original conditions.

A contemptuous attitude was also adopted by the Africans towards the recently freed negro slaves who shared similar feelings for the Africans. While slavery existed the Africans regarded themselves as a superior class to the negroes by virtue of their special privileges and exemption from the burdens to which the latter were subject. The slaves, on the other hand, had always conceived of the Africans as being inferior and looked forward to freedom to prove their self-dependence. Emancipation produced a nominal change in the relative position of the Africans and slaves but none in their attitudes, and it was feared that undesirable results might be produced. The need to integrate the two peoples was clearly evident.

It was towards the achievement of an industrious and thriving, non-exclusive and independent community firmly based on holdings with the appropriate security of tenure that the regulations of 1844 from the Secretary of State were directed.[63] Expenses hitherto borne by the British Government for medical assistance, education and special supervision were ordered to be discontinued. Henceforth the incapacitated and infirm were to be maintained in the local institutions, while other Africans were left to maintain themselves and·their families completely by their own labour. Orphans were to be supported until they were of age to be apprenticed or could obtain their own subsistence. Education also was to be provided for from local resources. In addition, titles to allotments were to be confirmed to those who could claim possession, the cost of survey and conveyancing to be met by the British Government.

The transfer of titles to the land threatened to founder on the rock of African suspicion and dissent. If deeds were accepted, the Africans were afraid that their provision grounds would become subject to taxation and that they would be deprived of the existing privilege of pasturing cattle and other stock, of cutting wood for sale, and for burning lime, on the waste or unallotted land. Thomas McCleverty, a spokesman for the Africans, expressed their dissent at a public meeting, 'Will the deeds make us better or worse, what will become of our privileges? The Deeds are going to make us worse, before they make us worse better send us back to Africa.' Amidst appreciative applause he and his associates staged a protest walk-out. Despite this reaction, however, the deeds were recorded by the Registrar and lodged in the

Colonial Secretary's Office.[64]

The regulations respecting the aged and infirm were never completely implemented due again to African opposition. Without exception, 16 adult paupers refused to enter the poor house as a pre-requisite for support. Six others were considered inadmissible as indoor paupers while nine out of thirteen orphans were allowed to remain under the care and protection of those under whom they had previously been placed. It was finally decided that an allowance of 5/− and 2/− per week should be given as outdoor relief to each adult and orphan respectively.[65] Medical attention was also provided at the rate of £25 sterling a year.[66] It was anticipated that with the orphans attaining a mature age and the invalids dying, the charge to the British Government would proportionally decrease. The proposed plan of lodging the aged and infirm Africans in the poor house was nevertheless urged to be kept in view and effected whenever possible.[67]

What was intended or expected to be a temporary expedient became a permanent charge upon the British Exchequer; the principle of maintaining the aged and infirm once accepted could not easily be relinquished. An attempt to form a friendly society in Kingstown in 1840 had failed to attract the support of a significant number of the settlers,[68] and with the persisting decline of the economy of the Virgin Islands making the Africans increasingly incapable of maintaining themselves, a large number was thrown upon the charity of the British Government.

By virtue of the continuing refusal of the Africans to enter the poor house, an attempt was made to unite the settlers further into the corporate life of the community. It was proposed in 1848, that in the first instance, in addition to the Africans already on the poor list, relief should be extended to others who were reported to be equally destitute and infirm, and incapable of earning their own livelihood, and in the second instance, that the charge of the Africans should be transferred from the Customs establishment to the guardians of the local poor.[69] A final decision was not reached until 1850; after a futile attempt to saddle the local authorities with part of the maintenance of the destitute and infirm Africans,[70] the Lords Commissioners of the Treasury were forced to reimburse the expenses incurred on their account by the local Board of Guardians,[71] as requested by that Board.[72]

The consent of the British Treasury was based on the understanding that the arrangement for relief was to be confined to those liberated

Africans only who had been captured and condemned and not to their descendants.[73] Even then, however, the numbers supported increased rapidly from nine at the end of 1850, to 46 towards the end of 1851.[74] No reason was given for this sharp increase and it was suggested that as few Africans had made any provision for old-age and infirmity there was not likely to be any considerable decrease for some time of the numbers requiring relief. The peak year was reached in 1859 when 74 Africans were supported; thereafter the numbers decreased though not with the velocity that was originally predicted.[75]

Acknowledgement of the responsibility to support the destitute and infirm did not mean a willingness to increase the extent of the responsibility. Whenever possible the intention was to reduce it. In 1856 when the Board of Poor Law Guardians was abolished,[76] the Africans were placed under the control of a contractor nominated by the Governor of the Leeward Islands. At the same time the weekly allowance of 4/6 for each destitute and infirm African, which had been authorised in 1850, was ordered to be reduced to 1/6 as allowed for other paupers in the Virgin Islands.[77] In 1861 a representation made by 63 inhabitants of Kingstown to the British Government for some financial aid to repair their chapel[78] was rejected, and they were advised to provide such amenities by their own industry.[79]

A similar denial of special privilege was made in answer to an application in 1868 from the contractor supplying the Africans to be relieved from the payment of the recently imposed import duties on articles imported by him for the use of the liberated Africans.[80] In an attempt to keep expenditure down, after 1862 certificates were required verifying the number of Africans subsisted and the period of their subsistence. Careful examination was instituted to certify the identity of Africans to ensure that they were definitely those originally captured and liberated. Their capacity to procure their own subsistence by a moderate exercise of industry was also ascertained. Finally, before any relief was afforded to married couples and widows, enquiry was made to determine whether they had ablebodied sons and daughters to support them.[81]

British policy had never produced the desired results. If the aim was to foster the development of an independent peasantry that policy was bound to fail. Even if the Africans had developed habits of agricultural enterprise, the lands which had been granted in 1831 and confirmed to them by fee simple in 1845 were nevertheless too small and too unproductive for the Africans to support themselves and their dependents, and to maintain the educational and medical institutions which catered for their needs. Their inability to achieve the latter was adequately demonstrated in 1861 when they memorialised the Queen for financial assistance to repair their chapel.

Again, the aim of the British Government to develop a permanent settlement of Africans in close relationship with the rest of the population also failed. Neither the Africans nor the negroes cultivated those habits of mutual understanding which were likely to draw them closer to each other. Reluctance to foster a more intimate relationship with the negroes, and the necessity to earn a living, compelled many of the Africans to resort to St. Thomas where more lucrative employment could be found. The extent of this migration is not known, but from the completely abandoned nature of Kingstown today, it is quite evident that what had begun as a temporary or occasional expedient, to supplement earnings obtained in the Virgin Islands, became permanent through necessity.

The liberated Africans in the Virgin Islands represented ideals of good which were not achieved. Their apprenticeship was intended to demonstrate to planters the advantages likely to be gained from an enlightened attitude towards the negro. The establishment of Kingstown was designed to show the capacity of the Africans to be productive when given the right conditions. And by throwing the Africans on their own resources it was intended to cultivate in them independence of outlook.

Failure to achieve these ends, however, should not obscure the fact that for some time the Africans positively held out the possibility of actual as distinct from potential good for the Virgin Islands. Their co-operative activity in the establishment of the settlement at Kingstown both in the clearing of the land and in the assistance given each other and the weaker members of their community promised to be an example worthy of emulation by the entire negro community. Their alienation from the negroes robbed it of whatever chances there were for its acceptance.

In contrast, however, was the example set by the Africans in the formation of a friendly or benefit society in 1840 under the guidance of the Methodist missionaries. The attempt though not very successful was effective in stimulating the negro population into similar efforts. Again, the suggestions of Robert Shew for the implementation of a system of metairie for the supposed benefit of the Africans should be noted. The detailed exposition of the system on this occasion not only clarified thinking on its operation but by doing so led to its easier adoption and implementation by other planters in the 1840's when declining economic conditions and the need to retain an adequate labour force on the plantations necessitated a reorganisation of the labour system.

[1] 47 Geo. 111, C. 36, Clause VII.
[2] P.C. 2/176. Orders in Council, 16 March, 1808.
[3] C.O. 152/105. Enc. in Ingram to Bathurst, 10 July and 26 Nov., 1815; P.P. 1825. Vol. XXV, pp. 5 and 600.
[4] C.O. 152/105. Enc. in Ingram to Bathurst, 10 July, 1815, and 26 Nov., 1815. Of the 1,070 Africans who comprised the cargoes of the Manuella, Venus, Candelaria and Atrevido, 625 were males and 181 females over 14 years of age, and 140 boys and 124 girls under 14 years.
[5] P.P. 1825. Vol. XXV, p. 600.
[6] P.P. 1825. Vol. XXV, p. 5.
[7] C.O. 152/105. Enc. in Ingram to Bathurst, 10 July, 1815.
[8] C.O. 324/103. Castlereagh to the Governor of the Leeward Islands, 11 April, 1808.
[9] P.P. 1825. Vol. XXV, pp. 500.
[10] P.P. 1825. Vol. XXV, p. 555.
[11] P.P. 1825. Vol. XXV, p. 556.
[12] P.P. 1825. Vol. XXV, p. 577.
[13] C.O. 239/7. Clement to Bathurst, 4 Aug., 1821.
[14] P.P. 1825. Vol. XXV, p.556
[15] C.O. 239/7. Clement to Bathurst, 4 Aug., 1821.
[16] P.P. 1825. Vol. XXV, p. 556.
[17] Ibid., p. 557.
[18] C.O. 239/9. Enc. in Maxwell to Bathurst, 1 July 1823. No. 64.
[19] P.P. 1825. Vol. XXV, pp. 528, 529 and 531.
[20] C.O. 239/9. Enc. in Maxwell to Bathurst, 1 July, 1823. No. 64; Colquhoun to Bathurst, 6 June, 1823.
[21] K. O. Laurence, 'The Settlement of Free Negroes in Trinidad before Emancipation.' (Caribbean Quarterly, Vol. 9, Nos. 1 & 2), pp. 26-47.
[22] C.O. 239/7. Maxwell to Bathurst, 1 July, 1823. No. 64; C.O. 318/81. Moody to Wilmot, 11 Feb., 1822; P.P. 1825. Vol. XXV, pp. 685-691.
[23] C.O. 319/28. Wilmot to Moody and Dougan, 8 Jan., and 25 Feb., 1823.
[24] C.O. 239/9. Enc. in Maxwell to Bathurst, 1 July, 1823. No. 24.
[25] C.O. 319/28. Horton to Herries, 8 Sept., 1826; and Horton to Hill 22 Dec., 1826.
[26] Circular Despatch: Sir George Murray to the Governor of the Leeward Islands, 16 Oct., 1828.
[27] C.O. 239/20. Enc. in Maxwell to Murray, 24 July, 1829. No. 22.
[28] C.O. 239/20. Maxwell to Claxton, 16 May, 1829.
[29] C.O. 239/20. Enc. in Maxwell to Murray, 24 July, 1829. No. 22.

[30] C.O. 239/21. Murray to Maxwell, 17 Dec., 1829, and enc.; C.O. 239/20. Maxwell to Claxton, 16 May, 1829.

[31] C.O. 239/20. Enc. in Maxwell to Murray, 24 July, 1829. No. 22.

[32] Ibid.

[33] C.O. 239/22. Enc. in Maxwell to Murray, 3 Aug., 1830. No. 36.

[34] Ibid.

[35] C.O. 239/26. Stewart to Howick, 2 March, 1831.

[36] C.O. 239/22. Maxwell to Murray, 3 Aug., 1830. No. 36.

[37] C.O. 239/25. Maxwell to Goderich, 6 July, 1831. No. 44; C.O. 239/26. Stewart to Howich, 14 Oct., 1831; C.O. 239/31. Stewart to Howich, 6 Jan., 1832.

[38] C.O. 239/25. Enc. in Maxwell to Goderich, 7 Sept., 1831. No. 56.

[39] C.O. 239/30. Enc. in Nickle to Goderich, 25 Sept., 1832. No. 26.

[40] C.O. 239/30. Ibid.; Stephen to Howick, 21 Nov., 1834.

[41] C.O. 239/32. Nickle to Goderich, 8 Feb., 1833. No. 74. and enc.; C.O. 239/35. Treasury to Stewart, 22 April, 1833.

[42] C.O. 239/35. Barret to Lefevre, 15 May, 1833.

[43] C.O. 239/26. Maxwell to Stewart, 29 July, 1831.

[44] C.O. 239/30, Nickle to Goderich, 26 Sept., 1832. No. 29, and enc.

[45] Ibid.; C.O. 239/26. Enc. in Stewart to Howick, 19 Oct., 1831.

[46] C.O. 239/31. Stewart to Howick, 14 Feb., 1832, and enc.; C.O. 239/30. Enc. in Nickle to Goderich, 26 Sept., 1832. No. 29.

[47] C.O. 239/39. Enc. in MacGregor to Aberdeen, 25 Feb., 1835. No. 59.

[48] C.O. 239/39. Aberdeen to MacGregor. (undated).

[49] C.O. 239/46. Enc. in Colebrooke to Glenelg, 29 Sept., 1837. No. 124.

[50] C.O. 239/31. Claxton to Goderich, 29 Sept., 1832.

[51] C.O. 239/46. Enc. in Colebrooke to Glenelg, 20 Aug., 1837. No. 90.

[52] C.O. 239/46. Enc. in Colebrooke to Glenelg, 21 Aug., 1837. No. 90 and 29 Sept., 1837. No. 124; Glenelg to Colebrooke, 13 Nov., 1837 and 26 Jan., 1838. No. 48.

[53] C.O. 239/46. Enc. in Colebrooke to Glenelg, 29 Sept., 1837. No.124; Colebrooke to Isaacs, 28 Aug., 1837. No.90.

[54] C.O. 239/46. Enc. in Colebrooke to Glenelg, 29 Sept., 1837, No. 124.

[55] Ibid.

[56] C.O. 239/47. Enc. in Colebrooke to Glenelg, 4 Nov., 1837. No. 154.

[57] C.O. 239/47. Minutes by Stephen, 21 Dec., 1837, and Taylor, 24 Dec., 1837, on Colebrooke to Glenelg, 4 Nov., 1837. No. 154.

[58] C.O. 239/50. Enc. in Colebrooke to Glenelg, 1 Sept., 1838. No. 203.

[59] C.O. 239/62. Enc. in Drummond Hay to Macphail, 19 Jan., 1841; Macphail to Drummond Hay, 13 Feb., 1841.

[60] C.O. 239/65. Enc. in Macphail to Russell, 16 Oct., 1841; Macphail to Stanley, 16 Dec., 1841. No. 111; C.O. 239/70. Enc. in Fitz Roy to Stanley, 9 March, 1843.

[61] C.O. 239/50. Colebrooke to Glenelg, 1 September, 1838. No. 203, and enc.

[62] Treasury 1/4898. Enc. in Fitz Roy to Stanley, 15 June, 1843. No. 42.

[63] C.O. 393/8. Stanley to Fitz Roy, 20 Jan., 1844. No. 112.

[64] C.O. 239/78. Enc. in Fitz Roy to Stanley, 10 Oct., 1845. No. 51.

[65] C.O. 239/75. Fitz Roy to Stanley, 9 Oct., 1844. No. 77.

[66] C.O. 239/75. Fitz Roy to Stanley, 26 Nov., 1844. No. 89.

[67] C.O. 239/79. Trevelyan to Stephen, 25 Jan., 1845.

[68] C.O. 239/60. S.M.'s Report for July, Aug., and Sept., 1840; P.P. 1845. Vol. XXXI, p. 206.

[69] C.O. 239/85. Higginson to Grey, 6 Nov., 1848. No. 57.

[70] C.O. 239/85. Grey to Higginson, 12 June, 1849. No. 159, and enc.

[71] C.O. 239/87. Grey to Higginson, 13 April, 1850. No. 214.

[72] C.O. 239/87. Higginson to Grey, 5 Sept., 1849. No. 54, and 2 Nov., 1849. No. 68.

[73] C.O. 239/87. Grey to Higginson, 13 April, 1850. No. 214.

[74] C.O. 239/90, Mackintosh to Grey, 27 Feb., 1851, and enc.; C.O. 239/51. Mackintosh to Grey, 30 Oct., 1851. No. 86.

[75] C.O. 314/21. Rothery to Treasury, 1 March, 1869.

[76] C.O. 315/8. Ordinance No. 17.

[77] C.O. 314/4. Hamilton to Labouchere, 12 Aug., 1856. No. 42, and Trevelyan to Ball, 6 Oct., 1856.

[78] C.O. 314/10. Hamilton to Newcastle, 25 Feb., 1861. No. 24, and enc.

[79] C.O. 314/10. Newcastle to Hamilton, 30 March, 1861. No. 164.

[80] C.O. 314/20. Hill to Buckingham, 4 Nov., 1868. No. 205.

[81] C.O. 407/11. Newcastle to Hamilton, 28 Oct., 1861. No. 319, and 25 July, 1862.

Chapter 6

The Aftermath of Slavery

Slavery was abolished in the Virgin Islands in 1834, but full freedom was not immediately instituted since a period of apprenticeship marked the transition from slavery to freedom. The system was affected by laws which governed the relationship between masters and apprentices, by the spirit in which those laws were implemented by the masters, and by the character of employment in the islands. In effect apprenticeship was nothing more than a modified form of slavery, with many of the essential features of the system which it replaced. Not even with the best of planning could it have been a panacea for the ills of slavery nor was it intended to be. It was an unnecessary period of marking time, since there were no immediate alternatives to plantation or domestic labour. Besides, apprenticeship did not contribute significantly to the developments of full freedom.

To many planters in the Virgin Islands apprenticeship threatened the beginning of utter ruin and destruction. The fears were expressed in terms of both the economy of the islands and the personal safety of the whites.[1] Because of these fears regulations were adopted to ensure the continuation of labour on the estates, and the prevention of disorder. For example, apprentices were subject to forty-five hours of compulsory free labour a week for their masters; thereafter they could, if they desired, contract to labour at agreed wages.[2] Their mobility was also restricted in so far as they were forbidden to change their residence without their masters' permission or to go beyond the estate without a written pass.[3] Elaborate precautions were taken against indolence, neglect and improper performance of work by apprentices. For the maintenance of order and discipline, regulations were made to ensure the punctual discharge of services, and for the punishment and prevention of insolence, insubordination, vagrancy, rioting, combined resistance and escape.[4] In certain respects, these regulations achieved a closer legal definition of the apprentices' subordination to their masters than under slavery.

Like slavery, however, apprenticeship could not depend solely on coercion. Because of the continued need for regular labour all the more necessary in view of the declining economy, and because of the now restricted nature of the labour available, compromise was vital to prevent dislocation and disorganisation. Consequently while planters continued to provide the customary allowances of food, housing and medical care, their power of coercion was considerably modified.[5] Assaults upon apprentices were made punishable offences, and apprentices could maintain civil suits for damages against their masters.[6] The acknowledgement by masters of a stipendiary magistrate to adjudicate or settle differences between themselves and the apprentices, and generally to supervise the operation and observance of the Act of Emancipation, was an essential feature of the new system.[7] Apprentices could not be worked on estates other than those on which they were employed prior to August 1, 1834, without the stipendiary magistrate's special permission, and the separation of husbands and wives, and parents and children was prohibited.[8]

The attempt at compromise between slavery and freedom was sometimes unhappy. The element of coercion present in the compulsory labour clauses created points of friction, and some planters failed to interpret apprenticeship in the spirit of the law.[9] Wherever this occurred it is not surprising that they should be resisted by apprentices suffering from recollections of past grievances, prompted by pride in their newly achieved freedom, or suffering from present unfair treatment. Resistance took the form chiefly of disobedience, destruction of property, neglect of and absence from duty and running away.[10] None of the cases was serious, and misunderstandings were more frequent in the early stages of apprenticeship while the system was yet unfamiliar to everybody. Later, when some adjustments had been made, and planters and apprentices had become more tolerant of each other's rights and less suspicious of each other's motives, apprenticeship worked better.[11] It was shown, for instance, in the decrease in the number of offences committed by apprentices from 467 in the first year of apprenticeship to 262 in the last year of apprenticeship.[12]

One of the major faults attributed to apprenticeship was its inflexibility, that is, its failure to introduce the apprentices progressively to the fuller responsibilities of freedom, and to narrow the gap between masters and apprentices. The system remained unchanged from the time it started to the time it ended. The British Government appeared to have been so concerned with the eventual achievement of freedom that it failed to make adequate provision for the intermediate stage of apprenticeship.

In the Virgin Islands the one stipendiary magistrate, William Gordon, for the entire group of scattered hilly islands insufficiently traversed with passable roads, was obviously inadequate to administer the system.[13] As such much was left to the good will of the masters. Nevertheless, Gordon was an efficient worker and gained a reputation for impartiality among both apprentices and planters.[14] The high regard in which he was held in the Virgin Islands was shown by the willingness of apprentices to submit grievances to him for adjudication, and his appointment to the Council in August, 1838, when he no longer held a special commission.[15] But in the performance of his magisterial duties, Gordon was severely handicapped by inadequate means of conveyance from one island to another, with the result that his activities were more or less confined to Tortola, and the outlying islands were rarely visited.[16]

Despite the inadequacy of supervision, apprenticeship in the Virgin Islands does not appear to have been excessively brutal, and certainly did not produce lasting bitterness. Planters or their representatives generally did not possess that viciousness of character which would upset the relatively smooth working of the system. Besides the labour system was sufficiently accommodating to make apprenticeship work without too much stress or strain. A contributory factor was the arrangement whereby masters and apprentices were allowed to make the agreements most convenient with regard to time of labour and the nature of the employment. Working hours varied from estate to estate but a nine-hour day was adopted.[17] The auxiliary Acts of the Virgin Islands authorised the planters to apportion the 45 hours through six days a week, but the power was rarely exercised, and following the practice of slavery, Saturdays and Sundays were allowed to apprentices to be used for their own benefit.[18]

A revolutionary aspect of apprenticeship was that the apprentices had become sellers of labour and their masters had become buyers of labour.[19] The methods of wage-bargaining, because of its recent innovation, were unfamiliar to both parties and many occasions did not arise for these to be learnt. In general, there was not much need for extra labour outside the statutory specifications so that it was not necessary for planters to offer unusually attractive incentives in money or allowances, or to coerce the apprentices to work on the estates. In any case the shortage of currency of small denomination posed a severe problem to the payment of wages.[20] For their part the apprentices were definitely not anxious to bargain away their newly attained freedom. These factors together with the existence of alternative and apparently more profitable work on provision grounds, which planters themselves were not anxious to restrict, enabled apprentices to 'dispose' of spare time as they chose.

Apprentices were not required to labour in their own time except at harvest time, and on these occasions they readily worked extra time on five week-days for a wage of 1d. sterling per hour.[21] Shortly after August, 1834 apprentices on a few estates volunteered to perform daily, a given portion of labour, on condition that when it was accomplished they should have the remainder of the day to themselves. No reason was given for its discontinuation soon afterwards, but it can be assumed that the apprentices who had an eye to their own interest did the job haphazardly to leave as much time as possible to devote to their own grounds. Later, attempts were made by several planters to hire their apprentices on Saturdays 'at a fair rate of wages,' but these also were unsuccessful due largely to a feeling among apprentices that they could earn more by working their grounds.[22]

Considerations other than economic conditions, personal attitudes and financial circumstances influenced the behavior of masters and apprentices. Geological variations due to topographical irregularities were also significant. Thus task work was not resorted to though it was often mooted; it was the opinion of some of the most experienced planters that the varied nature of the soil, not only on different estates but on parts of the same estates, made it almost impossible to introduce an equitable arrangement.[23]

A source of continual anxiety to some planters was the activity of 'speculators' from Demerara.[24] Under the auxiliary Acts, apprentices could purchase their freedom without the consent of and even in opposition to their masters. Consequently, the activities of the agents who resorted to the Virgin Islands could not legally be impeded. They paid between $100 and $200 for the unexpired term of the apprentices' services, and $200 to the apprentices themselves, and took them away as articled servants with the promise of high wages. It was feared that the practice would 'terminate the final ruin of (Tortola) much sooner.' The relatively large number of discharges, 226 in 1836,[25] compared with only 11 in the previous year,[26] was undoubtedly due to the activities of these speculators. Consequently, there were obviously some grounds for alarm. These, however, were subsequently removed when an Order in Council was issued on March 1, 1837, designed to prevent 'the abuse of such practice.'[27] By May, 1838, there were further discharges of only 14.[28]

So long as the apprentices remained in the Virgin Islands there was little or no inclination to living and working in any other than their customary employments. For those who preferred agriculture, land was not available simply for the taking, and unauthorised apprentices could not acquire a portion without trespassing. For those who wanted to be domestics they had to compete for employment in a very restricted area evidenced by the fact that domestic apprentices were themselves being employed in the fields. For those who remained in their masters' services, the lack of alternatives severely limited their bargaining power for wages. This would suggest that in any dispute over wages masters would be in a stronger bargaining position if they cared to exercise their power, and probably accounted for the small wages paid.[29]

Apprenticeship did not contribute in any tangible way towards the establishment of peasant farming in the Virgin Islands. So long as the apprentices remained in the colony, they seemed content to live and work on the estates, and showed no keen desire to purchase their freedom in order to establish themselves independently. The absence of an expressed desire, however, should not be construed to mean an unwillingness by negroes to improve their status. So long as they were confined by legal restrictions to labour for their masters for most of the time, and so long as they believed that the advantages of apprenticeship outweighed those of an uncertain existence elsewhere, they preferred to undergo their temporary qualified slavery. When circumstances permitted or warranted it, the negroes were only too eager to seek a substitution of means of livelihood. Full freedom instituted in 1838 was to provide the opportunities which eventually led to departures from the traditional mode of living.

With only 5,115 apprentices out of an estimated British West Indian total of 651,915,[30] it cannot be said that the Virgin Islands influenced the outcome of apprenticeship to any significant extent. Nevertheless, the Virgin Islands added their quota to the problems of the period. Here as elsewhere in the British West Indies, conditions gave rise to the belief that apprentices were not getting the training that would fit them for full freedom and that their treatment was not very different from what it had been during slavery. These views were held by all interested in the welfare of the apprentices, including the British Government and humanitarians in Britain.

The question was raised in the Virgin Islands in 1837 whether apprentices returned as domestics attached to estates but employed in the fields were praedial or non-praedial labourers.[31] The question threatened to disrupt the whole system of apprenticeship. If domestics accustomed to being worked on estates were freed in 1838, the regular field workers would demand a similar concession, inasmuch as the stipendiary magistrate was already encouraging them to expect this.[32] According to the law and established practice, domestics were non-praedials. Hence it was believed that the continuation of apprenticeship among the praedials after 1838 under the existing laws would be attended with increasing difficulties, and the hope was expressed that the legislature of the Virgin Islands would make provision for the general discharge of praedial apprentices at the same time as non-praedials.[33] Reluctantly, and 'after a strong opposition,' the legislature succumbed to pressures and passed a Bill in April, 1838 for a complete abolition of apprenticeship on August 1, 1838.[34]

Following the institution of full freedom, three alternatives of employment became available to the newly emancipated people – they could continue to work on the estates, they could emigrate, or they could set themselves up independently. One essential new feature was introduced by full freedom, namely, the substitution of wage labour for the 45-hour compulsory free labour. Henceforth, the retention of the negroes on the estates would be dependent upon the planters' ability to pay agreed wages or, failing this, to come to some equitable arrangement with the labourers, or otherwise to secure their services.

The demand for labour was dependent upon the general condition of the sugar industry, and vice versa, the state of the industry was dependent upon the supply of labour. If sugar cultivation expanded so would the need for labourers; conversely, contraction would mean a proportional diminution of the demand for labour. The sugar industry which had been on the decline even before the institution of apprenticeship was destined to decline even further after full freedom was introduced.

The decline of the sugar industry was a result of a number of adverse conditions. The first, and not necessarily the most important, was the unfavourable weather conditions. Beginning with a disastrous hurricane in 1837, which destroyed 17 sugar works,[35] the Virgin Islands, until 1847, experienced almost continuous drought, broken only by inter-mittent periods of rainfall inadequate to sustain sugar cultivation. In 1842 and again in 1852, the islands were visited by two more hurricanes which effected widespread damage to sugar cultivation, and to labourers' dwellings.[36] Further serious hurricanes occurred in 1867 and in 1871 which together destroyed all the existing sugar works in Tortola.[37] By then, however, sugar production was no longer an important industry in the Virgin Islands.

Another major factor contributing to the decline of the sugar industry, and one which finally led to its abandonment as an export commodity, was the passing of the Sugar Duties Act of 1846 by the British Parliament intended to equalise the duties on British colonial and foreign grown sugar imported into Britain.[38] The direct conse-quence of this measure, together with the commercial crisis in Britain in the mid-1840's and the fall of sugar prices,[39] was the collapse of the commercial and trading firm of Reid, Irving and Company. The Company had extensive planting interests in the Virgin Islands, con-trolling ten sugar estates with about 1,150 negroes in Tortola.[40] The withdrawal of the £50 which the Company paid weekly in wages could not, despite expressions to the contrary, seriously influence the wage system in the colony.[41] Of more importance was the fact that the cessation of the trading activities by the Company severed the only remaining line of direct communication with Britain. This factor carried the further complication that planters could no longer depend on advances of money or credit from Britain, since the Company normally allowed advances to be drawn on them.[42]

The lack of capital, credit and transportation proved to be the major obstacles to the continuation of the sugar industry. The President of the Virgin Islands reported in 1848 that 'there are now no properties in the Virgin Islands whose holders are not embarrassed for want of capital or credit sufficient to enable them to carry on the simplest method of cultivation effectively.'[43] The adequacy of labour in the colony, the difficult terrain which prevented the ready introduction of labour saving devices, and the already depressed state of the sugar industry made the introduction of immigration, mechanisation, or improved machinery unnecessary or impossible. The crses of the mid-1840's resulted in a marked decrease in the quantity and value of sugar exported after 1846 as can be seen from Table 5.[44]

Table 5

Amount and Value of Sugar Exported, 1839-1854

Year	Amount of Sugar Exported			Total	Value
	Hogsheads	tierces	barrels	barrels	£ Sterling
1839	423	20	1234	3429	11,981
1840	295	21	1217	2776	10,682
1841	425	20	1513	3718	14,922
1842	339	2	1027	2730	8,141
1843	259	45	1861	3336	11,393
1844	249	55	1008	2473	10,040
1845	421	133	1881	4518	12,060
1846	247	1417	42	6945	4,556
1847	374	45	1534	3584	9,174
1848	156	6	1247	2051	2,919
1849	120	1	1189	1793	3,038
1850	47	24	976	1307	2,170
1851	60	58	1226	1758	3,313
1852	-	4	128	144	199
1853	1	28	543	660	734
1854	34	1	426	600	836

The failure of the sugar industry generally caused a depreciation of the value of property in the Virgin Islands, and this facilitated the easier acquisition of land by the negroes by purchase and by rental. The decline of sugar not only resulted in a reorganisation of the plantation system, but directly contributed to the development of peasant farming.

After full freedom the important consideration in negotiations between employers and employees was the relative strength of each other's power of bargaining. The question was not just a numerical one in terms of numbers of labourers wanted and offering. Basically, the planters had to offer wages sufficiently high to attract labour. If there were few alternative choices of occupation open to labourers, then the planters could succeed with low wage-rates. If there were attractive alternatives open to the labourers the planters would have to bid higher wage-rates. In the Virgin Islands, the demand for labour was never high due to the depressed condition of the sugar industry; and several alternatives to living and working on the estates were open to the labourers. At the same time there were counteracting factors, such as the shortage of capital by the planters, and legal and other restrictions on labourers acquiring land. These factors necessitated continuous adjustments in the labour system in an attempt to achieve an equitable arrangement to suit changing conditions.

Children of labourers who were able and willing to work readily procured employment on the estates after 1838, but many others, especially the females, were withdrawn by their parents from field labour. Many women also showed a disinclination to work in the fields, and became domestics or housewives.[45] The main labour force, therefore, consisted of men. Working arrangements between labourers and employers were contractual — written or unwritten. Written contracts were provided for under an Act of the legislature which specified the rules to be observed.[46] Generally, however, written contracts did not appeal to either side, and preference was given to general hiring under verbal contracts.[47] The labourers were suspicious of restrictions, reminiscent of slavery, which would be imposed on their activities, while planters disliked being bound to conditions which might be impossible to keep, especially the payment of wages.

For the payment of wages, labourers were divided into three classes, as in slavery: the first class consisted of the best workers who received 6d. sterling a day; the second class of the younger and less experienced workers who received 4½d. a day; and the third class of the aged and the young who received 3d. a day.[48] In addition to these money wages, as part payment for their labour, labourers and their families were allowed to retain their houses and grounds, and were given medical facilities so long as the means allowed.[49]

During the depression of the 1840's culminating in the collapse of the firm of Reid, Irving and Company in 1847, the planters found it increasingly difficult to maintain the payment of wages. In view of the acute capital shortage planters turned to metairie in an attempt to save the sugar industry from complete extinction. Labourers accepted metairie primarily in order to retain their houses and grounds but also because it offered prospects of certain payment and more profitable employment since they could still have time to work their own grounds.[50] Metairie enabled planters to pay wages in kind rather than in cash, while the labourers shared with them the risks, expenses, and profits, if any, of sugar production. Under the system, secured by contracts, labourers provided the manual labour necessary for cultivation, reaping and manufacture, while planters supplied the land, the stock and the manufacturing facilities.[51] The sugar manufactured, and sometimes the molasses, was divided in fixed proportions between planters and labourers. Planters invariably purchased the labourers' share, a factor which gave rise to unfair dealings, and they were responsible for shipping.

Metairie was adopted as a last resort. Local antagonism to the system initially was not hard to explain: it was feared that metairie would make the labourers too independent and unamenable to discipline and control. Planters were opposed to any innovation which was likely to lessen their profits and to weaken their control over the disposal of land and the allocation of labour. But this attitude lasted only so long as planters were still optimistic about effecting a recovery in their declining economic position. Around the mid-1840's when complete ruin seemed a reality, they were driven by desperation to metairie. The system, which was at first adopted hesitatingly, spread rapidly after 1844, and by June, 1846, there was scarcely an estate on which it was not introduced.[52]

Metairie failed to save the sugar industry and the planters from ruin, partly because of the continued reliance on the traditional methods of production, and partly because planters were not stimulated to adopt more improved methods of agriculture. Both planters and labourers sought the cheapest and easiest means of fulfilling the respective parts of their agreements.[53] More important was the fact that by the 1850's, the planters had themselves become affected by the depression in the sugar industry and were incapable of making those exertions which were essential for the restoration of sugar cultivation, or of taking the initiative in the introduction of new industries in the Virgin Islands. Among them tradition died hard. The possibility of an eventual revival of the industry, and of the white population setting a worthwhile example to the rest of the community, was held only by the most optimistic.[54] This expectation was not realised, however. Census returns show a progressive decrease of the white population: in 1859 there were 201, in 1871 there were 123, in 1881 there were 52, and in 1899 there were only 32.[55]

The success of the free system depended largely on the feeling of security which the labourers experienced on the estates, and the confidence with which they thought their interests were being looked after. The operation of both the wage-labour system and the metairie system convinced many labourers that their welfare was being sacrificed to the planters' interests. Reports of uninterrupted mutual good understanding between planters and labourers were not accurate: in fact there were several points of conflict between the two, which though not continuously active, nevertheless operated occasionally to disturb relations between them. Even when there was apparent harmony, an awareness of the presence of these forces was a source of anxiety. From their still subordinate position on the estates, the labourers were more often the unfortunate recipients of the planters' high-handed and arbitrary actions.

The major source of continuous irritation between planter and labourer was the question of rent and labour. It arose primarily from the undefined position of the labourer in possession of a house and provision grounds on the estate, as a tenant-at-will. Instead of a money payment labourers satisfied rental charges by working on the estates. But they also received a small remuneration from the planters for their labour. The dual employer-employee, landlord-tenant relationship between planters and labourers, was the fundamental cause of differences between them. In return for their inadequate wages, labourers did as little work as they could,[56] and the planters were inclined when they observed a disposition by labourers to withhold their services from the plantations, even for the shortest time, to consider themselves defrauded. At first they were content to use threats of coercive action in order to remind labourers of their responsibility,[57] but by 1842 several of them were beginning to assert a right summarily to eject from his cottage and provision grounds, any labourer who absented himself from the service of the plantation, or who refused to renew his weekly contract.[58]

The labourer had all along been led to believe in his inalienable right to the produce of his grounds, in the event of the planter terminating his tenancy. His situation was indefensible from his inability to resort to legal action: it was the opinion of Crown law officers that cases of ejection could only be settled in the higher courts, a procedure which placed justice beyond his financial reach.[59] Under these circumstances it was of the utmost importance that the nature of the tenure by which the labourer held his house and grounds, either as 'tenant-at-will' or as 'tenant-on-condition', should be determined by a declaratory enactment, and that an inexpensive means should be afforded to landlords and labourers to maintain their mutual claims by law.

Accordingly, an Act was passed in 1851 to facilitate the 'more speedy and effectual recovery of the possession of premises unlawfully held over after the determination of the tenancy.' The Act, however, was intended primarily to help the planters, and the questions of tenancy and of cheaper adjustments in ejection cases were not resolved.[60]

The practice of charging an arbitrary rent was occasionally resorted to by 1842 as a means of compelling labourers to work, and as a punishment for the withdrawal of their services from the estates. Another source of labourers' dissatisfaction existed in the operation of the Criminal Code of the Virgin Islands whereby any person found with 'rum, sugar, sling, molasses, cotton or with one or more sugar-cane or canes' in his possession could be charged and punished.[61] In cases of imprisonment the punishment was extended beyond the term in jail, as the neglect of his grounds and the depredation of the crops by his fellow labourers made him, on his discharge from prison, solely dependent on his wages which alone were totally inadequate to support him.[62]

Metairie also led to dissatisfaction: labourers were ill-protected by the contracts, and they found little time to work their own grounds by which they could support themselves between crops.[63] The result was a heavy accumulation of debt which their share of the proceeds was often inadequate to liquidate[64] even if they were given their fair share; in several instances, this was neither promptly nor honestly given.[65] And as in the case of wage-rent disputes, the labourer was less able to afford legal action to secure redress.[66] In the final analysis, the employer possessed the ready weapon in the power of ejection to enforce recognition of his authority and command over the services of recalcitrant labourers. So long as the labourer paid rent by giving labour he was at the mercy of his employer.[67]

Two basic factors underlay the operation of the wage system during the early years: absenteeism, and the failure or refusal of employers to recognise the altered status of the ex-slaves in society. There were only four resident proprietors in the Virgin Islands by 1841, the plantations of others being directed by attorneys or managers. These men were more concerned with their own interests or with implementing orders, and were accused of being more preoccupied with returns than with the welfare of the workers.[68] With them the practices of slavery were too deeply rooted to allow for easy adjustment. Many of them continued to cling to the notions of their superior and dominant status in society, and while they were debarred from exercising the coercion of slavery, nevertheless sought to coerce, through the medium of the courts, by the power of ejection.

In contrast to the attitude of the employers who ascribed an inferior status to the labourers, the negroes themselves were infinitely jealous of their rights as free-men.[69] They interpreted the measures of coercion, both threatened and executed by their employers, as attempts to force their labour and to subvert their rights. Besides, by the 1840's planters were failing to provide such special amenities as medical assistance which had created some inclination among labourers to remain on the estates. Having a keen sense of their own interests, they sought, whenever possible, to escape from their unprofitable and exacting employment on the estates. Two avenues were open to them after emancipation: emigration and independent peasant farming.

It was the consistent policy of the British Government during apprenticeship that the apprentices could not be removed from one colony to another. Once they were free, however, either through manumission by the purchase of the unexpired period of apprenticeship, or through legal enactment terminating slavery altogether, no obstacle stood in the way of emigration; ex-slaves were at liberty to go to any of the British dominions on the same terms as any other British subject.[70] After the temporary ban on their activities by the restrictions of March 1, 1837, agents from Trinidad and Demerara renewed their attempts after August 1, 1838, to induce labourers to emigrate.[71] For this they used specious arguments of the superior advantages to be enjoyed in those colonies.[72] Their efforts do not appear to have been very successful; when they were, emigration did not assume the alarming proportions originally anticipated.[73]

In his emigration reports, the stipendiary magistrate did not consider periodical absences by labourers seeking temporary employment abroad, to be in the nature of true emigration.[74] However this might be, by 1848 labourers from the Virgin Islands were resorting in increasing numbers to nearby Vieques and St. Thomas, in search of employment. Such emigration, though temporary, was of greater disquietude to planters, since they coincided with the crop season.

The first emigrants to Vieques, who were skilled workers and porters from Road Town,[75] were followed by estate labourers who were induced by the high wages there.[76] Some of them eventually acquired land of their own, which the Spanish authorities, anxious to establish beyond dispute their right of sovereignty to the island by settlement, did not seem to prevent. Although Vieques was a slave society, labourers did not mind going there from fear of being enslaved. The Spaniards were apparently not anxious to raise the international question of right to the island with the result that nothing overt was done to curtail the civil liberties of immigrant Virgin Islanders. Because of the facilities offered, the British warning of the possibility of enslavement went unheeded.[77]

Emigration to St. Thomas was not difficult to explain. The Virgin Islands maintained strong trading connections with the Danish Islands even before emancipation.[78] From its more prosperous economy, its nearness and the absence of immigration restrictions, St. Thomas had a particular attraction for Virgin Islanders. Apart from the occasional vessel belonging to Reid, Irving and Company which visited the Virgin Islands until 1847, the only contact with the outside world, for a large majority of the people, was provided by St. Thomas. However, two factors tended to restrict free emigration during the early years of post-emancipation, namely, the absence of a worthwhile incentive apart from marketing opportunities there, and the existence of slavery in the island. The situation became more favourable within a decade of emancipation. When the Royal Mail Steam Packet Company received the contract to convey the mails between the West Indies and Britain and established a coaling station and rendezvous for the packet vessels in St. Thomas in 1842, emigrants found ready work at the coaling depot as porters and dock-workers. Also, with the abolition of slavery in the Danish Islands in July, 1848, Virgin Islanders could emigrate to St. Thomas without fear of being enslaved. At the same time attempts were made by planters in St. Croix to attract labourers there from the Virgin Islands.[79]

The coincidence of the abolition of slavery in the Danish West Indies, and the collapse of the firm of Reid, Irving and Company resulting in the failure of wage payments, provided an impetus for emigration. The abandonment of sugar cultivation on several estates made the requirement of a large labour force even less urgent.

Emigration provided one means of escape for the negroes from plantation labour and from the influence of planters. The attempt to set themselves up as small, independent proprietors was another. The attachment of the negroes to small cultivation had been encouraged during slavery through provision grounds, and after slavery they sought to secure land of their own. Among the major obstacles which stood in the way of easy acquisition was the fact that much of the land was legally owned even though uncultivated, and that a number of estates were in Chancery.

Shortly after full emancipation a few families in Jost Van Dyke and Virgin Gorda occupied lands in order to establish permanent settlements, but their occupancy was illegal.[80] To prevent unlawful occupation of lands, an Act was passed in April, 1839, empowering justices to exercise summary jurisdiction for the removal of those persons who acquired possession 'without any probable claim or pretence or title thereto.'[81] Another Act to impeded acquisition imposed a tax of 20/– per acre 'on all lands in cultivation otherwise than in the cultivation of sugar-cane, cotton or indigo.'[82] The discriminatory enactment in favour of planters was intended to curtail the size of peasant holdings and to reduce the rewards of small-farming. The expense of preparing and recording deeds, without which titles could not be confirmed, made purchase too expensive, while the difficulty of ensuring reliable bequeathal after death discouraged ready acquisition of land.[83]

Yet another impediment was created by the fact that much land was in the hands of the receiver of the Court of Chancery, and negroes were reluctant to purchase property to which their title could not be proved to be beyond question. As late as 1857, therefore, there remained 'immense tracts of land' still unoccupied.[84] Where lands had been purchased by labourers pooling their resources, these continued to be held in unequal undivided shares since the cost of securing individual deeds far exceeded the purchase price.[85]

One obstacle to the establishment of the peasantry was removed in June, 1841, when an Act was passed repealing the 20/– per acre land tax.[86] Another was overcome by the general economic and financial crises of the 1840's which made sugarcane cultivation increasingly difficult and unprofitable, and depreciated the value of property, thus making the planters more willing to sell, and the labourers more able to buy.

The remaining impediments to peasant land-ownership, namely, the expense of land-transfers and that of encumbered estates, were removed in 1864 by the adoption of two measures. The first was an enactment which authorised the printing of transfer forms to be sold to all intending purchasers at the Registry Office of the Virgin Islands, at 9d. each.[87] When filled in with all the necessary particulars, the forms could be registered at once, enabling a complete registered title to be obtained for only 4/6.[88] As a result of this action, titles became inheritable in perpetuity and provision was made for the clear demarcation of boundaries to prevent litigation.[89]

The second measure was the adoption by the Virgin Islands legislature of the West Indies Encumbered Estates Act which empowered the sale of encumbered estates by authorised Commissioners.[90] The effectiveness of this measure was seen when in 1864 eight estates totalling 780 acres were sold under decrees of the local Commissioner at a total cost of £979. Five of these estates (Cotton Bay, Spring Gut, Johnson's Gut, Appleby, and Cappoon's Bay) had been in Chancery for 35 years, while three others (Joe's Hill, Diamond, and Hawk's Nest) had been similarly encumbered for 44 years.[91] At an average cost of £1. 5s. per acre, the purchase of such lands was well within the financial reach of the negroes. The important point, however, was that the operation of the Encumbered Estates Act removed the uncertainty and suspicion among negroes which had previously made them sceptical about purchasing encumbered as well as unencumbered estates.

To a large extent these measures settled the problem of land transfer in the Virgin Islands other than Anegada, where different circumstances necessitated a different solution to the problem of land transfer and ownership. The soil of Anegada was principally waste and valueless, with patches of fertile land.[92] Plots of land had been held by different families and had been handed down from generation to generation without disturbance, but the greater part of the island was regarded as common property. For the purpose of taxation under a recent Tax Act, the question of land tenure was raised by President Price in 1859. The inhabitants themselves claimed possession of the lands, on the basis of original grants from the Crown, but no record of such grants could be found. At the same time it could not be proved that the whole island was Crown property.[93] As such, therefore, after the question had been submitted to the consideration of the Colonial Land and Emigration Commissioners in 1859, and recommendations received,[94] it was decided that the Crown's right to lands to which titles were said to exist, but which could not be validated, should be waived in favour of those who claimed titles. With regard to land held without title it was agreed that a title should be given where actual possession for 10 years could be proved, or where a considerable amount of capital had been expended on land possessed for less than 10 years. Where little or no capital had been expended it was decided that the land should be sold with the occupant having a presumptive right at the upset price of 4/-. No objection was made to unoccupied land being continued in common use except on the distinct understanding that the President of the colony would be at liberty at any time to withdraw any portion of it required for sale.[95] Despite repeated agitation of the question in 1871 and 1880 by the Anegadians themselves,[96] it was not until 1885 that an Ordinance was passed disposing of the lands in the manner decided on in 1859.[97] The final impetus to action was undoubtedly given by the proposal made by three Trinidadians in 1884 to purchase 1,000 acres of the island.[98]

Generally, the progressive rise of the peasantry coincided with the removal of the obstacles which impeded its advancement. From the commencement of freedom a general desire had been shown by the labourers to acquire lands and settle permanently,[99] but for the first few years after emancipation the labourers had to be content to remain on the estates.[100] Following the introduction of the Act of June, 1841, repealing taxes on negro lands, allotments of land were being rented by labourers from the small land-holders.[101] These proprietors were probably the first to be affected by the depression and were most willing to dispose of their lands.[102]

During the crises of 1846-7, several small settlements were established in various parts of Tortola on land probably bought by community effort.[103] If the labourers squatted this appears to have been unopposed for stipendiary magistrate Dyett reported that no case of squatting had been brought before him, and this was exclusively in his jurisdiction.[104] The acquisition of land by labourers proceeded rapidly after 1847, and reports present an increasing disposition to appropriate estates which were rapidly being thrown out of cultivation.[105] By 1865, the President could report that 'the greater part of the soil' was owned by negroes.[106]

By the end of the century, the Virgin Islands consisted primarily of small peasant holdings; in 1897, there was no property over 1,000 acres, there were 3 over 500 acres, and 45 between 100 and 500 acres. In contrast to these, there were 408 properties below 100 acres and of these 291 did not exceed 20 acres.[107] An important point to note was the relatively large size of these small holdings in comparison, say, with Jamaican peasant holdings most of which were under ten acres.[108] It is possible that the land of the Virgin Islands was less productive than that of Jamaica thereby requiring a larger acreage to produce an equivalent amount, but of more importance was the emphasis placed by Virgin Islanders on cattle rearing which was done extensively and required a large acreage.

The development of a peasant proprietary resulted in two fundamental changes in the Virgin Islands. The first was the development of

Table 6

Some Recorded Exports and Value, 1838-1887

PERIOD	CATTLE		OTHER LIVESTOCK		BUILDING LIME		CHARCOAL	
	Nos.	£. ster.	Nos.	£. ster.	Barrels	£. ster.	Barrels	£. ster.
1838-1842	1228	5823	670	1879	3006	253	170 (cwt)	46
1843-1847	1410	5283	2892	3035	6982	707	122 (bbl)	67
							693 (bags)	
1848-1852	2456	6226	4386	3792	3776	383	10890	1013
1853-1857	6345	20018	9759	5428	9217	664	33240	2360
1858-1862	5880	21976	12490	19025	19112	1561	69830	5862
1863-1867	6577	21593	12442	12111	7244	691	74083	4039
1868-1872	4909	17192	9303	5594	1250	175	40663	4755
1873-1877	4370	16971	12769	5574	100	9	43531	3208
1878-1882	4900	15076	11618	4644	–	–	52413	2955
1883-1887	5399	12904	8808	3541	132	6	43514	2269

small-scale farming on a family basis which was compatible with the financial position of the inhabitants, in preference to sugar production which required a larger capital outlay than they could afford. Sugarcane cultivation practically disappeared; by the 1860's, Blue Books were giving the information that, 'The Sugar cultivation in Tortola are nearly abandoned. The 20 manufactories not being equal to a single one in former years.'[109] In 1897 the area under sugarcane cultivation amounted to only 290 acres, equal to 4% of the cultivable area of the Virgin Islands, or 12% of all land under crops in the colony. From 1881 to 1896 only 875 barrels of sugar valued at £1,586. 15s. were exported.[110] By this time, sugar was being imported from other Presidencies within the Leeward Islands Federation.

As the sugar industry disappeared, greater emphasis was placed on the rearing of live-stock such as cattle, goats, sheep, pigs, and horses, and the planting of ground provisions such as yams and potatoes. This was the work of the peasants. Cattle was produced primarily for export, and ground provisions for local consumption. The Virgin Islands with fine pastures of guinea grass were ideally suited for cattle; [111] the only requirement was a more judicious selection of breeds.[112] In addition, the peasants engaged in the production of building lime, in the burning of charcoal, and in fishing for export. Table 6 shows the progress in the export trade of cattle, other livestock, building lime and charcoal, from 1838 to 1887, according to official statistics;[113] an unrecorded amount was also exported without being declared at the Customs because of the facilities for smuggling.

Since the 1820's cotton cultivation had lapsed in the Virgin Islands due to low, uneconomic prices offered in the European market and because of the increased competition from the Southern States of America.[114] During the American Civil War (1861-1865) when the production of cotton in the Southern States was severely disrupted, the price of cotton rose. It was in response to this high price that cotton cultivation was revived and expanded in the Virgin Islands towards the end of the war. The boom, however, was of short duration and by 1872 cotton production had reverted to the pre-Civil War level as prices fell. Thereafter, it formed only a small fraction of the export trade. Recorded cotton exports from 1856 to 1877 are given in Table 7. [115]

The second major change consequent upon the development of the peasant proprietary in the Virgin Islands, and proceeding directly from the shift from plantation agriculture to small-scale farming, was a swing in the direction of trade. The decline of the sugar industry made direct

Table 7

Recorded Exports of Cotton, 1856 to 1877

Year	Amount (lb)	Value (£. Ster.)
1856-1861	17,840	223
1862-1863	7,900	410
1864	25,225	1110
1865	35,533	998
1866	45,900	1546
1867	15,775	378
1868-1871	46,175	1164
1872-1877	20,876	265

trade with Britain no longer worthwhile; except for small quantities in 1851 and in 1854, the last sugar from the Virgin Islands was exported directly to Britain in 1848.[116] Thereafter until 1859 the commodity was shipped to the other British West Indian islands from where it probably found its way to Britain. After 1859 the trade in sugarcane and in manufactured sugar was confined solely to St. Thomas.

Between 1860 and 1862, exports valued at £16,224 were sent to Britain but these consisted solely of copper ore obtained from the reactivated mine in Virgin Gorda.[117] The quantities of the commodities produced by the small farmers — livestock, charcoal, lime and fish — were too small for profitable trans-Atlantic shipment to Britain. Only an inconsiderable amount, consisting primarily of a few heads of livestock, was occasionally exported to other West Indian colonies. A closer more adequate market was found in St. Thomas.

The import trade of the Virgin Islands tended to follow the same pattern as the export trade, with an important difference. Even after the direct export trade with Britain ceased, British merchandise continued to enter the Virgin Islands through the medium of St. Thomas where the articles were brought by the vessels of the Royal Mail Steam

Table 8

Official Imports and Exports, 1838-1887

PERIOD	IMPORTS (£ Sterling).				EXPORTS (£ Sterling).			
	Britain	British West Indies	Foreign Countries	Danish W.I.	Britain	British West Indies	Foreign Countries	Danish W.I.
1838-1842	7169	19266	31674	—	64786	7620	7295	—
1843-1847	2163	13219	31366	—	44595	11326	8018	—
1848-1852	1131	6131	21257	—	3890	10291	12382	—
1853-1855	4	445	10855	—	800	1953	16093	—
1856-1857	—	999	1178	9052	—	1962	191	19258
1858-1862	1928	1470	1174	36543	16224	1485	375	57536
1863-1867	35	618	2218	41445	—	459	64	46754
1868-1872	—	739	1653	30930	—	1990	1237	28940
1873-1877	—	223	592	20064	—	816	249	26827
1878-1882	—	112	87	23034	—	411	154	26387
1883-1887	—	3	193	36834	—	216	48	21512

Packet Company,[118] and through other British colonies which also provided an insignificant proportion of the trade of the Virgin Islands. According to the Blue Books, imports from Britain ceased in 1862, the items brought in during the previous three years being merely machinery to operate the Virgin Gorda mines. Some quantities of medicine were brought in from Britain in 1867 for victims of the hurricane of that year, but these cannot be regarded as part of regular importations.

The really important trade was with nearby St. Thomas. The scarcity of British vessels visiting the Virgin Islands even before emancipation had given impetus to this trend which was enhanced by the severing of trade connections with Britain. It was also facilitated by the buying habits of Virgin Islanders who resorted to St. Thomas in their small boats and canoes and purchased weekly supplies, and by the convenience of St. Thomas as a small market for small supplies. The changes in the direction of trade can be seen from Table 8. 19] Foreign states refer to St. Thomas, and the United States of America, as well as a number of Dutch and French West Indian colonies such as St. Martin, St. Bartholomew, St. Eustatius, Guadeloupe and Martinique which carried on a small trade, especially in livestock, with the Virgin Islands. Imports and exports from St. Thomas from 1856 are distinguished from those coming from other foreign territories.

Both as a source of employment for those who sought more remunerative occupation elsewhere, and as a market for the produce of the peasantry, St. Thomas figured prominently in the history of the Virgin Islands after emancipation. By attracting away the greater part of the able-bodied from the Virgin Islands, St. Thomas deprived them of the labour which was so vital to economic development. Only the less able-bodied remained to undertake agricultural projects which partly explains the heavy concentration on livestock production. The example of a freer and more profitable life obtained on the St. Thomas dockyards, in lieu of the hard agricultural life of the Virgin Islands, gave impetus to emigration farther afield, to Puerto Rico, Haiti and Colon, especially after the transfer of the mail station from St. Thomas to Barbados in 1885.[120] The net result of emigration was a sharp reduction in the negro population which fell from 5,892 in 1859, to 5,575 in 1861, to 5,235 in 1881, and to 4,607 in 1899.

When as a result of freedom, taxation was extended to the ex-slaves, association with St. Thomas facilitated the evasion of import and export duties by smuggling which proved detrimental to the Virgin

Islands largely dependent as they were on customs duties for revenues. The Virgin Islands had abandoned one market, Britain, and adopted another, St. Thomas, but the fundamental dependence remained. Reliance on the St. Thomas market meant that any disruptions there, as had been the experience with Britain, would seriously affect the trade of the Virgin Islands, especially since there was nowhere else to turn to conveniently. Two instances can be noted. During the last months of 1866 and early 1867 there was an almost complete cessation of trade due to the outbreak of cholera in St. Thomas and the imposition of a quarantine in the Virgin Islands to counter the spread of the disease.[121] Again, in 1885, the withdrawal of the Royal Mail steamers from St. Thomas resulted in a heavy fall in prices; cattle which normally fetched £35 to £45 each realised only £20 to £30. Exports of livestock were curtailed.[122]

The limitations imposed by an almost complete dependence on the St. Thomas market fixed production to what could be disposed of there, and alternatively fostered a strong disinclination to change. It meant, for instance, that the administration's project to introduce cotton, at the turn of the century, was accepted slowly and only after many inducements had been given, and the Virgin Islands continued to rely on cattle-rearing which eventually remained the primary industry of the islands.

Apprenticeship and emancipation emphasised the essential characteristics of the Virgin Islands which had developed during slavery, namely, a declining plantocracy, plenty of unused land, and a suppressed majority already experienced in small-scale farming on provision grounds and desirous of establishing themselves independently on their own land. The roots of the peasantry lay in slavery, but conditions after 1838 forced the pace of change. A succession of unfavourable weather conditions and a lack of capital and credit consequent upon commercial and financial crises in Britain did irreparable damage to the sugar industry which metairie failed to avoid. The unsatisfactory functioning of the wage-labour and metairie systems gave added impetus to emigration and peasant farming.

The Virgin Islands were probably unique among British West Indian colonies in that although they possessed little unfettered land and a relatively large labour force, they nevertheless realised the establishment of an independent peasantry. The answer lay in the existence of the necessary ingredient, namely, available land space, in the form of abandoned estates.

Seen in retrospect the emergence of the peasantry exerted a powerful influence on the political life of the Virgin Islands. Those who possessed the necessary property qualifications could henceforth participate in the politics of the colony. The trend was more marked in the 1860's. For those who had control over the political destiny of the islands, the entry of such a class of uneducated persons, suspected of being susceptible to the 'wrong' influence, threatened political chaos. This was one of the basic factors underlying the constitutional reforms of 1859 and the introduction of full Crown Colony Government in 1867.

[1] C.O. 239/38. Enc. in Colquhoun to Lefevre, 4 June, 1834; C.O. 239/37. MacGregor to Spring-Rice, 1 Aug., 1837. No. 157; P.P. 1835. Vol. L, p. 393.
[2] C.O. 315/5. Act No. 88. Clauses 41-49.
[3] Ibid., Clause 15.
[4] Ibid., Preamble and various clauses in the Act.
[5] Ibid., Clauses 29-34, and 37.
[6] Ibid., Clause 50.
[7] C.O. 315/5. Act No. 89.
[8] C.O. 315/5. Act No. 90. Clause 1.
[9] C.O. 239/47. Enc. in Colebrooke to Glenelg, 9 Oct., 1837. No. 139.
[10] P.P. 1836. Vol. XLIX, p. 397.
[11] C.O. 239/49. Enc. in Colebrooke to Glenelg, 16 April, 1838. No. 68.
[12] P.P. 1836. Vol. XLIX, p. 397; C.O. 239/49. Enc. in Colebrooke to Glenelg, 16 April, 1838. No. 67.
[13] C.O. 239/41. Thomas Marsh to Aberdeen, May 1835; P.P. 1836. Vol. XLIX, p. 396.
[14] C.O. 239/45. Light to Glenelg, 27 Feb., 1837. No. 114.
[15] C.O. 239/50. Colebrooke to Glenelg, 17 Aug., 1838. No. 190.
[16] P.P. 1836. Vol. XLIX, p. 395.
[17] C.O. 239/47. Enc. in Colebrooke to Glenelg, 9 Oct., 1837. No. 139.
[18] C.O. 239/46. Enc. in Colebrooke to Glenelg, 22 June, 1837. No. 34.
[19] D. G. Hall, 'The Apprenticeship Period in Jamaica, 1834-1838.' (Caribbean Quarterly, Dec., 1953, Vol. 3, No. 3.) p. 146.
[20] C.O. 239/41. Colquhoun to Aberdeen, 22 March, 1835.
[21] C.O. 239/46. Enc. in Colebrooke to Glenelg, 22 June, 1837. No. 34.
[22] C.O. 239/50. Enc. in Colebrooke to Glenelg, 16 Aug., 1838. No. 188.
[23] C.O. 239/46. Enc. in Colebrooke to Glenelg, 22 June, 1837. No. 34.
[24] C.O. 239/44. Reid, Irving and Co. to Glenelg, 5 Dec., 1836; C.O. 239/48. Reid, Irving and Co. to Glenelg, 9 Feb., 1837.
[25] C.O. 239/47. Enc. in Colebrooke to Glenelg, 14 Nov., 1837. No. 157.
[26] P.P. 1836. Vol. XLIX, p. 398.
[27] C.O. 239/48. Grey to Colquhoun, 10 March, 1837.
[28] C.O. 239/49. Enc. in Colebrooke, 5 April (No. 60), 16 April (no. 67), and 1 June, 1838.

[29] Hall, op. cit., p. 144.
[30] F. R. Augier, et. al: The Making of the West Indies. (Longmans, Green and Co. Ltd., London, 1960), p. 183.
[31] C.O. 239/45. Colebrooke to Glenelg, 20 March, 1837. No. 130; C.O. 239/46. Enc. in Colebrooke to Glenelg, 20 July, 1837. No. 53.
[32] C.O. 239/41. Enc. in Colquhoun to Stephen, 12 March, 1835.
[33] C.O. 239/46. Enc. in Colebrooke to Glenelg, 20 July, 1837. No. 53; Glenelg to Colebrooke, 22 Sept., 1837. No. 68.
[34] P.P. 1837-1838. Vol. XLVIII. Colebrooke to Glenelg, 18 April, 1838. No. 68, and enc.
[35] C.O. 239/46. Colebrooke to Glenelg, 12 Aug., 1837. No. 80, and 27 Sept., 1837. No. 116; Glenelg to Colebrooke, 14 Nov., 1837.
[36] C.O. 239/70. S. M.'s Report for Quarter ended Sept., 1842; P.P. 1852-3. Vol. LXII, p. 117.
[37] C.O. 314/17. Rumbold to Buckingham, 31 Oct., 1867; C.O. 314/18. Enc. in Rumbold to Buckingham, 13 Nov., 1867; Hill to Buckingham, 26 Nov., 1867. No. 192; C.O. 314/23. Enc. in Moir to Kimberley, 26 Aug., 1871; Moir to Mundy, 11 Sept., 1871; Moir to Baynes, 27 Oct., 1871. No. 204.
[38] Douglas Hall: Free Jamaica, 1838-1865. An Economic History. (New Haven, Yale University Press, 1959) pp. 88-92.
[39] Ibid., p. 270; Noel Deerr: The History of Sugar. (London, Chapman and Hall, Ltd., 1950) Vol. 11, p. 531.
[40] P.P. 1847-1848. Vol. XLVI, p. 136.
[41] C.O. 243/10. S. M.'s Report for the half year ended 31 Dec., 1847.
[42] P.P. 1845. Vol. XXXI, p. 577.
[43] P.P. 1847-1848. Vol. XLVI, p. 136.
[44] C.O. 317/10. to C.O. 317/25. Blue Books, 1839-1854.
[45] P.P. 1839. Vol. XXXVII, p. 322.
[46] C.O. 315/6. Act No. 112.
[47] P.P. 1839. Vol. XXXVII, p. 331.
[48] P.P. 1839. Vol. XXXVII, p. 322.
[49] P.P. 1839. Vol. XXXVII, p. 348.
[50] C.O. 239/71. S.M.'s Report for Oct., Nov., and Dec., 1842; P.P. 1845. Vol. XXXI, p. 577.
[51] P.P. 1845. Vol. XXXI, p. 577; W. K. Marshall, 'Metayage in the sugar industry of the British Windward Islands 1838-1865'. (*The Jamaican Historical Review*, Vol. V, No. 1, May, 1965), pp. 28-55.
[52] C.O. 239/75. S.M's Report for the half year ended 30 June, 1844; C.O. 243/10. S.M.'s Report for the half year ended 30 June, 1846.
[53] P.P. 1859. Vol. XXI, p. 525.
[54] Ibid.
[55] C.O. 314/7. Enc. in Hamilton to Lytton, 14 March, 1859. No. 22; C.O. 314/23. Moir to Mundy, 23 May, 1871. No. 104; C.O. 152/146. Enc. in Glover to Kimberley, 26 Dec., 1881. No. 405; Leeward Islands Blue Book, 1899.
[56] , P.P. 1845 Vol. XXXI, p. 577.
[57] C.O. 239/67. S.M.'s Report for Quarter ended 31 Dec., 1841.
[58] C.O. 239/68. S.M.'s Report for Quarter ended 30 June, 1842.

[59] Ibid.
[60] C.O. 315/8. Act No. 184.
[61] C.O. 315/5. Act No. 91.
[62] C.O. 239/59. S.M.'s Report for 1839.
[63] P.P. 1845. Vol. XXXI, p. 577.
[64] C.O. 234/10. S.M.'s Report for half year ended 31 Dec., 1848.
[65] C.O. 243/10. S.M.'s Report for half year ended 30 June, 1847.
[66] C.O. 243/10. S.M.'s Reports for half years ended 30 June, 1846 and 30 June, 1847.
[67] C.O. 243/10. S.M.'s Report for half year ended 31 Dec., 1847.
[68] C.O. 239/67. S.M.'s Report for half year ended 31 Dec., 1844.
[69] P.P. 1845. Vol. XXXI, p. 577.
[70] C.O. 239/48. Stewart to Reid, Irving and Co., 4 Oct., 1837.
[71] C.O. 239/50. Enc. in Colebrooke to Glenelg, 17 Aug., 1838. No. 191.
[72] C.O. 239/59. S.M.'s Report for Jan., 1840.
[73] P.P. 1839. Vol. XXXVII, p. 339; C.O. 239/50. Enc. in Colebrooke to Glenelg, 17 Aug., 1838. No. 191; C.O. 239/59. Drummond Hay to Colebrooke, 10 Feb., 1840; C.O. 243/10. S.M.'s Report for half year ended 30 June, 1846. Table A.
[74] C.O. 243/10. S.M.'s Report for half year ended 30 June, 1848. Table A.
[75] P.P. 1839. Vol. XXXVII, p. 331.
[76] C.O. 239/60. S.M.'s Report for July, August, and September, 1840.
[77] C.O. 239/60. Enc. in Macphail to Russell, 23 Nov., 1840. No. 79; Isaac Dookhan, 'Vieques or Crab Island: Source of Anglo-Spanish Colonial Conflict.' (The Journal of Caribbean History, Vol. 7, Nov. 1973). pp. 1-22.
[78] R. Montgomery Martin: History of the British Colonies. (London, 1834) Vol. III. pp. 494-495.
[79] C.O. 243/10. S.M.'s Report for year ended 31 Dec., 1848. Table A.
[80] P.P. 1839. Vol. XXXVII, p. 322.
[81] C.O. 315/6. Act No. 118.
[82] C.O. 315/6. Act No. 117; C.O. 239/60. S.M.'s Report for July, Aug., and Sept., 1840.
[83] C.O. 239/67. S.M.'s Report for Quarter ended 31 Dec., 1841.
[84] P.P. 1859. Vol. XXI, p. 376.
[85] P.P. 1866. Vol. XLIX, p. 376.
[86] C.O. 315/7. Act No. 128; C.O. 239/63. S.M.'s Report for March and April, 1841.
[87] C.O. 315/9. Ordinance No. 108. (No. 4 of 1864).
[88] P.P. 1866. Vol. XLIX, p. 376.
[89] Ibid., p. 379. Appendix A.
[90] P.P. 1866. Vol. XLIX, p. 378; C.O. 315/9. Ordinances Nos. 57 and 59.
[91] P.P. 1866. Vol. XLIX, p. 378.
[92] C.O. 314/7. Enc. in Robinson to Lytton, 8 April, 1859. No. 58; C.O. 152/147. Enc. in Glover to Kimberley, 23 Sept., 1881. No. 264.
[93] C.O. 314/7. Enc. in Robinson to Lytton, 8 April, 1859. No. 58.
[94] C.O. 314/8. Murdock and Rogers to Merivale, 27 May, 1859.

[95] C.O. 152/141. Kimberley to Berkeley, 15 Jan., 1881. No. 6; C.O. 152/158. Derby to Leeds, 30 Aug., 1884. No. 210.
[96] C.O. 152/141. Moir to Mundy, 24 July, 1871. No. 1; and, enc. in Berkeley to Kimberley, 11 Dec., 1880. No. 391.
[97] Virgin Islands Ordinances 1866-1889. Ordinance No. 3. of 1885; C.O. 152/162. Lees to Stanley, 1 Oct., 1885. No. 276.
[98] C.O. 152/158. Enc. in Porter to Derby, 9 Aug., 1884. No. 265.
[99] P.P. 1839. Vol. XXXVII, p. 322.
[100] P.P. 1839. Vol. XXXVII, p. 331.
[101] C.O. 239/64. S.M.'s Report for May and June, 1841.
[102] C.O. 239/67. S.M.'s Report for Quarter ended 31 Dec., 1841; and half year ended 31 Dec., 1843.
[103] P.P. 1845. Vol. XXXI, p. 577; C.O. 243/10. S.M.'s Reports for half years ended 30 June, 1847, and 31 Dec., 1847.
[104] C.O. 243/10. S.M.'s Reports for half years ended 30 June, 1847, and 31 Dec., 1847.
[105] P.P. 1856. Vol. XLII, p. 172; C.O. 314/4. Hamilton to Labouchere, 9 April, 1856. No. 7; P.P. 1864. Vol. XL, p. 94.
[106] P.P. 1866. Vol. XLIX, p. 378.
[107] P.P. 1898. Vol. LI, p. 245.
[108] Douglas Hall, Free Jamaica, pp. 160-162.
[109] P.P. 1866. Vol. XLIX, p. 378; C.O. 317/21. Blue Book for 1868.
[110] P.P. 1898. Vol. LI, p. 245.
[111] C.O. 314/4. Enc. in Hamilton to Labouchere, 9 April, 1856. No. 7; P.P 1860. Vol. XLIV, p. 102.
[112] P.P. 1859, p. 526.
[113] C.O. 317/9 to C.O. 317/58. Blue Books, 1838-1887.
[114] G. R. Porter: The Tropical Agriculturist: a practical treatise on the cultivation and management of various productions suited to tropical climates (London, Smith, Elder and Company, 1833) pp. 12-13; P.P. 1859. Vol. XXI, p. 528.
[115] C.O. 317/27 to C.O. 317/48. Blue Books, 1856-1887.
[116] C.O. 317. Blue Books after 1847.
[117] C.O. 314/7. Enc. in Hamilton to Lytton, 14 March, 1859. No. 43; C.O 314/11. Enc. in Hamilton to Newcastle, 22 April, 1862. No. 178 and 23 June 1862. No. 199.
[118] P.P. 1867. Vol. XLVIII, p. 100.
[119] C.O. 317/9 to C.O. 317/58. Blue Books, 1838-1887.
[120] C.O. 152/145. Enc. in Glover to Kimberley, 23 Sept., 1881, No. 264; P.P 1888. Vol. LXXII, p. 964.
[121] P.P. 1867-1868. Vol. XLVIII, p. 107; P.P. 1868-1869. Vol. XLIII, pp 93-94.
[122] P.P. 1886. Vol. XLV, p. 509; P.P. 1888. Vol. LXXII, p. 967.

Chapter 7

Problems of Financial Adjustment

The emancipation of slaves in the Virgin Islands constituted a social as well as an economic revolution in the colony. Socially, it converted slaves into free people entitled to all the rights of that class, while economically it resulted in a swing from large-scale plantation agriculture to independent small-scale farming. These two factors necessitated wide changes in the fiscal policy of the colonial legislature, with regard both to expenditure and revenue. The financial problems of the post-emancipation period stemmed from the attempts of the legislature to adjust to the new situation and, to some extent, the people's reaction to them.

After 1838 the government of the Virgin Islands became involved in additional expenditure. By the Tax Act of 1839, fees to officers of government were abolished and a system of salaries was instituted instead due primarily to the fact that the returns from fees of offices provided inadequate payment of the officers concerned.[1] After 1838, also, it became incumbent upon the legislature to provide the social amenities hitherto provided by slave-owners and missionaries who were in financial difficulties. Besides, there were certain services which were more specifically the responsibility of the legislature, such as the provision of poor-relief, and assistance to the aged and infirm and the mentally handicapped. So also was the maintenance of the jail, the care of prisoners, the provision of public offices and the establishment of a police force.

Among the expenses of government after 1838, must be mentioned the liquidation of the consolidated debt contracted during the period of tax abeyance, 1819 to 1832. The accumulation of this debt was due to the failure of the legislature to meet both its ordinary expenditure of administration, such as the payment of the part salaries of government officials, and its extraordinary expenditure such as the formation and equipping of a militia following the slave revolt of 1831, and the rental of buildings used for public purposes following the destruction of government offices by the hurricane of 1819. In 1832, the consolidated debt amounted to £19,938, and by 1838 it had not yet been liquidated.

While the legislature of the Virgin Islands was faced with increased expenditure after 1838, the sources of revenues had noticeably shrunk. It was no longer possible to levy a capitation tax on slaves since slavery had been abolished. Other sources, for example, sugar and cotton, were now much weaker, due to the decline in production of these commodities. Moreover, the planter-legislators were not yet prepared to accept a tax on their lands. In addition to these, considerable revenue was lost through the practice of smuggling.

In order to satisfy its financial requirements the legislature of the Virgin Islands resorted to various schemes by which these could be satisfactorily achieved. These included attempts to curtail smuggling, modifications in the system of taxation, and changes in the system of government to secure more reliable Assemblies. Also of importance were the union of the colony in the federation of the Leeward Islands in 1871, and certain extraordinary measures to increase revenue and reduce expenditure. Without exception these schemes failed to produce the desired result.

Before emancipation all classes of imports both for domestic consumption and for re-export were smuggled and after emancipation, smuggling was extended to include exports also. Facility was given by the neighbouring island of St. Thomas described as 'a point of easy daily resort.'[2] Not only was it the 'grand ware-house' but it was conveniently situated to provide a suitable market for the produce of Virgin Islanders who operated small crafts and canoes. Trips to St. Thomas could be made as occasion arose. Unlike the exportation of sugar which could be transported to Britain only once a year, that is, at the end of the crop, and as facilities for transportation allowed, the buying and selling of the peasants, dealing in small quantities at a time by direct payments, necessitated frequent trips to St. Thomas.

The natural formation of the Virgin Islands gave opportunity to the smugglers to evade the payment of duties which no Customs House establishment, however efficient, could entirely prevent. In the Virgin Islands in 1840, there were only two customs officers, the Collector, and the Landing Waiter and Searcher. These officers were far from adequate, and smuggling was indulged in by nearly everybody with very little molestation from the Customs House.

Smuggling continued throughout the nineteenth century and while it was impossible to calculate the extent of the loss to the colonial revenues, it was generally acknowledged to be considerable. It was even suggested that, had smuggling been non-existent, the revenues from customs duties lost would have been sufficient to meet expenditures, without the need to revert to extraordinary methods of raising the requisite amounts.

After 1838 several unsuccessful attempts were made to suppress smuggling. In September, 1839, President Drummond Hay secured an agreement from the people not to smuggle or to encourage or deal with known smugglers, but the agreement was not observed.[3] Five years later, fifteen percent of the revenues collected under the Import Duties Act of that year was allocated for the employment of vessels to be used as patrols against smugglers. However, it was unlikely that the sum so obtained would suffice to promote an efficient system. The five percent import duty was only a fraction of what it should be because of smuggling. Therefore the greater the activity of smugglers, the less provision would there be for their apprehension. In effect the fifteen percent – £24 in 1844, £78 in 1845 and £68 in 1846 – was inadequate for the adoption of efficient measures.[4]

It was not until December, 1846, that the Assembly was led to adopt more appropriate measures. The first provided for the establishment of a revenue protection force to assist the Customs Officers, the Treasurer and other revenue collectors in the detection of fraudulent evasion of the revenue law. The second provided for the establishment of a port of entry on the western coast of Tortola, or on one of the adjacent islands.[5] These measures, however, did not produce any appreciable benefits.

To prevent smuggling altogether, it was often suggested whether customs duties should not be repealed or drastically reduced, and replaced by other taxes. The suggestion was dismissed in the 1840's because direct taxation was already considered burdensome.[6] It was not that direct taxes would not supply the actual deficiencies, since the import duties yielded so little, but that they could not be made so burdensome as to provide what the import duties should yield if smuggling were controlled. Additional taxation was opposed on the grounds that 'new burdens could scarcely be imposed without undue pressure on already decaying interests.' Instead, modifications in the fiscal structure were suggested in order to achieve increases in the revenue, and in order to remove the temptations to defraud the revenue, the President proposed the enactment of legislation to authorise the creation of certain points along the coast to be legal places of entry.[7]

Later in the nineteenth century, further efforts were made to suppress smuggling. Thus in 1856, a sub-treasurer was stationed at West End, Tortola, to inspect and clear vessels trading to and from that neighbourhood.[8] A decade later, the police and other constables were made revenue protection officers, and separate sub-treasurers were provided for Road Town, Anegada, Virgin Gorda and Jost Van Dyke.[9] Further measures were adopted in 1881, when a small-decked schooner of six tons, hitherto hired to convey mails between Tortola and St. Thomas, was bought for the exclusive use of government and partly employed in patrolling the seas around the Virgin Islands, for the detection, capture and discouragement of smugglers.[10]

Since almost the whole of the export and import trade of the Virgin Islands towards the end of the nineteenth century was with St. Thomas, it was evident that that island possessed the key to any effective control over smuggling. This was particularly true of imports from that island since the Danish authorities there could put the officials of the Virgin Islands in possession of the amount of all cargoes shipped in Virgin Islands boats, by means of itemised clearances. It was necessary for some understanding to be reached with the Danish authorities whereby, for example, clearance specifying the amounts of individual items of all cargoes shipped could be furnished weekly to the British authorities. Such advised clearances would thus give the administration of the Virgin Islands a fair knowledge of goods legitimately shipped from St. Thomas.[11] The Danish Government was at first willing to co-operate and in June, 1897, a proclamation was issued requiring a specific declaration at the Customs House from all vessels clearing from St. Thomas for any of the Virgin Islands, indicating the nature and content of their cargoes.[12] However, these regulations were severely modified in September, 1897; the Danish colonial government expressed inability to make the production of detailed certificates of cargoes obligatory, since this would entail an amount of labour and expense out of proportion to its resources.[13] This declaration in effect left the situation unchanged.

Virgin Islanders, however, showed a consummate disregard of all efforts made to restrict smuggling. An incident occurred in 1856 which showed the extent to which they were prepared to go in violation of the law.[14] On being informed on November 24, that a boat belonging to an inhabitant of Thatch Island was trading without a licence, the sub-treasurer of Tortola proceeded to seize it. He soon had to abandon the seizure, however, when he was assaulted and the crew of his boat badly beaten. Two days later, a force consisting of four constables was despatched by the stipendiary magistrate to arrest the offenders. On landing they were obstructed by forty to fifty people, and when they persevered and made their arrest were also severely beaten. On the following day, a larger force comprising thirty men, principally rural constables, twelve of whom were armed, was despatched to quell the spirit of insubordination and to apprehend the offenders. Despite this show of force, it was only the assistance of the Wesleyan missionaries who were influential among the inhabitants, which enabled sixteen arrests to be made without active opposition.

The resistance of the people of Thatch Island was a manifestation of the general spirit of unrest which was pervading the Virgin Islands in the 1850's. It demonstrated the co-ordinate relationship between unpopular taxation, smuggling and violence which were characteristic of the Virgin Islands at the time.

Before emancipation the free tax-paying population had been reluctant to submit to any taxation beyond what was necessary to support immediate public expenditure. There was general dislike for a broadly-based system of taxation, and the most acceptable sources of revenue were taxes on slaves, buildings and retail liquor. Except in the case of the first Money Bill of 1783, there was no general tax on land until 1859.[15] The legislature adopted a dual policy with regard to taxation: it sought to modify the system of taxation to suit the economic conditions of the colony and, in addition, to apply taxation to as many classes of the population as possible.

Of more importance in determining attitudes to taxation after emancipation was the second condition which aimed at distributing taxes among as many classes as possible. Early taxation undoubtedly fell exclusively on the small class of white Virgin Islanders. A shift was noticeable when in 1809 the tax on mills was replaced by a special tax of £6. 10s. a year on each free male inhabitant, white or coloured, between the ages of 20 and 60 years, who did not pay either the existing slave, building or horse tax. This action was evidently an attempt to incorporate the rising class of free coloureds into the body of tax-payers. Although the tax was dropped in the Act of 1817, all hawkers and pedlars, who were chiefly free negroes and coloureds were required to take out a licence for £6.12s. every twelve months.

The Tax Act of 1832 reveals a continuing attempt to extend taxation to the several sectors of the community and to impose it in the least burdensome manner consistent with the declining economy of the colony. In that year the tax on slaves was not levied, and the incidence of taxation was extended to the free negroes and coloureds in greater measure since they had been accorded extended privileges the year before. Thus, in addition to the reintroduction of the licence of £6. 12s., but for every six months, on hawkers and pedlars, retail traders of sugar and spirituous liquors, and bakers, who were essentially people drawn from the free negro and coloured group, were required to operate under licence, bakers at 16/6 for every three months.[16]

The institution of full emancipation in August, 1838, entitling the ex-slaves to all the rights and privileges of free people, also carried with it certain recognised responsibilities including contribution towards the expenses of government. This meant sharing in the payment of taxes in so far as ex-slaves held taxable property, consumed dutiable goods, or required licences for various purposes. After 1838, the legislature of the Virgin Islands attempted to impose the duty of tax-payers on the newly freed population. From being merely an item for taxation, the ex-slaves became taxpayers in their own rights. In extending the limits of taxation to them, the legislature instituted some fundamental changes. The principles of 'light' and 'equitable' distribution were, of course, retained as far as the traditional tax-payers, that is, the large land-owners, were concerned. But henceforth, taxation was also used to influence the economic behaviour and occupation of the ex-slaves.

Freedom enabled the ex-slaves to establish themselves in employment divorced from plantation agriculture, and away from the authority of their previous masters. To ensure a sufficiency of available labour for the plantations, the tax system was adjusted to prevent or discourage the ex-slaves from establishing themselves in independent employments, and in cases where this happened, to reduce the profits of such employments thereby making them less attractive. The double use of taxation as a means of raising revenue and as a determinant of occupation, imposed a greater strain on the ex-slaves' ability to pay. The change in principle was evident in the Tax Acts of 1837 and 1844.

In the Tax Act of 1837, a land tax of 20/− an acre was imposed on cultivated lands other than those devoted to the cultivation of sugar and cotton.[17] As the tax did not extend to the owners of estates, the aim was obviously to extend the system of taxation to include those negroes who sought to establish themselves as independent proprietors. The fact that negro lands belonging to estates were exempt from the tax emphasised the intention of the planter-legislators to prevent the drift away from the estates by the ex-slaves.

Through the initiative of the stipendiary magistrate, the 20/− land tax was repealed in 1841,[18] but by 1844 it became necessary to adopt measures to curtail the increasing number of negroes seeking to set themselves up independently. This aim was evident in the nature of the articles taxed in 1844. According to one Act, vessels registered in the colony were required to be licensed, and unlicensed vessels were liable to be seized.[19] The Act affected in particular those people who were engaged in fishing or who were accustomed to conveying their products in their own vessels to market in St. Thomas, that is, the newly emancipated negroes. Two other Acts affected the ex-slave population also, though not exclusively. The first levied taxes and export duties on their primary produce, namely, cattle and sheep;[20] and the second placed an impost of 5% on all houses valued at £10 and over and on all incomes of £50 and over except those of public officers paid from Britain.[21] All these were direct taxes on the property of Virgin Islanders; another enactment imposed indirect taxes also, by requiring a duty of 5% advalorem on all goods, wares, merchandise and chattels imported into the Virgin Islands.[22]

The Tax Acts of 1844 were continued and sometimes extended during the following decade. For instance, in 1847, the taxes on incomes and houses were doubled,[23] and in 1852 the tax on vessels was extended to include not only vessels kept in the Virgin Islands, but all others used there.[24] At the same time provisions were made for the more efficient collection of taxes. Half-yearly assessments on houses and lands were substituted in 1847 for quarterly assessments which were found inconvenient and harassing both to the people and to the revenue officers. No returns had hitherto been required from tax-payers on their liability to the colony but an arbitrary assessment had been made by the Treasurer from which appeal could be made to the House of Assembly. There every person either in writing or personal appearance could swear off any amount of taxation. This system was abolished in 1847[25] when, also, the Treasurer was authorised to appoint one or more sub-treasurers to assist him in the collection of taxes.[26] By an Act of 1852 extending the tax on vessels, it was expected that the inclusion of a second category of vessels would make the collection easier, reduce the possibility of evasion and increase the revenues.[27]

Smuggling and violence were both aspects of a resistance against the system of taxation generally. Discontent was especially widespread since the failure of the legislature to tax lands, thereby throwing the greater share of the taxation upon those least able to bear it, was regarded as an attempt by its members to escape what they demanded from others. Resistance was not confined to ex-slaves. It extended to all classes of the community including even members of the legislature. The activity of one class tended to give encouragement to another. These factors were evident in the disturbances of 1848 and 1853.

The initiative in the attack of 1848 was taken by the coloured population of Road Town, following the revolt of the slaves in St. Croix and the declaration of slave emancipation in the Danish Islands. A serious grievance of the coloured people of the Virgin Islands was their exclusion from public offices. In this respect they were charged with being 'desirous to rule' and were 'ambitious of public appointments.'[28] However, their complaint of exclusion from office could be justified, though not in point of colour, since they wanted appointments for themselves rather than for 'foreigners'. Of the sixteen offices held by coloured people in 1848 all but one were held by non-Virgin Islanders.

The reason for the disorder of 1848, however, has to be seen more properly in connection with smuggling. Previously smuggling had been conducted with almost perfect impunity, and in a few instances where seizure of goods had been made confiscation was the only penalty incurred for a breach of law. Under more recent enactments, however, pecuniary penalties were also imposed on smuggling offences, and enforced by imprisonment with hard labour in cases of non-payment. The willingness of the magistrates to carry out the provisions of these laws, and to enforce their decisions, antagonised the small dealers and their friends and connections about Road Town who stood to gain most from smuggling. It was not surprising, therefore, that the ire of the coloureds who were small shop-keepers was directed and vented against the magistrates.

When the coloured population of Road Town attacked the magistracy it was genuinely believed that their action would signal a general revolt of the masses. The concentration of their attack against the stipendiary magistrate, Isidore Dyett, however, deprived them of sympathetic support, especially of the rural population among whom

Dyett was popular. Many appreciated the protection he offered them against unscrupulous planters, his generous advice, and his impartial adjudication of disputes. When news of a physical assault upon him reached them, they offered him their protection in case of another attack.

The very personal aspects of this case offered no security against eventual general revolt. In this particular instance the people had come to the defence of a friend. It was still quite possible that they might be led to attack real or supposed injustice. Fear was all the more acute because of the absence of an adequate police force. An Act of the legislature in 1837 had provided for the appointment of a police magistrate, a superintendent or chief officer of police, four sergeants and eight constables.[29] Nevertheless in 1848 the civil defence force was composed of only a number of rural constables. Their inadequacy to deal with even a minor disorder necessitated the swearing in of a sufficient number of special constables. Besides, the rural constabulary could not always be summoned readily in an emergency and it was doubted that their loyalty would survive many direct clashes with groups of disaffected people.[30] Since the repeal of all the laws relating to the establishment and regulation of a militia in 1839,[31] the legislature had taken no further action to set up such a force.

The connection between public disorder and taxation was more discernible on the occasion of the uprising of August, 1853. Agitation centered upon the close attachment between the Methodist missionaries and the people, over three thousand of whom were members and attendants of the Methodist chapels. The activities of the missionaries contributed to a large extent to the outbreak of the riot, though dislike of taxation was a long standing grievance among the people.

A petition from Robert Hawkins and Joshua Jordan, the Methodist missionaries resident in Tortola, to the Assembly in March, 1853, requested that they should be relieved from all taxes on horses, houses, boats, and servants, as well as on their salaries. The missionaries also asked that an annual grant should be made to them from colonial funds for educational purposes.[32] The Assembly, however, rejected the petition on the general assumption that it was 'not in circumstances to grant it.'[33] More specifically, the grant for education was denied because it was feared that if allowed the annual grant of £300 sterling which was placed at the disposal of the Bishop of Antigua for use by the Established Church in Tortola would be withdrawn.[34] The reaction of the missionaries was indicative of future developments: on being informed of the rejection of their petition Jordan replied, 'we will raise the people against you.'[35]

The direct consequence of the denial of the petition and of the implied threat of the missionaries was their encouragement of public protest. A public meeting was held in the Methodist Chapel in Road Town on May 24, to consider the necessity and propriety of memorialising the Queen for a grant in aid of general education in the Virgin Islands, and for the exemption of the Methodist Society 'from an unparallelled system of Taxation imposed upon it.'[36] The tenor of the meeting was reflected in a petition to the Queen, which pleaded the general lack of educational institutions in the Virgin Islands, and the inability of the people, in view of unremunerative employment and high taxation, to satisfy the deficiency. The petition called for an annual grant in aid of education and for the interposition of the Queen 'on behalf of the Wesleyan Church . . . that the obnoxious system of taxation under which it has long groaned may be removed.'[37]

The discontent of the inhabitants was undoubtedly fostered by the proceedings of the missionaries and the spirit of protest was maintained by a subsequent meeting held at Chateau Bellair by two Virgin Islanders. The legislature seemed oblivious to these proceedings, and further aggravated the situation by imposing an extra tax of 6d. on each head of cattle in the Virgin Islands in June, 1853. As cattle rearing was primarily the occupation of the rural negro population, this tax fell principally on them. And to their injudicious levy, the legislature added bad timing when they scheduled the Act to come into operation on August 1, 1853, the anniversary of emancipation.

That there was no violent protest when the Act was passed in June would suggest that rioting could have been avoided if the legislature had been more circumspect in enforcing it. Similarly, had they shown a willingness to compromise when a large body of rural labourers entered Road Town on August 1, with an evident determination to resist the law, trouble could have been prevented. Instead, even before violence was shown, the Riot Act was read, and two arrests made. Nothing more could prevent the outbreak of violence and several constables and magistrates present were beaten.[38] As a result of continued rioting, the greater part of Road Town was burnt down and a number of country houses were sacked during the following three days.[39]

President Chads undoubtedly possessed considerable personal courage and this probably led him to attempt to meet physical force with moral suasion. He obviously had the confidence of the people since they repeatedly referred to him to act on their behalf; but he also possessed very little judgment and tact in handling emergencies. When on August 2, a large crowd numbering between 1,500 and 2,000 labourers reentered Road Town and approached him he could only promise, if properly memorialised, to lay their grievance over the cattle tax, before the legislature.[40] Further action highlighted by the shooting of one of the protesters, and the spread of widespread destruction in revenge, prevented conciliation since all the members of the legislature had fled to St. Thomas along with the greater part of the white population. The only whites who remained were the President, the Collector of Customs, a Methodist missionary and the doctor.[41]

The riot of August, 1853 was eventually suppressed with military assistance from St. Thomas, and reinforcements of British troops despatched by the Governor of the Leeward Islands from Antigua.[42] Subsequently twenty of the principal offenders were sentenced to various terms of imprisonment, and three others to death.[43]

The riot was due primarily to disaffection among the rural labouring population, but the protest against taxation was not confined to them. When in July, 1857, a mercantile Ordinance was passed by the Legislative Council requiring all mercantile houses to take out first class licences at an annual cost of £15 each,[44] it was opposed by some of the leading inhabitants of Road Town. Having obvious interest in retail trading, they based their protest on the ground that the Ordinance was adopted to the circumstances of a few people in Tortola who could afford to monopolise trade.[45] In November, 1857, also, the same inhabitants, and including some others, requested the repeal of the Road Ordinance of 1855 under which all male inhabitants were required to work on the highways four days a year, or in lieu, to pay one shilling a day.[46] They asserted that such measures could only 'disturb the peace of society, excite contention and multiply instead of diminishing offences.'[47] The petition was rejected but when labour was demanded shortly after, there was a considerable number of defaulters.[48] Legal proceedings were instituted, and fourteen persons, including some holders of petty government offices, were imprisoned for four days. Their liberation was followed by threats of violence against the jailer, the trial magistrate and the President.

Legislation with regard to taxation after 1853 shows the continuous preoccupation of the legislature to adjust the system to make it more acceptable to the population. One of the earliest actions taken was the abolition of licences on livestock in an attempt to conciliate the peasantry on a point on which they felt strongly.[49] In order to make the system more equitable, a general tax on all lands in the Virgin Islands was imposed for the first time in 1859, though a graduated scale was adopted to discourage evasion or to prevent undue hardship in paying. Thus, in 1859 and 1860, all lands in Tortola were required to pay 3d. an acre, lands in the other inhabited islands were to pay 2d. an acre, while lands in the uninhabited islands were to pay 1d. an acre. After 1860, the payments were to be 2d., 1d., and ½d. an acre respectively.[50] Other legislation sought to give further relief; in March, 1859 income tax was abolished,[51] and in 1864, the tax on sugar, rum and molasses made in the colony was repealed.[52]

After the 1860s only two attempts were made to impose additional taxation in the Virgin Islands. In order to meet an estimated deficit of £135 in the budget, an additional ten percent was added in May, 1872 on all existing taxation.[53] This merely resulted in decreased revenue as was evident in the returns from import duties. From May to August, 1871, before the tax, revenue from this source amounted to £181, but for the same period in 1872, even with the additional rate, the duties realised only £128.[54] The ten percent tax was soon abolished,[55] and the export duty on horses and mules was increased from 1/− to 4/− a head.[56] These were insignificant items.

Public opinion expressed in petitions protesting against existing rates of taxation was a very persuasive factor in the Virgin Islands. To this was added a willingness of the people to resort to physical violence. In 1887 they were reportedly arming themselves for a general destruction of the islands and again, in 1890, smugglers openly defied the customs officer in Road Town to seize their boat and threats of violence were made amidst the firing of guns. On both occasions, disorder was prevented by reinforcements from Antigua, and in 1890, from St. Thomas also.[57] In the absence of any adequate controlling medium locally, and in the face of concerted opposition, the legislature was most willing to pay deference to expressions of local sentiment.

The accommodations offered by the constitutional reforms of 1854 and 1859 in reducing the opposition of recalcitrant Assemblies enabled several useful measures to be adopted with regard to taxation. It was the success achieved which partly suggested the institution of full Crown Colony Government since there existed the possibility of the emergence of destructive influence in the Legislative Council. If the adoption of Crown Colony Government presupposed the greater participation of the Crown in the conduct of the affairs of the colony this was not reflected in any tangible attempt to develop the economy, especially through agriculture. The inhabitants were forced to depend on their own resources which resulted in a perpetuation of traditional practices of cultivation based upon the needs of St. Thomas.

Successive studies were made of the financial condition of the Virgin Islands in 1883 and 1896 by officials from the Colonial Office, with a view to the augmentation of finances.[58] Repeatedly, recommendations were based on the assumption that the existing economic structure would be maintained. No attempt was made to suggest a remodelling of that structure in order to achieve a realignment of economic forms. In common with the Colonial Office, successive Governors of the Leeward Islands, and Presidents of the Virgin Islands were unable to formulate any constructive policy to improve the agricultural condition of the Virgin Islands. To some extent the institution of measures was hampered by the Crown Colony system which required that all proposals, financial and otherwise, should receive the approval of the Secretary of State for the Colonies prior to implementation.

Proposals to improve agriculture suggested locally were always negated.[59] Not until 1900 after the British Government had decided to establish a Department of Agriculture in the West Indies to encourage agricultural diversification and the development of colonial resources,[60] was an Experiment Station established in Tortola for the same purposes.[61] The achievements of the Station, however, belonged more properly to the period after 1902; it had little or no effect in stimulating an interest in agriculture among the people before that date.

Crown Colony Government had resulted from a belief that it would lead to the maturity of measures to develop the economy of the Virgin Islands. In order to reduce administrative expenses the colony was associated with other British Leeward Islands in the federation of 1871.[62] The initial financial contribution of the Virgin Islands to the Federal Government was one-sixteenth of the federal expenditure. Coming at a time when the Virgin Islands were further burdened by the necessity to maintain the salaries of the President and the Chief Justice, at a total annual cost of £978, hitherto paid by the British Government, this extra financial requirement though small imposed a severe strain on local resources. As early as July, 1872, the fear was expressed that the Virgin Islands would not be able to meet the charge.[63] Computed on the federal expenditure for 1872, the Virgin Islands' contribution amounted to £385. 12s. 6d. Nevertheless, it defaulted to the tune of £121. 17s. 6d.[64] The contribution was reduced by half in 1873, the other half being borne by Anguilla previously exempted from such payments though enjoying the services of federal officers.[65] The amount was subsequently reduced to one-forty-eighth of the whole.[66] Despite these arrangements there was a gradual accumulation of the federal debt which in 1875 totalled £319.[67] Some effort was made thereafter to meet the payment but in 1883 the debt amounted to £390, the Virgin Islands for some time past having ceased to pay its required quota.[68] Ensuing inability to pay resulted in a massive debt to the federation of £1,310 in 1892,[69] and of £1,670 in 1896.[70] This trend stressed the need for economy which was sought in the reduction of the civil establishment.

The importance of the reductions made in the civil establishment lay in the financial inability of the Virgin Islands to maintain the institutions of government, and partly because of this, the difficulty of securing properly qualified persons to fill the several offices. The answer to this two-pronged problem was the amalgamation or abolition of offices in response to the declining economy. The combination of several offices under a single incumbent was nothing new in the Virgin Islands but could be traced to the time of the institution of the legislature in 1773. In the period after 1866, however, the practice was considerably accelerated as a result of the policy to curtail expenditure to suit revenue.

Following the death of the Chief Justice in April, 1866, approval was given to the proposal to combine the offices of Judge and Magistrate.[71] In 1868 and 1869 the offices of stipendiary magistrate and of Queen's Council respectively were abolished.[72] More important than these was the abolition of the office of Colonial Secretary in 1869, and the transfer of his duties to the Provost Marshal, in whom was vested the duties of Registrar, clerk to the magistrate, and clerk to the President.[73] Further changes were effected during the same year following the dismissal of the Treasurer-Postmaster who was implicated in the illegal sale of a foreign vessel the *Telegrapho*. The Inspectorship of Police was abolished and in the holder of that office was vested the duties of Clerk in the Treasury, and Landing Waiter of Customs.[74] Because of the vacancy in the Postmastership, advantage was taken of these changes to transfer the business of the Post Office to the Treasury.[75] Towards the end of 1870 the offices of jailer and clerk to the Provost Marshal were united to allow the saving of £25 a year to be appropriated to the superannuation of the Colonial Surgeon.[76] Yet further changes were made in 1872: the duties of the Treasury devolved upon a sub-Treasurer under the superintendence of the President; the offices of coroner and crown prosecutor were united, later to be fused with that of surgeon; the salary of the rector was abolished and this was followed by the disendowment of the Established Church;[77] and finally the office of the jailer was abolished and the salary of the turnkey reduced.[78]

Prompted by the low state of the economy, the legislature was led to resort to an extraordinary measure to raise necessary revenue. The normal returns from the sale of postage stamps was quite small but capable of stimulation by the introduction of a special issue. Between 1887 and 1889 when such an issue was resorted to, there was considerable augmentation in sales to philatelists. For example, whereas sales in 1885 and 1886 were £87 and £55 respectively, in 1887 and 1889 they amounted to almost £146 and £216 respectively. However, when in 1890 a common stamp was issued for the entire Leeward Islands this advantage ended. A windfall of £953 obtained in 1894 from the sale of the remainder of old issues of Virgin Islands stamps encouraged a new issue in 1898, and by the end of 1899, revenues totalling £1,450 were produced.[79]

Nevertheless, it was not the intention of the Colonial Office to make the sale of stamps the perpetual medium of special revenue. The special issue of 1898 had been opposed on the grounds that it was an abuse of the function of the post office, that it would create a precedent for other West Indian colonies to demand similar privileges, and that it was a retrograde step from the principle of federation. When in 1901, a fresh issue of 2/6 stamps to raise an additional revenue of about £200 was proposed, the suggestion was rejected.[80]

The Virgin Islands failed to achieve the revenue necessary to meet increased expenditure. It was shown, for instance, in the difficulty in liquidating the consolidated debt, finally settled by a composite agreement, in the failure to balance annual budgets thereby leading to recurrent deficits, and finally in the need for an imperial grant to liquidate all outstanding debts at the end of the century.

Until 1832, no attempt was made to pay off the outstanding consolidated debt. Appeals to the Crown could produce no fruitful result since the constitution of a legislative colonial government did not permit the Crown to exercise any power in the levy or distribution of public money in the colony. This was the exclusive function of the local legislature. In the financial Acts of 1832, some provision was made for the liquidation of the debt, 'by an annual dividend to each creditor.' The arrangements were, however, to say the least, very unsatisfactory since the debt was made the seventeenth and last charge upon the revenue.[81]

The recognised principle for discharging the debt was enunciated in a subsequent Act to the effect 'that the consolidated debt of the Virgin Islands shall be paid from any balance of monies remaining in the Treasury at the end of the year.'[82] The depressed state of the economy, dependent as it still was on the sugar industry, did not always permit a surplus of revenue over current expenditure. No dividends were paid in 1832; a payment of just over £719 was made in 1833; and in 1836 and again in 1841 there were budgetary balances of £906 and £601 respectively which went towards the liquidation of the debt. In 1839, 1842 and 1843 fixed and contingent expenditure exceeded revenues from all sources; it is, therefore, not likely that any expenditure was made towards the debt. Another difficulty in meeting payments was shown when in 1844 an additional floating debt of £700 was incurred because the legislature failed to renew the revenue laws until nine months after they had expired.

The delay in liquidating the debt resulted in constant pressures for payments.[83] These were generally supported by Lord Stanley, the Secretary of State for the Colonies, though the final responsibility rested with the local legislature. He considered that it was impossible for the British Government to acquiesce silently 'in such an abandonment of the legislative bodies of a British Colony of one of the most sacred trusts with which they are invested.'[84] He was not to be persuaded by the allegation of the inability of the colony to sustain further taxation which he regarded as the invariable plea of fraudulent communities. In 1845 he ordered the immediate adoption of appropriate measures to satisfy claims so as to prevent him from taking 'any ulterior steps in reference to that body, for the protection of the Colony from the discredit attaching to their acts.'[85]

The Assembly, which had control over finances, was not to be intimidated by external pressures. It was not until May, 1847, that it could be induced to pass the required legislation which provided that each creditor should be paid at certain periods each year an amount in proportion to the total claim.[86] In addition to the surplus of revenue over expenditure, the total revenue derived from a stamp duty Act and an Act to regulate the gathering of salt on Salt Island,[87] passed previously, was appropriated exclusively towards the payment of the debt. Even so, the President was unable to give any assurance that there was a prospect of a large payment.[88] That proceeds were small and payments insignificant was evidenced in the case of one creditor to whom was due £1,711. 6s;[89] it was not until 1849 that the first dividends were paid on this debt, and even then they amounted to only £46. 1s. 4d.[90]

The increasing inability of the legislature to meet its financial obligations was stressed when by 1854, the colony became further burdened with a floating debt of £1,584 due as salaries to public officers. The debt was liquidated, after the officers had generously agreed to relinquish the sum of £692, by a loan of £700 from Robert G. Pedder, a local planter. The accumulation of this debt and the nature of its liquidation suggest that no surplus was obtainable from the ordinary revenue for the discharge of the consolidated debt. This was a recurrent difficulty. It was only through the incidental revenue totalling £6,015 derived from the duties on wrecked goods exported in 1860, that the nine months arrears on the salaries of public officers could be paid.[91]

The need for further measures to liquidate the consolidated debt was recognised by President Longden in 1862,[92] when the total debt amounted to £4,183. But since the annual revenue of the colony averaged about £2,000, all of which was appropriated otherwise, there appeared little hope of claims being satisfied. While upholding the claims of the creditors, Longden did not consider the condition of the people 'of a kind from which can be wrung the means of paying (at least within any definite period) the debts of a past generation.'[93] The Legislative Council consisting of two white immigrants and five coloured residents opposed the payment of a debt for which they did not consider themselves responsible.[94] In the end, however, a solution was found in a composition payable by annual instalments. In January, 1864, the Legislative Council unanimously adopted a resolution providing for the payment of £206. 9s. 8d. that year, and half that sum during the following two years.[95]

The difficulties experienced over the liquidation of the consolidated debt, and the fractional payment by which it is was finally settled, revealed the low state into which the economy of the Virgin Islands had sunk. As Longden explained, even the meagre provision could be made only 'by starving down the public service to the lowest point and delaying some of the most necessary public works.'[96] The inability of the government to devise measures to develop the economy, its unwillingness to institute higher taxation, and the evasion by the people of their responsibility to contribute fully, meant that sufficient revenue was rarely collected to defray expenditure. The Colonial Office's repeated injunction to equalise revenue and expenditure,[97] and later to keep revenue in excess of expenditure,[98] failed to produce satisfactory results. The result was yearly deficits in the colonial budget. This was particularly so after 1872 when the Virgin Islands were required to pay the salaries of the President and the Chief Justice, and to contribute to the maintenance of federal institutions. The financial state of the islands after 1887, when it became more acute because of the impossibility of devising measures to curtail expenditure, is shown in Table 9.[99] By the end of the century it was necessary to obtain an imperial grant to liquidate a debt of £2,206.[100]

Table 9

The Financial Condition of the Virgin Islands, 1887-1895

Year	Excess of Expenditure over Revenue £ s. d.	Surplus of Revenue over Expenditure £. s. d.	Deficit on 31 December £. s. d.
1887	- - -	- - -	225. 15. 6
1888	249. 0. 6.	- - -	474. 9. 6.
1889	- - -	247. 6. 6.	227. 9. 6.
1890	249. 0. 10.	- - -	511. 10. 4.
1891	729. 17. 1.	- - -	1241. 7. 4.
1892	828. 17. 3.	- - -	2070. 5. 8.
1893	118. 15. 9.	- - -	2198. 1. 3.
1894	225. 19. 9.	953. 0. 0.	1562. 1. 0.
1895	489. 8. 8.	- - -	1901. 9. 5.

During the post-emancipation period reliance was placed on agriculture as the basis of the economy of the Virgin Islands but nothing was done to develop it. Rather, economic decline led to difficulties in raising sufficient revenues to meet increased expenditure. The spirit of dissatisfaction and protest expressed in smuggling, refusal to pay taxes, and open violence, both in its origin and its manifestation, has to be seen within the context of the entire social, economic and political framework of the Virgin Islands.

The emancipation of slaves and the collapse of the sugar industry removed or modified the returns from two main items of taxation, namely, slaves and sugar, and made it necessary to extend the system of taxation. The manner in which this was done was bound to cause discontent, and probably justified the extreme measures which were adopted to oppose it. The apparent inclination of the legislature to shift the incidence of taxation from land on to the personal property of the ex-slaves was open to the charge of discrimination. The resort to physical violence illustrates the extent to which the inhabitants were prepared to go to secure recognition of their demands for a more equitable distribution or less oppressive system of taxation.

The nineteenth century was one of political instability highlighted by recurring disputes between the Assembly and the President and Council. In their near similarity of views on taxation the Assembly and the labouring population generally supported each other. After 1833 the President was responsible for initiating tax proposals and his views on taxation were shared by the Council. In this situation social turmoil could not but encourage or result from political crises. The nineteenth century was characterised by repeated attempts by the local executive supported by the British Government to find an acceptable formula for the government of the Virgin Islands.

[1] C.O. 315/6. Act No. 117.
[2] C.O. 239/58. Enc. in Colebrooke to Russell, 26 March, 1840. No. 16.
[3] Ibid.
[4] C.O. 239/59. Enc. in Colebrooke to Russell, 22 July, 1840. No. 44; C.O. 315/7. Act No. 148; C.O. 317/15-17. Blue Books, 1844-1846; P.P. 1845. Vol. XXXI, p. 206.
[5] C.O. 315/7. Acts No. 162 and 167.
[6] C.O. 239/58. Enc. in Colebrooke to Russell, 26 March, 1840. No. 16; C.O. 239/82. Enc. in Higginson to Grey, 19 Feb., 1847. No. 10.
[7] C.O. 239/86. Enc. in Higginson to Grey, 9 March, 1849. No. 18.
[8] P.P. 1857-58. Vol. XL, p. 131.
[9] Virgin Islands Ordinances 1866-1889. Ordinance No. 115. (No. 2 of 1866)
[10] C.O. 152/145. Enc. in Glover to Kimberley, 23 Sept., 1881. No. 264; Kimberley to Glover, 23 Sept., 1881. No. 185.
[11] C.O. 152/216. Enc. in Fleming to Chamberlain, 16 Feb., 1897. No. 101.
[12] C.O. 152/226. Scott to Villiers, 13 April, 1897. No. 22; Scott to Salisbury, 31 July, 1897. No. 39.
[13] C.O. 152/226. Scott to Salisbury, 27 Sept., 1897. No. 42.
[14] C.O. 314/4. Enc. in Hamilton to Labouchere, 8 Dec., 1856. No. 62.
[15] C.O. 315/1. Act No. 8; C.O. 316/1. Minutes of Assembly, 26 Nov., 1776.
[16] C.O. 315/6. Act No. 79.

[17] C.O. 315/6. Act No. 99
[18] C.O. 315/7. Act No. 128.
[19] C.O. 315/7. Act No. 143.
[20] C.O. 315/7. Act No. 144.
[21] C.O. 315/7. Act No. 145.
[22] C.O. 315/7. Act No. 148.
[23] C.O. 315/7. Act No. 174.
[24] C.O. 315/8. Act No. 194.
[25] C.O. 239/82. Enc. in Higginson to Grey, 21 July, 1847. No. 44.
[26] C.O. 315/7. Act No. 172.
[27] C.O. 239/93. Enc. in Mackintosh to Pakington, 11 Sept., 1852. No. 59.
[28] C.O. 239/85. Enc. in Higginson to Grey, 2 Nov., 1848. No. 55.
[29] C.O. 315/6. Act No. 101.
[30] C.O. 239/85. Enc. in Higginson to Grey, 2 Nov., 1848. No. 55.
[31] C.O. 315/6. Act No. 111.
[32] C.O. 239/95. Enc. in Mackintosh to Newcastle, 27 July, 1853. No. 63.
[33] C.O. 239/95. Enc. in Chads to Newcastle, 29 Aug., 1853.
[34] C.O. 239/95. Enc. in Mackintosh to Newcastle, 27 July, 1853. No. 63.
[35] C.O. 239/95. Enc. in Chads to Newcastle, 29 Aug., 1853.
[36] C.O. 239/95. Enc. in Mackintosh to Newcastle, 27 July, 1853. No. 63.
[37] Ibid.
[38] C.O. 239/95. Enc. in Mackintosh to Newcastle, 10 Aug., 1853. No. 69.
[39] C.O. 239/95. Enc. in Chads to Newcastle, 14 Aug., 1853.
[40] C.O. 239/95. Enc. in Mackintosh to Newcastle, 10 Aug., 1853. No. 69.
[41] Ibid.
[42] C.O. 239/95. Enc. in Mackintosh to Newcastle, 10 Aug., 1853. No. 69; Chads to Newcastle, 14 Aug., 1853.
[43] C.O. 239/96. Enc. in Mackintosh to Newcastle, 29 Sept., 1853. (Separate), and 21 Dec., 1853. No. 92.
[44] C.O. 315/9. Ordinance No. 26.
[45] C.O. 316/9. Minutes of Legislative Council, 16 Sept., 1857, and enc.
[46] C.O. 315/8. Ordinance No. 9.
[47] C.O. 316/9. Minutes of Legislative Council, 2 Dec., 1857, and enc.
[48] C.O. 314/6. Enc. in Hamilton to Bulwer Lytton, 9 Nov., 1858. No. 118.
[49] C.O. 315/8. Act No. 215.
[50] C.O. 315/9. Ordinance No. 52.
[51] C.O. 315/9. Ordinance No. 62.
[52] C.O. 315/9. Ordinance No. 110.
[53] Virgin Islands Ordinances: 1866-1889. Ordinance No. 1. of 1872.
[54] C.O. 152/109. Baynes to Kimberley, 25 Sept., 1872. No. 153.
[55] C.O. 152/109. Kimberley to Pine, 31 Dec., 1872. No. 197; C.O. 152/113. Baynes to Kimberley, 9 May, 1873. No. 128.
[56] Virgin Islands Ordinances: 1866-1899. Ordinance No. 5 of 1872.
[57] C.O. 152/170. Enc. in Gormanston to Holland, 3 Jan., 1888. No. 4; C.O. 152/169. MacGregor to the Under-Secretary of State, 15 Nov., 1887; C.O. 152/178. Haynes-Smith to Knutsford, 22 Oct., 1890. No. 282.
[58] C.O. 884/5. West Indian No. 80, pp. 94-95.

[59] C.O. 152/224. Enc. in Fleming to Chamberlain, 8 Nov., 1897. No. 650; C.O. 152/228. Fleming to Chamberlain, 5 Jan., 1898. No. 20; C.O. 152/247. Enc. in Melville to Chamberlain, 21 July, 1899. No. 439.

[60] C.O. 152/241. Chamberlain to Fleming, 6 Sept., 1898. No. 349.

[61] C.O. 152/247. Lucas to Morris, 2 Sept., 1899; C.O. 152/257. Enc. in Fleming to Chamberlain, 23 July, 1900. No. 482.

[62] P.P. 1871. Vol. XLVIII, p. 625.

[63] C.O. 152/108. Pine to Kimberley, 24 July 1872. No. 105.

[64] C.O. 152/109. Baynes to Kimberley, 12 Oct., 1872. No. 174.

[65] C.O. 152/112. Pine to Kimberley, 21 March, 1873. No. 56.

[66] C.O. 152/187. Haynes Smith to Ripon, 25 March, 1896. No. 111; C.O. 152/203. Fleming to Chamberlain, 16 March, 1896. No. 111.

[67] C.O. 152/122. Berkeley to Carnarvon, 25 March, 1875. No. 91.

[68] C.O. 152/155. Porter to Derby, 17 Dec., 1883. No. 335.

[69] C.O. 152/186. Haynes Smith to Ripon, 6 Feb., 1893, No. 30.

[70] C.O. 152/203. Fleming to Chamberlain, 16 March, 1896. No. 111.

[71] C.O. 314/16. Pine to Cardwell, 5 May, 1866. No. 79, and No. 82; and 18 June, 1866. No. 109; and Carnarvon to Pine, 24 July, 1866. No. 6.

[72] C.O. 314/19. Enc. in Hill to Buckingham, 23 June, 1868. No. 114; C.O. 314/20. Hill to Buckingham, 8 Oct., 1868. No. 176, and enc.; C.O. 314/20. Hill to Buckingham, 5 Dec., 1868. No. 227; C.O. 314/21. Granville to Pine, 6 Feb., 1869. No. 28.

[73] C.O. 314/19. Buckingham to Hill, 14 Nov., 1868. No. 262; C.O. 314/20. Hill to Buckingham, 5 Dec., 1868. No. 262; C.O. 314/21. Granville to Pine, 3 April, 1869. No. 54; and Hyde to Pine, 6 July, 1869. No. 38.

[74] C.O. 314/21. Hyde to Pine, 2 Aug., 1869. No. 154; Pine to Granville, 25 Aug., 1869. No. 156.

[75] C.O. 314/21. Hyde to Pine, 2 Aug., 1869. No. 155.

[76] C.O. 314/22. Pine to Kimberley, 9 Sept., 1870. No. 116; Kimberley to Pine, 8 Oct., 1870. No. 35.

[77] C.O. 314/24. Enc. in Pine to Kimberley, 24 Feb., 1872. No. 34; Kimberley to Pine, 23 April, 1872. No. 21; Pine to Kimberley, 24 Feb., 1872. No. 36; Kimberley to Pine, 27 March, 1872. No. 213.

[78] C.O. 314/24. Enc. in Pine to Kimberley, 24 Feb., 1872. No. 34.

[79] C.O. 152/245. Fleming to Chamberlain, 18 March, 1899. No. 180; C.O. 152/253. Fleming to Chamberlain, 3 Jan., 1900. No. 17.

[80] C.O. 152/265. Melville to Chamberlain, 29 Oct., 1901. No. 616; Chamberlain to Jackson, 26 Nov., 1901. No. 505.

[81] C.O. 315/5. Act No. 79. Clauses 45-49.

[82] C.O. 315/6. Act No. 117 (1839). Clause 143.

[83] C.O. 239/75. Enc. in Fitz Roy to Stanley, 5 Dec., 1844. No. 90.

[84] C.O. 407/6. Stanley to Fitz Roy, 10 April, 1844. No. 136.

[85] C.O. 407/8. Stanley to Fitz Roy, 27 Jan., 1845. No. 191.

[86] C.O. 315/7. Act No. 177.

[87] C.O. 315/7. Acts Nos. 160 and 176.

[88] C.O. 239/84. Enc. in Higginson to Grey, 11 April, 1848. No. 19.

[89] C.O. 239/83. Robertson and Olivier to Grey, May, 1847.

[90]   C.O. 239/87. Enc. in Higginson to Grey, 26 Nov., 1849. No. 70.
[91]   C.O. 314/15. Hill to Cardwell, 6 Sept., 1865. No. 125, and enc.
[92]   C.O. 314/12. Enc. in Hamilton to Newcastle, 26 July, 1862. No. 226.
[93]   C.O. 314/12. Enc. in Hamilton to Newcastle, 27 Oct., 1862. No. 273.
[94]   C.O. 314/12. Enc. in Hamilton to Newcastle, 26 Nov., 1862. No. 286.
[95]   C.O. 314/14. Enc. in Hill to Newcastle, 5 Feb., 1864. No. 12.
[96]   C.O. 314/14. Hill to Newcastle, 5 Feb., 1864. No. 12.
[97]   C.O. 314/19. Buckingham to Hill, 14 Nov., 1868. No. 262; C.O. 314/24. Kimberley to Pine, 23 April, 1872. No. 21; C.O. 152/165. Stanhope to Gormanston, 3 Nov., 1886. No. 60.
[98]   C.O. 152/253. Chamberlain to Fleming, 7 Feb., 1900. No. 63; C.O. 152/259. Chamberlain to Fleming, 24 Feb., 1900. No. 525.
[99]   C.O. 884/5. West Indian No. 80, p. 94.
[100]   C.O. 152/234. Fleming to Chamberlain, 3 Aug., 1898. No. 402.

Chapter 8

The Social Services

While slavery yet existed in the Virgin Islands, and when there was apparently the means, social services suffered to a greater extent from neglect by the legislature or rather, its dependence on other interested or responsible bodies. After emancipation, in view of the difficulties experienced by the legislature in meeting the ordinary expenses of administration, the institution of social services was governed by the poverty of the islands.

During slavery the welfare of the enslaved negroes was the responsibility of the slave owners who provided the slaves with their food, clothing, housing and medical facilities. In so far, also, as their permission was necessary before the missionaries could enter the estates, or before the slaves could go to church, they accepted the responsibility for and regulated their educational and religious instruction. In slavery, therefore, the welfare of the negroes was dependent upon the paternalism of their owners.

The maintenance of social services among the free population, namely, the whites and free-blacks and coloureds, was the responsibility of the colonial legislature. But as the Church undertook the task of education, its role was more or less confined to the maintenance of the poor, the aged and the infirm. Even so, by forbidding the manumission of slaves unless they were capable of maintaining themselves, it sought to reduce its obligation to a minimum. The retention by the Assembly of the power of selection of those whom it considered fit subjects for public charity was directed towards the same end. So too did the arrangement whereby the maintenance of the poor was financed from the receipt of special taxes the collection and disbursement of which rested with the vestry of the Established Church, and not made a direct charge upon the public chest.[1] It was not until 1832, by which time emancipation was almost a foregone conclusion, that the disbursement of poor relief was transferred to the Treasurer to be paid out of public funds.

As much as possible the legislature sought to avoid the financial responsibility of maintaining social services. As far as popular education was concerned, for instance, it gave as much moral support as possible to the missionaries, but restricted expenditure to the maintenance of a single clergyman of the Church of England. Courts were established but magistrates were unpaid Justices of the Peace, who probably received small inducements by being allowed to retain fines. The Virgin Islands were indeed served by a Chief Justice but he was paid by the British Government.

A jail was also maintained at the local expense but the extent of the costs involved is not known since a number of factors would have made for minimal expenditure. Slave owners were mainly responsible for the discipline and punishment of their own slaves, and even when slaves violated the colonial law the emphasis was on flogging rather than on imprisonment. In view of the solidarity among the whites and their decreasing numbers it is not likely that imprisonment was much resorted to with respect to them. Finally, the Virgin Islands have ever been marked by an absence of major crime requiring the sentence of imprisonment.

Available evidence does not mention the existence of any police force or a rural constabulary during slavery. Slave owners disciplined their slaves and as far as the free population was concerned order was maintained by the local militia if and when it existed. Provision for the organisation of militias, however, was only made during periods of war or following the outbreak of major social disturbances such as the slave revolt of 1831.

After emancipation all classes of persons requiring assistance were entitled to be maintained as destitute poor. But there were no changes in the procedure for the award of relief: no law was yet in existence for the appointment of guardians or for the mode of regulating the distribution of relief. The system adopted continued to be application by petition to the House of Assembly where a standing committee for that purpose enquired into the merits of each case. Where it was thought fit to grant such relief an order was made for a daily, weekly or monthly allowance, according to the circumstances of the case, to be paid by the Treasurer from the general revenue of the colony.[2] Provision was made also for disbursement of these expenses in the Money Act currently in force, and its importance was recognised when it was placed at the head of all expenditures.

While the relief of the poor was to some extent satisfied, no proper arrangement was made with regard to the aged and infirm who were liable to be ejected from the estates. An uncertain provision for the relief of such persons was made in the Tax Act of 1837,[3] and after August, 1838, the old and infirm on estates were placed on a poor list by a Committee of the Council and Assembly.[4] Contribution to beneficiaries, however, ranged between 1/– and 3/– only per week, government being compelled by low finances to rely on private contribution.[5] Planters were encouraged to provide relief by being allowed to use verified statements of their expenditure on their old and infirm tenants in payment of taxes.[6] The arrangement was unsatisfactory not only because it encouraged tax evasion, but also because it left the recipient at the will of the landlord. Besides, it afforded no relief to the town paupers for whom no such arrangement could be made. The immediate post-emancipation years brought several attempts to correct the deficiencies in the granting of relief without direct government financial involvement.

To make more appropriate provision for the aged and infirm, attention was directed towards the establishment of benefit or friendly societies. The essential principle on which such societies operated was that members make regular monetary contributions in return for financial assistance in time of illness or old age.[7] Following the example of the liberated Africans resident on their exclusive settlement at Kingstown in Tortola, among whom a friendly society was formed in 1840, efforts were made by the Rector to establish similar organisations under his supervision and direction on several estates in Tortola.[8] Despite his enthusiasm and energy, however, no success was achieved. The failure was partly due to indifference among labourers who did not fully understand the advantages of a system calling for a regular outlay of one shilling a month, but promising only a prospective and indefinite relief. It was also partly due to the jealousy of the Methodist missionaries who withheld their support since they interpreted the action of the Rector as an attempt to alienate the labourers' support from the Methodist Society.[9]

It was not until 1846 that renewed attempts were made to encourage the formation of friendly societies. By the mid-1840's when economic conditions had deteriorated the necessity to make better provision for the future was becoming increasingly apparent to the labouring population. The withdrawal of allowances formerly granted on estates for medical attendance provided the impetus, while the liberated Africans at Kingstown once more set the example.[10] The first attempt was made towards the end of 1846. That it drew its members principally from among adherents of the Methodist Society was tacit testimony that the missionaries had to some extent overcome their earlier opposition to the formation of such societies.

From the beginning the success of the society appeared extremely doubtful. It consisted of about one hundred members and to the stipendiary magistrate it did not seem that the society was enthusiastically supported by them.[11] Progress was slow. During the half year ending June 30, 1847, there was an addition of only twenty members,[12] and during the following six months only thirteen. In December, 1847, the stipendiary magistrate reported that the total funds collected amounted to about £40 sterling.[13] In the light of past experience this looked like success, but an association which contained a membership of only 145 out of a potential clientele of over 2,000 in two years, could not reasonably claim to be either progressive or prosperous in a real sense.[14] The subsequent history of the friendly society is vague, and by 1871 it had ceased to exist.[15]

So long as the financial position of employers made it possible for them to contribute towards the support of the indigent, the legislature of the Virgin Islands did not see the imperative need for active participation. It is true that in May, 1839, the legislature adopted resolutions directing that a Committee of Public Buildings should examine the out-offices attached to the Court House, and report on the feasibility of converting them into an infirmary of two wards and apartments for a nurse.[16] However, no immediate action was taken.

The first measure for poor relief was adopted in August, 1844 when provision was made for the rental of premises (until a suitable public building could be provided) to be used as a workhouse and infirmary. It was to be staffed by a master, a matron and a surgeon, with the Rector responsible for religious instruction. The immediate management of the establishment including the selection of inmates was vested in a Board of Guardians. In the composition of this Board the colony was deemed one Union and divided into four Districts, one or more guardians to be appointed from each. Any pauper who refused to be lodged in the workhouse was not entitled to any support though the guardians could order temporary relief to out-door poor with contagious diseases or to children who because of accident could not conveniently be removed to the workhouse.[17]

In keeping with the provisions of the Act, a combined poor-house and infirmary was opened for the reception of the indigent and infirm on December 21, 1844. In a few years the original premises were too small to accommodate the steadily increasing number of residents and in 1846 a larger building was purchased with the sum of £300. 8s. 5¼d remaining unawarded from the slave compensation fund.[18]

The original expenditure on poor relief was reduced in 1854 by dismissing the matron and reducing the salary of the master. In order to facilitate tighter control over funds expended on poor relief the Board of Guardians was reconstituted — the representatives of the four Districts of the 'Union' comprising the Board of Guardians were replaced by five Presidential nominees and these were empowered to appoint resident guardians for each outlying island to report on the relief requirements of each. Provision was also made for the apprenticing of children of paupers to prevent them from becoming dependent upon public charity.[19]

Widespread changes were effected in the administration of poor relief in 1856 the most important being the substitution of a system of outdoor for the system of indoor relief. The poor house was abolished and only an infirmary was retained for the medical and surgical treatment of destitute persons. Entry was dependent upon the production of certificates from a reputable authority and the amount of relief allowed to each pauper on any occasion was limited to 1/6 a week and was to cease if the circumstances of the recipient permitted it. The stipulation that allowances were to be paid weekly pre-supposed that they could be varied or stopped at short notice, while a burial allowance of 16/− was dependent upon the inability of friends and relatives to bear the cost. A slight economy was achieved in the establishment by the appointment of a matron at a yearly salary of £15, instead of a master at £26. Despite the various authorisations of disbursement, a ceiling of £26 a quarter was imposed on expenditure both on outdoor paupers and on persons received in the infirmary.[20]

The financial measures imposed in 1856 were too stringent, and in 1859 the amount that could be drawn upon the Treasury for poor relief was raised to £156 a year.[21] However, in 1864, the amount was reduced to £130 a year while the Board was empowered to expel inmates from the infirmary, who no longer needed medical assistance.

To ensure the most efficient functioning of the establishment in order to reduce costs, regular inspection by the President, the Board of Guardians and members of the Legislative Council was authorised. The surgeon was required to attend inmates twice weekly, and submit monthly reports.[22]

The greater part of outdoor relief granted after 1864 was given in small allowances of 9d, 1/– or 1/6 a week.[23] Around ten percent of the gross revenue was expended, but ten percent of a small amount of total revenue was inadequate. For the purposes of economy, tight control was exercised over the selection of candidates. No assistance was granted unless the applicant was quite incapacitated for work, and without relatives who could give assistance. In 1871 there were 56 outdoor paupers;[24] by 1881 these had been reduced to 28. Even the relief given at a weekly cost of £1. 0s. 3d., or £52. 13s. a year exceeded substantially the £40 placed on the estimates of expenditure for 1881. President Churchill held the opinion that at least £100 a year more was required to relieve the destitution in the Virgin Islands, 'supposing assistance to be given only to those who are absolutely helpless and without resource and at the rate of only 6d. per week or £1. 6s. a year for the maintenance of each pauper.'[25]

The support of paupers in the infirmary was equally deficient; allowances averaged only 2½d. a day, food was scant, and equipment and utensils inadequate. Apart from the matron who was too old and inefficient, there was no other nurse or attendant attached to the institution, and the inmates were obliged to look after each other's everyday wants.[26] Most of the people suffered from extreme old age, and from such incurable diseases as chronic rheumatism, chronic ulcers, asthma and syphilis.[27] Wherever possible treatment was given, and though complete cures were never possible some were discharged.

Reform in the infirmary was not in the direction of greater financial contribution to the institution. Rather the paupers suffered further in the drive to reduce the expenses of administration. The number of inmates was reduced in 1897, and they were put on the same status as outdoor paupers though they were allowed to reside in the infirmary.[28] Final action was taken in 1907 when the infirmary was closed and the three remaining inmates were provided with cheap housing when no one could be found to board them.[29]

The same preoccupation with reducing cost and limiting the scope of operations seen in the case of poor relief was shown towards the adoption of public health measures. Basically, the economic backwardness of the colony dictated severe parsimony in methods to deal with the health problems of the community.

In an attempt to suppress an outbreak of smallpox in 1843, vaccinators-general were appointed to vaccinate the entire population. For each successful vaccination they were paid 4/– while patients were treated in a special smallpox hospital attended by a doctor and nurse.[30] Once the emergency was past, however, the legislature sought to reduce the expenditure involved for vaccinations.[31]

Together with the geographical separateness of the islands, the fact that each island consisted of pocket communities separated by hillspurs and inadequately connected with passable roads, aggravated the problems of planning. Unless supervisory officers were to be appointed in each community, it meant that there would be inefficiency or non-extension of services. In most instances the latter prevailed, sometimes with disastrous consequences as seen with regard to the health regulations adopted in 1851. A Board of Health of seven members constituted that year[32] formulated a number of rules and regulations designed to prevent the outbreak of diseases and to avert their spread. Executive authority was vested in a paid health officer. The most elaborate precautions were taken for the disposal of refuse in Road Town for which a single street warden was appointed. Regulations were also prepared for the reporting of any outbreak of disease in the town to the Board of Health or to the health officer. For the reception of patients, provision was made for a hospital where also passengers coming from infected ports could be examined.[33]

The regulations introduced in 1851 pertained principally to Road Town, and seen after the event, they betrayed a remarkable lack of foresight. The only regulation governing the other parts of Tortola and the remainder of the Virgin Islands was one which authorised the application of the rules to those parts 'as occasion may require.' It can only be interpreted to mean that the regulations would be extended to the various parts of the Virgin Islands, after discovery had been made of a contagious disease. In view of the frequency and regularity of communication between the Virgin Islands and the Danish Islands where epidemic diseases were known to prevail, it is surprising that greater precautions were not taken to examine all those who communicated between the two groups of islands. It is possible that the legislature was guided by considerations of the heavy cost such measures would have entailed at a time when the colony was unable to meet the current expenditure of government, and by the difficulty of enforcing the regulations given the shortage of supervisory personnel. The failure to extend to the entire Virgin Islands such measures as were introduced in Road Town resulted in a disastrous outbreak of cholera in December, 1853.

Cholera broke out at several points in the Virgin Islands after it had made its appearance in St. Thomas.[34] The first cases occurred in Jost Van Dyke and West End of Tortola, that is, at points not directly covered by the 1851 regulations. Had proper facilities for dealing with the disease existed in the out-ports it is possible that it might have been limited in its scope. From the West End the disease spread to Road Town and from there to other rural areas and to the neighbouring islands, with the exception of Beef Island and Salt Island.

The Board of Health sought to blame 'the ignorance and supineness of the people' for the cause of the disaster. The fact was that the medical aid available even in Road Town was small, and the Board failed through lack of facilities to implement appropriate quarantine regulations. Its activities were confined principally to the burial of the dead. Though the disease was followed by epidemic diarrhoea which itself persisted for several months, the majority of deaths occurred within a few days of the initial outbreak. Over eighty percent of those attacked died, including a large number of able-bodied men, giving further evidence of the inadequacy of the measures to safeguard the public health. The number of deaths in relation to the estimated total population of the several islands is shown in Table 10.

Table 10

Number of Deaths from Cholera, December, 1853

Island	Estimated Population	Number of Deaths
Tortola	4337	574
Thatch		34
Jost Van Dyke	1235	196
Peter	153	22
Virgin Gorda	825	44
Anegada	369	72
TOTAL	6,919	942 or 13.9%

The outbreak of smallpox in Tortola and Jost Van Dyke in 1861 resulting in thirty-three deaths,[35] once more focussed attention on the need to make better provision for the vaccination of the inhabitants. In 1862 a system of compulsory vaccination by a panel of vaccinators appointed to specific districts was introduced. For his services, each vaccinator was entitled to 1/– for each person successfully vaccinated and, in addition, was allowed 16/8 for each day he was out of Tortola for the purpose of vaccination.[36]

To prevent sickness another expedient was resorted to after 1862, namely, the adoption of quarantine regulations to prevent the introduction of infectious diseases from abroad. In 1866, 1867 and 1868 there were outbreaks of epidemic smallpox, cholera and yellow fever in St. Thomas.[37] To prevent their spread to the Virgin Islands, a strict quarantine was enforced against St. Thomas, and later extended to St. John and other adjacent islands when these places were used as ports of entry.[38] The policy of quarantine regulations undoubtedly facilitated changes in the policy of vaccinations in 1888. The number of public vaccinators was reduced and the Government Medical Officer was declared the ex-officio public vaccinator. Henceforth, vaccinations were to be given twice a year in Road Town and in the other localities of Tortola 'from time to time . . . as may be deemed expedient', and visits were to be made to Virgin Gorda, Anegada and Jost Van Dyke at least once a year. Fees for successful vaccinations were abolished and the only expense incurred was a daily allowance to the doctor of 5/– when on trips to Virgin Gorda and Jost Van Dyke, and 10/– to Anegada.[39]

Because of heavy dependence upon expatriates for the operation of essential services, the ability of the Virgin Islands to attract qualified people or to retain their services was dependent upon their ability to pay. The situation can be adequately illustrated with reference to the medical services. The Virgin Islands had never been blessed with an abundance of doctors even during the more prosperous days of slavery, and by 1850 there was only one. There was always a heavy demand upon his services and in cases of emergencies such as the smallpox epidemic of 1861 the need for more medical assistance was severely felt. The impoverished state of the Treasury posed insuperable obstacles in the way of getting doctors. By 1872 the salary attached to the medical appointment was £100 a year, though the incumbent was entitled to a further £25 a year as coroner, and derived a small sum of about £100 a year from private practice. However, these returns were considered inadequate to meet the high cost of living in the Virgin Islands.

Small remuneration added to the difficulty of obtaining doctors after 1871 when Doctor Ogilvie accepted a more remunerative appointment in Jamaica.[40] Early in 1873, Dr. Herbert Norton who had practised in Dominica for over a year was appointed by Governor Pine as a public medical officer and coroner of the Virgin Islands.[41] However, he stayed there for only a few months before resigning for a more lucrative appointment in St. Lucia.[42] For the next four years the functions of a doctor were performed by a relatively inexperienced individual who had neither diploma nor licence to practice medicine or surgery.[43] He was tolerated because of the lack of any alternative, and in case of emergency, special arrangements had to be made. For example, on the outbreak of a fever in Road Town in January, 1878, Governor Berkeley despatched Dr. Chipman of Dominica to offer temporary relief on condition that his travelling expenses and an allowance of £35 a month would be met by the legislature of the Virgin Islands.[44]

The basic poverty of the Virgin Islands remained after 1878, but the colony was continuously served by a doctor. It was made possible only by reducing the contribution of the Presidency to the federal government which enabled the legislature to offer a medical officer's salary of £200 a year. Later when there was need for further economy, by combining the office of President with that of doctor at a salary of £300 a year, the legislature sought to ensure the availability of a doctor in the islands. However, it was inconvenient for the doctor-commissioner to leave his administrative work as Commissioner to attend to patients in the outlying islands. Consequently, an assistant medical officer was appointed in 1901.

The avoidance of public expenditure and the attempt by the legislature to shift responsibility for the maintenance of social services from itself to another body was also evident with regard to education which was left largely to the clergyman of the Established Church assisted by a lay-reader, and to the Methodist missionaries. Initially the lead in education was taken by the Anglicans over the Methodists, although the latter continued to influence a greater following in religion. Between 1838 and 1842 denominational schools and attendance expanded rapidly: the Anglicans increased from three schools with 243 pupils to ten with 659, while the Methodists increased from one with 80 to three with 199.[45] In addition to these regular day schools, the denominations operated a number of Sunday schools for religious education.

While the Anglicans and Methodists were introducing education at a lower level, an only attempt was made by the legislature to foster higher education. Authority was given for the establishment in Road Town of a school to be called 'The Virgin Islands Endowed School for Boys.' The President was empowered to appoint a master nominated by the Bishop of the diocese, at a salary of £250 a year. Provision was also made for the constitution of a Board of Visitors with representatives from the legislature, the Bench, and the religious denominations, for its management. Emphasis was placed on a classical education though other subjects were not to be neglected if facilities offered.[46] The most important provisions relating to the school were those which pertained to the financing of the institution. Instead of being provided with regular legislative grants, the school was dependent for support upon student fees, ranging from £10 to £20 currency a year to be paid quarterly in advance. The failure or success of the experiment was dependent upon the ability or willingness of parents to meet the financial exactions. Under the tuition of T. P. Todman with assistance from Rev. Alexander Bott, the endowed grammar school was opened in September, 1844, with a total enrolment of seventeen students.[47] However, the need to make payment easier for those who were already in, and to encourage others to enter the school, soon became evident. By February, 1845, several persons were beginning to withdraw their sons from the school and others were contemplating similar action. To prevent this, it was made possible to pay fees not only in coin but also in bills of exchange.[48] Even so, the school was a luxury the islanders could not afford; by October, 1846, there were no pupils and the school was closed.[49]

The failure of the legislature to secure the establishment of an institution for higher education was followed by a quasi-official attempt to introduce a system of industrial education the need of which for the labouring classes was felt soon after emancipation.[50] On the initiative of President Drummond Hay an industrial school was established in 1847,[51] and located in Anegada probably for no other reason than that the island lacked any other school. Its secular nature was emphasised: it was intended to be open to the community in general without reference to religious persuasion; and although the Church of England catechism was taught, it was only to children whose parents desired it.[52] The school seems to have been well attended at first and to have made appreciable progress. The daily attendance averaged sixty-five, and industrial training was offered by the occasional employment of the pupils in cultivating a garden, and more regular teaching in plaiting straw hats, and in making fishing nets.[53] These were all local occupations and the fact that children were taught and did at home the very things in which they were instructed in school made the latter superfluous, and accounts for the lack of lasting enthusiasm among parents.

The religious denominations experienced a shortage of funds for education in the 1840's, but financial support from the local legislature was almost non-existent. The British Government had contributed £200 a year which was administered by the Bishop who naturally gave preference to the Anglican Church,[54] but in 1841 it introduced a phased withdrawal of its grant which ceased completely in 1845.[55] The capacity of the Methodists and Anglicans to maintain their educational services was dependent on the extent of the support they received from their adherents and from the parent and other societies in Britain.

The attempts made to persuade the people to pay fees met with varying success. The Methodists, because of their greater following and because they took more care in educating the people on the necessity of paying fees, were more successful than the Anglicans. For instance, parents participated in a scheme proposed by W. T. Weymouth, the Superintendent of the Wesleyan Mission in the Virgin Islands, in March, 1847. According to Weymouth's proposals, the Methodist Society would provide half of the expenses of operating a day school in every chapel if the parents agreed to pay the other half. Parents' contribution would be by means of fees, totalling 9d. a week for each child learning reading, writing and cyphering; parents who sent more than two children to school would pay for only two. The scheme resulted in a local contribution of from one-third to four-fifths of the cost of supporting the schools which permitted the expansion of the Methodist school system during the next two years.[56]

So long as payment was not hard, the Methodists could expect general support. Towards the end of 1848, no doubt emboldened by their recent success, the missionaries endeavoured to enforce a semi-annual payment at the rate of between 4/2 and 8/4 a year for each child. It resulted in an immediate decrease in school attendance.[57] The protest was not against the amount required which would not have been more than the original levy, but against the enforcement of payment in advance. In view of the general poverty and inability of the people to pay, a crisis developed in 1853, when the grant offered by the Methodist Society in London and averaging over £168 a year was withdrawn.[58] The only possible way of meeting the deficit was by an additional levy on the people.

The riots of August, 1853, put an effective stop to all teaching activities in the Virgin Islands, and it was not until May, 1855 that the first schools were reopened.[59] Only gradually were others resumed, and considerable caution was exercised in establishing new ones. The initial enthusiasm exhibited by parents at the re-opening of the schools, however, soon petered out; attendance became very irregular because of the continuing need to pay fees.[60] The regularity and perseverance exhibited by the Methodist missionaries in the promulgation of their religious and educational views enabled them to overcome the atten-dance barrier to some extent. It accounted, too, for their greater success compared with the Anglicans who, except for a school in Virgin Gorda, concentrated their activities in Road Town and its immediate environs. The activities of the Methodists were more diffused and systematic encouraged by the steady support of the rural population.

In common with the Anglicans, the Methodists suffered from a lack of sufficient finance to undertake their educational activities. The need became more acute as the work expanded, and was largely responsible for the slow progress made. Assistance in the form of a regular outlay was necessary, but it was not until January, 1859, that the legislature granted £50 a year to be apportioned, on the basis of the recommen-dations of three Commissioners of Education, among existent and prospective schools irrespective of their religious persuasion. The grant was made only after several appeals by the President, and even when approved was not scheduled to be brought into effect until January 1, 1860.[61]

The education grant was increased in February, 1863 to £80 a year to be distributed in quarterly payments to existing schools 'in proportion to the actual attendance at such schools,' and it was to be administered by a Board of five Commissioners.[62] The grant was increased but the number of children who could benefit from it was restricted by the age limit of five to twelve years imposed on those attending school. In addition, no school with an average attendance of less than twenty was entitled to a grant, and new schools could not be established without the prior approval of the Commissioners. Examinations by the Board were instituted to ensure that the money was beneficially used.[63]

The Virgin Islands suffered considerably from the lack of qualified administrative and professional skills which to a large extent had to be imported since the education system was not geared to produce people of high educational attainments. As outlined in 1866, education was confined to the most elementary type and the school-leaving age was limited to twelve years in an attempt to suppress deliberately the standard of education in schools.[64] Except when Boards were formed education policy was administered by the clergymen of the Church of England and by the Methodist missionaries. Their function, however, was more or less supervisory and even this suffered since they were not themselves trained teachers. Their role in education also explains the continued religious flavour given to the varied curricula followed in the schools. It was only with the formation of the Leeward Islands Federation that some attempt was made to introduce a secular and unified curriculum throughout the Virgin Islands.

With federation also, the general administration of education in the colony was entrusted to an Inspector General of Schools in the Leeward Islands. Even so his visits to the Virgin Islands were rare and confined chiefly to the examination of schools to determine their grades and suitability for grants-in-aid. As such, therefore, the direct responsibility for superintending the operation of schools rested with the Anglican and Methodist ministers. In addition to their lack of professional competence they were hampered by inadequate travelling facilities among the islands. Supervision was infrequent, and hurried, even when conducted. The result was that teachers were left more or less with a free rein in the management of their schools. Consequently, school records were improperly kept, discipline was deplorable, and the standard of instruction was low.

On the basis of the results of the annual examination held by the Inspector General, schools were placed in three classes: first, second and third. The deficiencies of education in the Virgin Islands thereby became glaringly obvious. Of nine schools examined in 1877 only the Methodist school in Road Town secured a grade in the third and lowest class due to better teaching and supervision.[65] In the following year, of the eleven schools examined only one Methodist and one Anglican school in Road Town obtained places in the third class. On both occasions, the others failed to achieve any grade. None of the schools which failed was entitled to grant-in-aid but they were considered sufficiently important to the districts in which they were located to merit the award of exceptional aid.[66]

The continuation of exceptional aid merely perpetuated some of the evils of the education system without producing any beneficial results. So long as teachers received the customary allowances, little initiative and energy were displayed in teaching. To correct this attitude the payment of exceptional aid was discontinued in 1881.[67] Marked improvement in teaching resulted: of the nine schools examined in 1884, four qualified for aid, though they were all of the third class;[68] and similar results were reported for the following three years. Of these schools, one was in Anegada, another in Virgin Gorda, and the remaining two were the Methodist and Anglican schools in Road Town.[69]

Withdrawal of exceptional aid partly corrected some of the inefficiencies of some of the schools, but the education system as a whole remained unchanged. The operation of the legislative grant, itself never paid in its entirety, continued to be supervised by the denominational ministers. The results remained unsatisfactory: teachers were inadequately remunerated and were scarcely of the standard required to produce good results; schools were ill-provided with books and aids; and the performance of the pupils showed only limited progress.

Some measure of tighter control was obviously necessary to lift standards. To Commissioner Cookman whose energy and enthusiasm in administration was marked by impatience with inept institutions, the remedy for the educational ills of the Presidency lay in the complete withdrawal of grants from the denominational schools and their use for the construction of a government school. Governor Fleming was 'not in favour, as a rule, of withdrawing state aid from denominational schools in countries where the clergy of different denominations take an interest in the cause of education.' Under the special circumstances of the Virgin Islands, however, he was constrained to agree.[70] The Secretary of State for the Colonies, Joseph Chamberlain, had other suggestions. He was probably not convinced that the measures would produce a more efficient school system, and he was unwilling to introduce any controversial element in his plan for agricultural reform in the Virgin Islands. Consequently, he counselled a more moderate course and advised that ministers should be required to institute the necessary changes within a reasonable time. If they failed, the grant might then be withdrawn.[71] Nothing was done to implement this suggestion, and the defects of the education system continued into the twentieth century.

Events after 1838 made it necessary for the legislature to make some provision to maintain education and poor relief, and to cater for public health. In other respects, where its responsibility could not be transferred to a subordinate colonial body, it was compelled to take direct action. Even so, it followed a policy of conscious withdrawal and sought wherever and whenever possible to transfer its obligations elsewhere. Its attitude was most clearly seen in the related subjects of police, the administration of justice, the maintenance of a jail, the care of prisoners and, under the peculiar circumstances of the Virgin Islands, of the mentally incapacitated.

The first attempt to establish a police force in the Virgin Islands was in March, 1837, when the legislature passed an Act for the formation of a police force to consist of a superintendent or chief officer of police, four sergeants and eight constables, at a total annual cost of £660.[72] It does not appear that this Act was brought into operation; Blue Books, showing expenditures, do not suggest that any financial provision was made. It was not until 1859 in view of the British Government's refusal to guarantee police protection by British troops that a second attempt was made.[73]

On the basis of legislative enactment in 1859, an Inspector of Police and two policemen were appointed, and to them was added in 1860, another policeman.[74] Financial provision showed wide variations from year to year and this inevitably affected the composition of the force. In keeping with the policy of limiting expenditure to suit revenue, the office of Inspector of Police was abolished in 1869. By 1887 there were only two policemen in the islands, and one was seventy-one years of age while the other was sixty.[75] Their activities were confined to Road Town, and the claim that they performed 'good service' was obviously exaggerated and designed to evade further financial commitments. In the rural parts of Tortola and in the outlying islands, order was maintained by a number of rural constables. They received no regular salary but were paid only for the occasional services performed. In times of emergency, they were assisted by special constables.

The absence of an organised and disciplined law enforcing medium would suggest a favourable opportunity for the perpetration of much crime, and alternatively, the lack of detection of crimes committed. In the small communities of the Virgin Islands, detection would not have been difficult especially in view of the strong social stigma attached to crime. With regard to detection and rejection, only smuggling was the exception, since it had become so institutionalised as to be regarded as a way of life. It ceased to be regarded as an offence by the populace at large, notwithstanding official attitudes to the contrary.

Apart from smuggling, the islands had only a small number of criminal offenders probably due to the common experiences of the people under adverse circumstances, and their intimate relationship fostered by living in separate communities and by intermarriage. Most of the cases were for trivial offences — common assault, and the use of indecent, threatening and abusive language arising out of personal quarrels, questions of trespass, and the unlawful impounding of stock — and many were by persistent offenders.[76]

The judicial system comprising unpaid Justices of the Peace, and a Chief Justice and stipendiary magistrate paid by the British Government did not survive beyond 1872. The Justices of the Peace were the first to be affected, their extinction stemming from the cliqueishness which existed in the colony. Justices were selected from among known supporters of the President, and the decrease in the number of these men resulted in the eventual dissolution of that body. The offices of Chief Justice and stipendiary magistrate were abolished between 1866 and 1872, and magisterial functions were concentrated in the President who was mainly responsible for cases of summary jurisdiction. With the creation of the Leeward Islands Federation, a circuit court was established in the Virgin Islands, for the adjudication by judges of the Supreme Court of the Leeward Islands, of civil and criminal cases transferred from the lower courts.

As before the emancipation of slaves the administration of justice was inefficient after it. When he visited the Virgin Islands around 1823, Trelawney Wentworth observed that 'even *Justice,* long since reputed *blind,* had here all her other faculties impaired.'[77] The continuing maladministration of justice resulted in 1844 in public resolutions condemning the 'injustice and oppression and . . . disgraceful transactions in the public courts.'[78] The irregularities were due not only to the lack of training in law of the individuals performing the duties of judge and magistrates, but also because of the direct or indirect interest which they had in law suits brought before the courts. The charge levied against the acting President, the Chief Justice and several justices with partiality in the administration of justice in 1844, exemplified the dichotomy in society which existed between the 'rulers' and the 'ruled' and resulted, for instance, in the attempt to deprive the colonists of the use of the jury system in civil cases in 1867.[79] Had it been successful, it would have deprived the people of a major bulwark against oppression by interested judges and justices.

The attempt to deprive the colony of the benefits of jury was part of the process whereby it was sought to deprive it of the benefits to be obtained from the presence of a Supreme Court. Complaints by federal judges of the few and unimportant cases to be tried there, and the inconveniences and expenses caused in travelling to and from the colony, and in living there, resulted in frequent requests to abolish the Court, and to transfer its business to the St. Kitts circuit.[80] Despite the decrease in the number of cases tried in the Virgin Islands, the pressure was resisted as long as possible on the grounds that the retention of the Court was necessary to inspire confidence in the administration of justice and because of its good moral effect. Besides, the greater inconvenience to litigants and witnesses, especially when administrative officers were involved, and the greater cost to the Virgin Islands, did not deem such action advisable.[81] However, the reactionaries were eventually successful; the circuit court which had guaranteed fairer adjudication of disputes was abolished in 1902, and justice was executed by an untrained Commissioner-magistrate.[82]

There were considerable differences between the numbers of offences committed, convictions in the law courts and committals to prison. For example, out of 166 offenders tried in 1844, there were 83 convictions and of these only 24 were committed to jail.[83] The number of persons condemned to imprisonment was never large, and it decreased as the century progressed; by 1887 the number of prisoners confined in the jail averaged only about one daily.[84] Even so, living conditions were far below required standards. The jail though kept clean by regular scouring and white-washing by the prisoners themselves was more often than not in a state of disrepair. It was unhealthy on account of improper roofing which caused dampness especially in rainy weather, inadequate ventilation and lack of sanitary facilities.[85] Even when a new jail was constructed after the destructions of the hurricane of 1867, conditions remained unchanged. Rather, it was reported of the new jail that 'the architect must have been reading a description of the black-hole in Calcutta, and derived his plan from his reading.'[86] Reconstruction was postponed pending the establishment of a central federal prison, in one of the Leeward Islands. By the end of the century the jail was in an almost complete state of dilapidation, and attempts to secure imperial aid of about £300 by way of a grant or loan to effect necessary repairs failed.[87]

Despite the small number of prisoners, there were insufficient buildings for the purposes of a prison, and arrangements were defective with respect to the classification, treatment and discipline of prisoners. For example, irrespective of the nature of their crime, several inmates were usually lodged in the same cell; except when the cells used for solitary confinement were available, sick prisoners had to remain in the cells they occupied with other prisoners; and the smallness of the jail yard forced male and female prisoners to be exercised within sight of each other. [88]

The prison was used solely as a place of confinement, and no attempt was made to reform prisoners, since officers were untrained for that purpose. The financial contribution towards the provision of food was insufficient, despite the fact that, like poor relief, the provision for prisoners was placed at the head of appropriations in the colonial budget. Distress was particularly acute before 1854 when food was supplied by contractors.[89] Debtors were required to provide their own food, and only if they were unable were they supplied the usual prison allowance.[90] The attention accorded prisoners also deteriorated when as a result of the economy measures adopted in 1872, the jail establishment was reduced with the abolition of the separate office of jailer whose duties were transferred to the Provost Marshal. The only regular attendants left were the turnkey and matron, while the colonial surgeon attended sick prisoners as circumstances warranted.[91]

Closely associated with the care of prisoners was that of lunatics or the mentally incapacitated the known cases of whom were not many, never exceeding four in any one year after 1838. From the fact that towards the end of the century numbers tended to increase, and that sometimes lunatics were forced to take the initiative in order to get treatment, it is possible that cases existed which were treated privately and were unknown to the authorities.[92] But even the known cases were not treated in a separate asylum; rather, lunatics were housed in the jail. Since the jail was ordinarily too small for its legitimate purposes, the greatest inconvenience arose both to prisoners and to lunatics when the latter were added. The suffering of the lunatics was increased since they were looked after by the ordinary jail attendants who were untrained in handling such cases. Medical treatment was provided occasionally by the surgeon to the jail.[93] Only in special cases requiring closer attention were lunatics removed to the infirmary. Even there the lack of adequate facilities limited treatment.

Following the establishment of the federation of the Leeward

Islands, a change was instituted in the manner of treating lunatics. While mild cases of mental disorder continued to be treated locally in the common jail, the more acute cases were transferred to a central asylum in Antigua.[94] It was not a federal service, and the expenses incurred were charged directly upon the local treasury rather than being included in the federal contribution. But like the federal contribution, the expenses were never fully met, and part of the parliamentary grant given in 1898 was used to liquidate this debt.[95]

The attempt by the legislature before 1902 to provide for the social well-being of the Virgin Islands was not successful. Despite some progress made, the standard of education was low, and its administration confused: schools were financed by the local legislature, examined by the federal Inspector, and managed by local ministers. The formulation of an educational policy, much less its consistent and vigorous execution was difficult. Public health measures were limited to vaccinations, the declaration of quarantines, and the sanitation of Road Town. With reference to a pure water supply, for example, reliance was placed on rainfall and probably on shallow wells; no reservoirs were constructed or deep wells sunk. The administration of justice bore most heavily upon litigants forced between the inefficiency of the local magistrate and the high costs of trials in St. Kitts. The infirmary was nearing extinction, and the few prisoners and lunatics suffered from inattention and poor food, while the police force was reduced further to only one.

The scale of priorities when applied to social services generally was extremely limited, and the principle of placing expenses for the support of the poor, the aged and infirm, and of prisoners, at the head of annual budgetary expenditures, did not apply to education, though this was of equal if not of more importance.

Political pressures exercised little, if any, influence on the adoption of measures for social services. Even until 1867 while the principle of representation existed, measures were not introduced because of their appeal to the electorate. Even when Crown Colony Government was introduced, no greater initiative was shown by the legislators. Indeed, there was a conspicuous absence of marked deference paid to social services; the general attitude indicates no attempt to become further and more deeply involved. This is not surprising since the prevailing doctrine was *laissez faire* by which the individual was held responsible for his own general welfare with minimum government involvement.

A fundamental weakness of the system of social services was that in the Virgin Islands after emancipation there did not exist people with the requisite knowledge and ability to plan, introduce and execute detailed and comprehensive schemes for more general development. To a large extent the defects were inherent in a political system where the executive power was held until 1872 by a President who was subject to frequent change, and thereafter by an external authority in the Governor of the Leeward Islands. A continuous policy was impossible in the absence of a permanent civil executive authority.

The deficiencies of the system, too, have to be examined against the background difficulties against which the legislature had to operate. The basic problem was one of finances, that is, the institution of social services was dictated by considerations of economy. Even when, as in education, specific sums were allocated, extreme difficulty was experienced in meeting the obligation to pay.

The entire initiative and burden for the introduction of the measures rested with the legislature in Road Town which also had to perform functions of co-ordination in the absence of other responsible bodies. Its problems were enhanced by the evident distrust which the people felt for the legislature and by the isolationism which existed and which was bred of life on separate islands in secluded communities. Life in pocket communities unrelieved by regular communication due to improper roads, and to the absence of organised boat services, could not lead to easy co-operation or concerted action. It partly explains the inability of the legislature to introduce uniform measures.

The Christian denominations gave valuable assistance in the establishment and management of schools, but their record was somewhat tarnished by the jealousies which existed between Anglicans and Methodists. As shown in their attitudes towards friendly societies, their suspicions of each other prevented concerted action. Neither were the activities of the two co-ordinated. In the absence of such organisations as community welfare groups, the bulk of the social activities was left to them, but they did not at all times live up to the trust reposed in them. The failure of the legislature to grant the clergyman his stipend regularly resulted in his withdrawal to St. Thomas in 1853. In the same year the Methodists promoted a public meeting which contributed to the riots of August. In both cases, there was a prolonged suspension of their educational activities.

Social services showed heavy dependence on the initiative of the legislature, and were not supported by even a semi-educated or middle class able to direct or execute them. If the educational system was designed to prevent the one, the economy of the islands did not produce the other. Neither was there any voluntary assistance forthcoming. In health matters, for instance, there was little that the health officer and street warden could accomplish without the active support of the entire population. The legislature lacked the ability to win that support due to its tendency to place reliance only on a small clique of individuals, a factor which played a significant part in its disintegration after emancipation.

[1] C.O. 239/10. Maxwell to Horton, 17 Feb., 1824, and enc.
[2] P.P. 1839. Vol. XXXVII, p. 25.
[3] C.O. 315/6. Act No.99; P.P. 1839. Vol. XXXVII, p.1.
[4] P.P. 1839. Vol. XXXVII, p.331.
[5] Ibid.
[6] P.P. 1839. Vol. XXXVII, p.347.
[7] C.O. 239/55. S.M.'s Report for June, 1839.
[8] C.O. 239/60. S.M.'s Report for July, Aug., and Sept., 1840.
[9] C.O. 239/74. Fitz Roy to Stanley, 23 April, 1844. No.66, and enc.
[10] C.O. 239/75. S.M.'s Report for half year ended 30 June, 1844; P.P. 1845. Vol. XXXI, p.577.
[11] C.O. 243/10. S.M.'s Report for half year ended 31 Dec., 1846.
[12] C.O. 243/10. S.M.'s Report for half year ended 30 June, 1847.
[13] C.O. 243/10. S.M.'s Report for half year ended 31 Dec., 1847.
[14] C.O. 243/10. S.M.'s Report for half year ended 30 June, 1848.
[15] C.O. 314/23. Moir to Baynes, 11 Dec., 1871. No.231.
[16] C.O. 316/4. Minutes of Assembly, 4 May, 18 May, and 6 July, 1839.
[17] C.O. 315/7. Act No.138.
[18] C.O. 315/7. Act No.156.
[19] C.O. 315/8. Act No.216.
[20] C.O. 315/8. Ordinance No.17.
[21] C.O. 315/9. Ordinance No.54.
[22] C.O. 315/9. Ordinance No.107. (No.3 of 1864); P.P. 1866. Vol. XLIX, p.375.
[23] P.P. 1866. Vol. XLIX, p.375.
[24] P.P.1873. Vol. XLVIII, p.161.
[25] C.O. 152/145. Enc. in Glover to Kimberley, 23 Sept., 1881. No.264.
[26] C.O. 152/162. Enc. in Lees to Stanley, 1 Oct., 1885. No.282.
[27] Ibid.; C.O. 152/165. Enc. in Gormanston to Granville, 13 July, 1886. No.182; C.O. 152/168. Enc. in Porter to Holland, 16 Aug., 1887. No.216.
[28] C.O. 152/216. Enc. in Fleming to Chamberlain, 20 Feb., 1897. No.112; C.O. 152/215. Chamberlain to Fleming, 31 May, 1897. No.202.
[29] C.O. 152/291. Sweet-Escott to Elgin, 17 Oct., 1906. No.417; Elgin to Sweet-Escott, 4 Dec., 1906. No.290; C.O. 152/295. Sweet-Escott to Elgin, 27 March, 1907. No.139, and several enc.
[30] C.O. 239/74. Enc. in Fitz Roy to Stanley, 21 May, 1844. No.34; C.O. 315/7. Act No.139.
[31] C.O. 315/8. Act No.179.

[32] C.O. 315/8. Act No.183.
[33] C.O. 239/90. Enc. in Mackintosh to Grey, 29 May, 1851. No.45; Grey to Mackintosh, 30 Aug., 1851. No.65.
[34] C.O. 314/2. Enc. in Mackintosh to Newcastle, 10 April, 1854. No.59.
[35] C.O. 314/10. Enc. in Hamilton to Newcastle, 10 Dec., 1861. No.12; C.O. 314/11. Enc. in Hamilton to Newcastle, 11 March, 1862. No.159.
[36] C.O. 315/9. Ordinance No.92.
[37] C.O. 314/16. Enc. in Pine to Carnarvon, 16 Nov., 1866. No.169, and 5 Dec., 1866. No.177; C.O. 314/17. Enc. in Pine to Buckingham, 18 May, 1867. No.81; C.O. 314/19. Enc. in Hill to Buckingham, 3 Jan., 1868. No.8.
[38] C.O. 314/17. Enc. in Pine to Buckingham, 18 May, 1867. No.81.
[39] Virgin Islands Ordinances: 1866-1889. Ordinance No.4 of 1888.
[40] P.P. 1873. Vol. XLVIII, p.161. Moir to Pine, 25 May, 1872; C.O. 152/113. Enc. in Baynes to Kimberley, 10 April, 1873. No.84.
[41] C.O. 152/113. Baynes to Kimberley, 10 April, 1873. No.84.
[42] C.O. 152/113. Baynes to Kimberley, 10 May, 1873. No.134.
[43] C.O. 152/131. Berkeley to Carnarvon, 25 Jan., 1878. No.12.
[44] Ibid.
[45] P.P. 1838. Vol. XLVIII, p.163; C.O. 239/71. S.M.'s Report for Oct., Nov., and Dec., 1842.
[46] C.O. 315/7. Act No.142.
[47] C.O. 317/15. Blue Book for 1844.
[48] C.O. 315/7. Act No.151; C.O. 239/77. Enc. in Fitz Roy to Stanley, 23 May, 1847. No.43.
[49] C.O. 317/17. Blue Book for 1846.
[50] C.O. 239/59. S.M.'s Report for March and April, 1840; Colebrooke to Drummond Hay, 19 June, 1840.
[51] C.O. 243/10. S.M.'s Report for half year ended 30 June, 1847.
[52] Ibid.
[53] C.O. 243/10. S.M.'s Report for half year ended 31 Dec., 1847.
[54] C.O. 239/79. Drummond Hay to Stanley, 1 Nov., 1845, and enc.
[55] Shirley Gordon: A Century of West Indian Education. (Longmans, 1963) pp. 38 ff.
[56] C.O. 243/10. Enc. in S.M.'s Report for half year ended 30 June, 1847.
[57] C.O. 243/10. S.M.'s Report for half year ended 31 Dec., 1848.
[58] C.O. 239/95. Enc. in Mackintosh to Newcastle, 27 July, 1853. No.63.
[59] P.P. 1856. Vol. XLII, p.172. Enc. in Mackintosh to Russell, 22 May, 1855.
[60] P.P. 1859. Vol. XXI, p.523. Price to Hamilton, 23 March, 1858.
[61] C.O. 315/9. Ordinance No.55.
[62] C.O. 315/9. Ordinance No.96. (No.2 of 1863).
[63] C.O. 314/13. Enc. in Hill to Newcastle, 4 May, 1863. No.40.
[64] P.P. 1867. Vol. XLVIII, p.98; C.O. 314/16. Cardwell to Pine, 10 July, 1866. No.2; and, enc. in Pine to Carnarvon, 3 Sept., 1866. No.147.
[65] C.O. 152/132. Enc. in Berkeley to Hicks-Beach, 19 June, 1878. No.148.
[66] C.O. 152/134. Enc in Berkeley to Hicks-Beach, 26 March, 1879. No.86.
[67] C.O. 152/143. Enc. in Berkeley to Kimberley, 15 Feb., 1881. No.54; P.P. 1883. Vol. XLV, p.102.

[68] P.P. 1884-5. Vol. LV, p.421.

[69] P.P. 1886. Vol. XLV, p.508; P.P. 1888. Vol. LXXII, p.513.

[70] P.P. 1898. Vol. LIX, p.977.

[71] C.O. 152/229. Chamberlain to Fleming, 15 April, 1898. No.15.

[72] C.O. 315/6. Act No.101; C.O. 239/45. Light to Glenelg, 21 March, 1837. No.134.

[73] C.O. 315/9. Ordinance. No.51.

[74] C.O. 317/30 and C.O. 317/31. Blue Books for 1859 and 1860.

[75] C.O. 152/168. Enc. in Porter to Holland, 12 Oct., 1887. No.256.

[76] C.O. 239/67. Enc. in Hay to Macphail, 9 Feb., 1842. No.14; C.O. 314/3. Enc. in Mackintosh to Grey, 1 March, 1855. No.17; C.O. 314/15. Enc. in Hill to Cardwell, 4 May, 1865. No.18; C.O. 152/152. Enc. in Glover to Derby, 11 Jan., 1883. No.11; C.O. 152/16. Enc. in Lees to Derby, 26 March, 1885. No.110.

[77] Trelawney Wentworth: The West India Sketch Book. (London, 1834.) Vol. 1, p.199.

[78] C.O. 239/77. Enc. in Fitz Roy to Stanley, 5 Feb., 1845. No.6.

[79] C.O. 314/17. Memorial of Inhabitants of Virgin Islands to Queen, 25 June, 1867; C.O. 314/18. Pine to Elliot, 9 Sept., 1867. Minute by Taylor, 10 Sept., 1867; Buckingham to Hill, 20 Sept., 1867. No.79.

[80] C.O. 152/138. Berkeley to Hicks-Beach, 9 April, 1880. No.116 and enc.; C.O. 152/188. Haynes-Smith to Ripon, 14 Nov., 1893. No.228; C.O. 152/217. Fleming to Chamberlain, 29 March, 1897. No.199, and enc.

[81] C.O. 152/138. Berkeley to Hicks-Beach, 9 April, 1880. No.116; Kimberley to Berkeley, 1 June, 1880. No.43; C.O. 152/188. Ripon to Haynes Smith, 4 Dec., 1893. No.182; C.O. 152/217. Fleming to Chamberlain, 11 Sept., 1897. No.543.; Chamberlain to Fleming, 2 Nov., 1897. No.453. C.O. 152/224. Chamberlain to Fleming, 28 Dec., 1897. (Confidential).

[82] Leeward Islands Act No.5 of 1902.

[83] C.O. 152/60. Enc. in Lees to Derby, 26 March, 1885. No.110.

[84] C.O. 152/168. Enc. in Porter to Holland, 12 Oct., 1887. No.256.

[85] C.O. 314/3. Enc. in Mackintosh to Grey, 1 March, 1855. No.17; C.O. 314/10. Enc. in Hamilton to Newcastle, 24 July, 1861. No.6.

[86] C.O. 314/23. Enc. in Mundy to Kimberley, 26 April, 1871. No.71; C.O. 152/152. Enc. in Glover to Derby, 11 Jan., 1883. No.11.

[87] C.O. 152/236. Enc. in Fleming to Chamberlain, 6 Oct., 1898. No.538; Chamberlain to Fleming, 10 Nov., 1898. No.437; C.O. 152/239. Fleming to Chamberlain, 21 Dec., 1898. No. 719 and 23 Feb., 1899. No.115; Chamberlain to Fleming, 16 Jan., 1899. No.16 and 28 March, 1899. No.122.

[88] C.O. 239/67. Enc. in Drummond Hay to Macphail, 28 Jan., 1842. No.8; C.O. 239/90. Enc. in Mackintosh to Grey, 26 April, 1851. No.31; C.O. 239/92. Enc. in Mackintosh to Grey, 14 Feb., 1852. No.5; C.O. 239/95. Enc. in Mackintosh to Pakington, 28 Jan., 1853. No.7; C.O. 314/3. Enc. in Russell to Mackintosh, 5 June, 1855. No.12.

[89] C.O. 314/3. Enc. in Mackintosh to Molesworth, 11 Sept., 1855. No.69.

[90] C.O. 239/55. Enc. in Thomas to Colebrooke, 4 Jan., 1839; C.O. 314/3. Enc. in Mackintosh to Grey, 1 March, 1855. No.17.

[91] C.O. 314/24. Enc. in Pine to Kimberley, 24 Feb., 1872. No.34; C.O. 152/178. Enc. in Smith to Knutsford, 14 July, 1890. No.202.

[92] C.O. 152/176. Enc. in Evans to Knutsford, 7 Nov., 1889. No.306; C.O. 152/168. Enc. in Porter to Holland, 17 Aug., 1887. No.220.

[93] C.O. 239/62. Enc. in Roger to Drummond Hay, 5 Jan., 1841; C.O. 239/67. Enc. in Drummond Hay to Macphail, 28 Jan., 1842. No.8; C.O. 239/80. Enc. in Fitz Roy to Gladstone, 7 Feb., 1846. General No.4; C.O. 239/95. Enc. in Mackintosh to Pakington, 28 Jan., 1853. No.7.

[94] C.O. 152/168. Enc. in Porter to Holland, 12 Oct., 1887. No.256; C.O. 152/176. Enc. in Evans to Knutsford, 7 Nov., 1889. No.306.

[95] C.O. 152/229. Cookman to Chamberlain, 28 Feb., 1898. No.37.

Chapter 9

The Disintegration of the Legislature

The difficulties experienced in adjusting to the financial problems of post-emancipation, and the failure of the legislature to institute any proper system of social services, were two aspects of the economic decadence of the Virgin Islands during the nineteenth century. Another was seen in the retrogression from the principle of political representation in the constitutional life of the islands, though this was not, in turn, without its social and economic implications. The constitutional problem was complicated and aggravated by recurring crises between the constituent parts of the legislature and by weaknesses inherent in the political system.

By the time the legislature was introduced in the Virgin Islands in 1773, legislative government had already been established in other British West Indian colonies. The system, therefore, was clearly patterned on those existing which themselves had earlier derived from the British model. The triple form comprising a Lieutenant-Governor, a Council, and an Assembly, was a replica of the British frame comprising the monarch, the House of Lords and the House of Commons. The similarity of form was followed by an assertion of a similarity of function, which was especially true of the Assembly, and to a less extent, of the Council. Their assumption of and adherence to the practices and privileges of the corresponding bodies in Britain, largely determined the tone of legislative proceedings in the Virgin Islands.

The Lieutenant-Governor, or in his absence, the President or senior member of the Council, was responsible for summoning and adjourning the Assembly, and presiding at meetings of the Council. To these legislative functions were added administrative duties including the issuing of orders for the performance of public works and superintending the execution of laws. With respect to these matters he was assisted by the Council, a body of twelve members nominated by the Governor of the Leeward Islands. The Council had a dual responsibility: as an Executive or Privy Council it advised the Lieutenant-Governor or President on important matters touching on the welfare of the colony; as a legislative body, it deliberated as the upper chamber of the colonial legislature. The legislative body 'par excellence' was the House of Assembly consisting of fifteen members elected triennially. Members could claim immunity for their acts as representatives of the people, and had ultimate control over finances.

The legislative system suffered from several weaknesses which were partly inherent in it, and partly due to the arrangement whereby the Virgin Islands formed part of the administration of the Leeward Islands. The executive power in the colony was really vested by Royal Commission in the Governor of the Leeward Islands who determined the composition of the Council by his provisional powers of appointment and the reserve powers of suspension. Control over the Assembly was exercised by powers of convocation, prorogation and dissolution. The Governor also possessed the initial power of assent, and definitive power of veto over all legislative enactments. In addition to his executive and legislative powers, the Governor had judicial and administrative functions such as the right to establish courts of justice, dispose of officers, arrange fees of office, pardon offenders, and authorise the organisation of militias.

The denial by the Governor of his powers to the Lieutenant-Governor as head of the administration of the Virgin Islands in his absence, except for those of convocation and adjournment of the legislature, reduced the latter to a mere figurehead. Consequently, Lieutenant-Governors rarely assumed office in the Virgin Islands, and their position was taken by the Presidents. Partly because he was unpaid, partly because he was disinclined, and partly because he tended to share the sentiments of the ruling class, the President exercised even less influence than a Lieutenant-Governor.

Much of the weakness of the system of government stemmed from the absence of a strong central executive who could adopt a firm line with recalcitrant legislatures. Some of the periods of most constructive activity of the legislature coincided with the visit of the Governor. Unfortunately, most of the visits of Governors were induced by crises in the colony, which demanded their attention. On such occasions their stay was invariably short, and confined more or less to the solution of the problems which necessitated their presence.

The greatest weakness in the legislative system existed in the differences which it encouraged between the Council and Assembly. For instance, the separate functions of the two bodies were never clearly defined, and there was inadequate provision for consultation between them, communication being limited to messages from one to the other. But a message could scarcely contain all the explanations necessary for the full understanding of a subject, and the result was misunderstanding and distrust. The point on which there was frequent conflict was the question of finance. By and large, the Council conceded the primacy of the Assembly in this respect,[1] but it retained the right of participation in financial matters to an extent which was sometimes resisted by the Assembly as an infringement of its own prerogative.

Taxation was the subject upon which disagreement between the Council and Assembly hinged and turned, so much so that between 1796 and 1817 they sought to escape from the annual wrangle over the money bill by passing bills covering a period of years, and to pass subsidiary legislation to finance any extraordinary project. Another expedient to avoid disputes was the adoption of the committee system. Members of the committee were drawn from both houses to examine and report on controversial financial matters, and reports were invariably accepted though subject to modification. Not even these methods of convenience could completely prevent disputes between Council and Assembly.

Differences between the two branches of the legislature were aggravated by the advisory role of the Council. It not only enabled the Lieutenant-Governor, or President, to secure the support of the Council, but by so doing convinced the Assembly that it could not depend on the Council in a contest with the head of the administration. One way by which the Assembly sought to express its disapproval with the Council was by refusing to meet to transact business with it. Often it used the Council as a target for the expression of its opposition against the Governor as the local representative of or against the British Government itself. In either case the result was a growing animosity between the Assembly and Council.

After the hurricane of 1819 and the refusal of the British Government to grant requests for assistance, the Assembly adopted a restrictive attitude. It expressed its discontent by refusing to pass tax legislation, and by creating an artificial dispute with the Council. Finally, it passed a resolution in January, 1826 designed to resist the practice hitherto observed whereby the President summoned and adjourned the legislature, by ascribing such functions to the Speaker.[2]

In their role as the duly constituted representatives of the people, members of the Assembly prided themselves on being the watch-dog over the public purse. Not only did they claim the right to sanction the disbursement of public funds, but also the manner and efficiency with which it was collected. These claims led to the development of undesirable traits expressed in a tardy and negligent attitude to devise measures with regard, for example, to taxation and the payment of debts. For example, President Isaacs was forced in 1835 to take the unusual and objectionable step of appointing the Rector to a paid assistant-commissionership of slave compensation, since no provision had been made by the Assembly for the payment of his salary.[3] Again, in January, 1837, the Assembly declared itself in abeyance for six months on the frivolous pretext that it was not legally constituted since the original Act to which it owed its existence could not be found.[4]

Not even the reorganisation of the legislature by acting-governor Henry Light in March, 1837, was productive of much good; and it was not until March, 1838, that an Assembly prepared to act was obtained.[5] Even so several of the measures it passed had to be disallowed, their repugnance, to Henry Taylor of the Colonial Office, being indicative of the inability of the legislature to adopt measures for the good of society.[6] Shortly after, in May, 1838, a serious dispute between the Council and Assembly over the right of financial control brought a complete cessation to the transaction of public business. The impasse was broken only by the dissolution of the Assembly and the holding of new elections.[7]

By its attitude to legislation and its assertion of privilege, the Assembly had succeeded by 1838 in creating the impression that its existence was no longer desirable. Further evidences of a similar character after emancipation resulted directly in changes in the system of representative government. Until 1838, the resistance of the legislature to increased taxation stemmed from the refusal of the British Government to grant the assistance requested. After 1838, the behavior of the legislature or more properly, the Assembly, can be ascribed to its support of the rural population against the extension of taxation.

Without the Assembly no legislation could be passed, and it was only by the use of frequent dissolutions and extended prorogations that Assemblies were secured to pass the required legislation. Thus between 1841 and 1849, the Assembly was dissolved six times and prorogued for long periods at least on two occasions. Even when Assemblies were prepared to legislate, they sometimes hedged on the question of taxation being content either to defer action or to continue existing laws for definite periods.

The temper of the Assembly with regard to taxation was exemplified by the disturbances of 1848 which were partly stimulated by the realisation of the participants that they had its sympathetic support. The direct involvement of the members of the Assembly in the riot was widely accepted, and evidence was produced implicating the majority of being ringleaders through whom subscription lists circulated for the purpose of collecting funds to meet any pecuniary penalties which might be imposed on the perpetrators.[8] These charges seem to have been justified for after the end of the disturbance the Assembly retaliated by dismissing the Clerk of the Assembly, one of the magistrates who had interfered to prevent it, and by appointing a participant in the outrage to that office.[9]

To the dilatory attitude and passive and active resistance to taxation of the Assembly was added continued differences between it and the Council and President. Disputes stemmed largely from the fact that after 1837 the President was responsible for initiating tax proposals and had the support of the Council. They were due also to the evident disdain with which President Drummond Hay, who held his office from 1839 to 1851, regarded members of the Assembly.[10]

Against the Council, the Assembly could only retaliate by refusing to co-operate with it in the transaction of public business. It was otherwise with the President who was accused of 'discourteous and ungentlemanly conduct'[11] and of being racially prejudiced against the black and coloured inhabitants, and of favouring the white population.[12] Furthermore, he was accused in October, 1849 with the irregular importation of wine and other articles.[13] In defiance of the President's authority, in January, 1850, the Assembly revived the right previously claimed in 1845[14] to order the attendance of public officers at the bar of the House and their production of papers without the intervention of the Executive.[15] Finally, in February, 1851, the Assembly succeeded in securing the transfer of Drummond Hay from the Presidency.[16]

The deliberate opinion of the Council, which it purported to derive from an intimate knowledge of the society, was that it was 'impossible in the present state of the population to bring together the requisite number of qualified freeholders competent to exercise the Legislative functions of the House of Assembly,'[17] a verdict which was shared by the President. In support of this notion it was pointed out that the few persons who from position and education were capable and qualified to legislate were either members of the Council or private individuals who preferred to remain aloof from political activities. It is true that through death, emigration and absenteeism the numbers of those capable of legislating were depleted. However, the assertion of the President and Council cannot be justified since in the 1840's members of the Assembly could be obtained able and willing to legislate. The fact was that the President and Council would brook no opposition to legislative proposals no matter how heavy the demands were. Failing to secure unquestioning co-operation from the Assembly, they sought to disparage its ability. Even the participation of some members of the Assembly in the plunder of the American merchantship *Wilhamet* wrecked on the reefs of Anegada in 1850 was used as another pretext to prove their incapacity to legislate.[18]

The need for reform could have been better justified with reference to the electorate which showed marked apathy in the exercise of its voting rights. The election results of March, 1837, illustrate this point adequately. Of a census of 143 only 34 electors chose the members for the Assembly in which there was still one vacancy because the only elector for the district could not be found. In Tortola, only 17 persons voted of the 92 registered, while in Virgin Gorda only 7 of 33. The best proportion was obtained in Jost Van Dyke where 10 of the 18 persons registered voted,[19] though the inhabitants of that island were not always ready to register and vote. Around 1830 a visitor to the island, who witnessed the election of two members of the Assembly, observed that they were unanimously chosen by 'three sun-dried mortals . . . (who) composed the whole body of constituents.'[20]

The inconveniences arising from the absence of a strong local executive, the differences between the Assembly and Council, and the general impression that the Virgin Islands lacked the human resources to maintain the existing system of government, were factors responsible for early administrative and constitutional changes in the colony.

The administrative changes effected sought to correct some of the weaknesses in the system of legislative government. In an attempt to prevent disputes between the Council and Assembly over summoning and adjournment, a procedural arrangement was made in 1826, whereby the legislature was to meet on the first and fourth Friday of each month, notice to be issued by the Clerk of the Crown under the authority of the Governor. Notices of meetings were to be served on the members of the Council by the deputy Provost Marshal and those on the members of the Assembly by the sergeant-at-arms. If either branch of the legislature found it necessary to request a meeting between the regular days, permission was to be obtained by an application in writing from either the President of the Council or the Speaker of the Assembly, as the case might be, to the Clerk of the Crown.[21]

In order to secure more direct supervision of the affairs of the colony, and to correct some of the shortcomings inherent in the absence of a strong local executive, the administration of the Leeward Islands was divided into two parts in 1816, one part to be governed from Antigua, the seat of the existing government, and the other, in which was included the Virgin Islands, from St. Christopher. For a while, the arrangement worked better, helped by an interested Governor Thomas Probyn, and between 1817 and 1818, seven acts were passed, compared with only one for the previous six years.[22] During the regime of Governor Maxwell extending from 1819 to 1832, however, very little attention was given to the Virgin Islands, and the result was legislative inertia and recurring disputes and crises.[23]

Further changes were effected in 1833 when the Leeward Islands were reunited under one Governor. He was directed to visit the Virgin Islands at least once a year and to remain there for a short time, 'in order to acquire local information and give such directions as may be impracticable at a distance.'[24] In addition, immediate personal visits were required in cases of emergency. At the same time, the President was given greater authority as Officer Administering the Government of the Virgin Islands. Among his legislative duties were the initiation of legislation, the acceptance and rejection of Bills, appointment to the Council, the dissolution of the Assembly, the issue of writs of election and the summoning and prorogation of the legislature. His administrative duties included the remission of death sentences, the discharge of the functions of chancellors, the appointment of administrative officers, the supervision of the stipendiary and local magistracy, and the issue of the Commission of the Peace. The President, in short, was charged with all the functions and duties hitherto performed by the Governor, which were 'multifarious in kind and some of them important upon occasion.'

Defects in the administrative system persisted due to the continuation in office of an unpaid resident as President who was highly susceptible to influence from local agricultural and commercial interests. To remedy this situation the policy was adopted in 1837 of appointing Presidents from outside the colony and paying them a salary of £800 a year.[25]

The first constitutional reform stemmed from the widely accepted assumption that a sufficient number of persons could not be found to form an Assembly and to discharge its functions. Some cognizance was also taken of the apathy of voters. According to the Constitution Act of 1837, the qualifications of voters and candidates for election remained unchanged, but all existing residential qualifications were removed and the numbers of elected members were reduced from fifteen to nine. Henceforth, also, voters were given as many votes as the number of members required for the Assembly. To ensure regular attendance a fine was imposed on representatives who refused to serve, and no member could resign without the consent of the Assembly.[26]

Various schemes proposed after 1837 sought either to limit the legislative function in the Virgin Islands, or to eliminate the legislature altogether. Among those suggested to achieve the first was one to include the colony in a general legislature of the Leeward Islands, which would enable the transfer of some subjects of legislation from the local body.[27] However, Sir William Colebrooke, Governor of the Leeward Islands, failed to convince all the island legislatures of the efficacy of the measure, and the plan was abandoned. To achieve the second aim, it was proposed to amalgamate the Virgin Islands with a neighbouring Leeward Island, the legislature of which would contain representatives from the Virgin Islands.[28]

The Colonial Office generally agreed that the Assembly was incompetent and that it lacked the public spirit of a legislative body. But it did not accept any of the suggestions made for its removal, either in whole or in part. It was not fully convinced of the uselessness of the Assembly since it often made good laws.[29] It was believed that the Assembly had done no considerable mischief, and that 'the peculiarity of the place is not so much the want of competent legislators, as the universal consciousness of that want so that nobody will undertake to legislate.' A very real constitutional point, however, was the possible implications for the other colonies. The Virgin Islands were only a minor colony, but to abrogate its Assembly was to establish a precedent there which might have very large consequences elsewhere.[30]

Moreover, it was hoped that with time and experience, the legislature would improve.

Basing his case on the consideration that the state of British West Indian society was inadequate to maintain a representative system, Henry Taylor, in charge of the West Indian division of the Colonial Office, recommended in 1839 the abolition of existing Assemblies and the substitution of Councils, modelled on those existing in Crown Colonies, where the Crown could have paramount control.[31] Taylor's suggestion was discussed subsequently at three Cabinet meetings but it failed to receive support.[32] Even if it had, it is doubtful if it would have secured parliamentary approval necessary for its adoption. When in 1839, the Melbourne Government sought to suspend the Jamaican Assembly for five years, it was bitterly opposed and forced to resign.[33] The temper of Parliament compelled acquiescence in the old system of representative government but the idea of the necessity for eventual Crown control was not abandoned. When in 1854, the Virgin Islands started the process of constitutional retrogression in the Leeward Islands, it was in the direction of Crown Colony Government.

The riots of 1853 provided the opportunity to effect further constitutional changes in the Virgin Islands. By that time the Colonial Office was engaged in limiting the power of Assemblies in other British West Indian colonies such as in Jamaica where an Executive Committee system was adopted in 1854.[34] While the colony was yet unrecovered from the shock of the disturbances, Governor Mackintosh secured the agreement of both branches of the legislature to devolve their functions upon a single mixed body, consisting of one-third nominated, and two-thirds elected members.[35] The Colonial Office, however, thought differently. Accession to the requests for continued military and other parliamentary assistance was made conditional upon 'the institutions of the colony being placed on such a footing as to enable the Crown to guard against the recurrence of such disasters and . . . appeals for indemnification.'[36] It required the enactment of legislation by the local government investing the British Government with political control in the colony.

Consensus was reached on the point of Crown control, but the method by which it would be achieved was uncertain. Henry Taylor believed that the existing legislature should be replaced by a Legislative Council of which half was to be elected and the other half nominated, with the President having a casting vote.[37] It would give the

Government the necessary preponderance in the legislature by which it could effectively conduct affairs. However, in the instructions issued to Governor Mackintosh in September, 1853, the directions were vague and ambiguous. The legislature was asked to devolve its functions upon a Legislative Council partly nominated and partly representative in which the President should have a casting vote.[38]

The Secretary of State's instructions were received when Mackintosh's proposals were already being considered by the legislature. Because of their ambiguity, Mackintosh was convinced that he had adopted the correct course. In any case, he refused to distract the attention of the legislature from the measures under consideration lest any new amendment should result in the failure of the Bill. Rather, he suggested, amendments should be looked for from the new legislative body.[39]

The Constitutional Amendment Act finally passed in August, 1854, abolished the existing system of government by Council and Assembly and substituted a Legislative Council instead. A Privy or Executive Council of four members was provided for by Order in Council, and its functions were made entirely advisory. Nevertheless, through the President, it was able to wield legislative influence.

Under the Act, the Legislative Council was to consist of ten members including the President who was to be ex-officio the presiding member, three nominated and six elected members. Nominated members were to be appointed by the Crown while the elected members were to be selected by registered voters. No qualification was required of candidates for election except that they should be adult British subjects. Voters, however, had to satisfy some property qualification. Only male adults who were £5 freeholders, £10 leaseholders, or £5 house-holders could vote.[40]

The qualifications for voters were a reduction on those hitherto required and aimed at including as many as possible of the white voters whose properties had depreciated due to the current economic depression. The retention of any qualification whatever was evidently to exclude as many as possible of the rising class of peasants.

Another essential provision of the constitution was that the responsibility to register rested with the voter himself. The Provost Marshal was required to keep a book called the 'Register of Voters' in which he was to enter the names of all qualified voters in the Virgin Islands. The list was to be revised annually by 'striking off the names of all such persons as shall not appear in person or by deputy and prove their title to be continued on such register and entering the names of all such persons as shall prove their title to be admitted on the said Register.'

The legislature was induced to pass the Constitutional Amendment Act of 1854 on the understanding that the British Government would guarantee the responsibility for maintaining order in the Virgin Islands.[41] However, because the new constitution did not introduce the changes required by the British Government, it was decided to withdraw the detachment of British troops then stationed in Tortola, in March, 1855.[42] The legislature naturally regarded this decision as a 'deliberate act of breach of faith,'[43] but the British Government stuck to the decision of not retaining British troops in Tortola to perform police duty, unless its responsibility could be measured by an equivalent power of control in the colony.[44] In effect it meant that continued British protection was dependent upon Crown control of the legislature by a majority of nominated over elected members.

The resistance against arrest by the inhabitants of Thatch Island in November, 1856, and the temporary excitement by some malcontents of Road Town in 1858, provided the impetus for further reform. Governor Hamilton's refusal of a request for troops to cope with the anticipated out-break of violence in 1858 convinced the legislature that it must concede the required constitutional reform if the Virgin Islands were to secure British military support when necessary.[45] A further amendment in March, 1859, therefore, provided for a Legislative Council of seven members besides the President, three of whom were to be nominated by the Crown, and four to be elected by the qualified registered voters. To prevent deadlock in the Legislative Council, and to ensure that under normal conditions legislative proposals were passed, the President was given both a deliberative and a casting vote.[46] Provided the nominated members supported the President, measures could be assured of a majority vote.

Under normal circumstances the changes in the constitution effected in 1859 would have been sufficient to satisfy local conditions and requirements. The Ordinance enabled some necessary social and financial legislation to be undertaken,[47] though these were more important for the ease in which they were passed than for any high social value. As indicated by the measures dealing with taxation and the manner in which the consolidated debt was liquidated, the basic attitudes still remained, influenced by the poverty of the colony.

Whatever the achievements that could be claimed by the Legislative Council, the system of government was nevertheless severely modified. The representative element contained in the constitution was abolished in 1867, and full Crown Colony Government was instituted instead.

The essential feature of Crown Colony Government was that executive power and the control of general policy and legislation were vested in the Governor (or in his absence, the President) assisted by a Legislative Council consisting of officials, and some colonists nominated by the Governor. Since these men were required to give him their support, he could look forward to the successful implementation of policies.

Two factors were responsible for the change to Crown Colony Government. Many of the 'old guard', that is, men who had supported or were willing to support the President in the Executive Council when that body existed and who had continued to give their support in the Legislative Council, were either dead or leaving the colony.[48] As such, therefore, there were fewer men on whom the President could rely for unstinted support; even those who remained were either advanced in years or were in declining health.[49] Of more importance was that by the mid-1860's some members were not prepared to adopt the policies laid down by the President. It was felt that eventually political power would pass into the hands of an 'illiterate' class of people incapable of legislating.[50] The anticipated result was political chaos,[51] a quite over-worked excuse by this time. The real point was that Presidents were intolerant of opposition and sought to avoid or to remove it. There was nothing to prove that the Virgin Islands possessed men less capable and willing to legislate in the 1860's than they were at any time previously. It was probably hoped that Crown Colony Government would preserve the existing political status quo.

The character of the electorate was also made the reason for further reform, and in this regard an illogical and far-fetched argument was resorted to. It was shown that since property was rapidly passing to a local peasantry who would thus be qualified to vote, but who, instead looked to St. Thomas for their future welfare, it could not be pretended that the retention of the franchise would awaken a sense of responsibility. Consequently it was considered advisable to exclude the elective element from the government, until the general spread of sound education enabled the people to use it properly.[52]

It is probable that the majority of all those persons qualified to vote never bothered to register and that this was done, on receipt of the necessary written authorisation, by those who sought their support. It would account for the wide disparity in the number of registered voters from time to time: in 1858, there were forty-two; in 1862, thirty-six; in 1865, sixty-three; and in 1867, only six, five of whom were public officers. Voting showed even less acknowledgement of civic responsibility: in 1858, only ten persons exercised the franchise; in 1862, twenty-seven; in 1865, twenty-seven; and in 1867, four.[53] The results of registration and voting are not surprising, since under the Constitution Ordinance of 1859, registration was not compulsory but left to the determination of claimants, and voting was held only in Road Town during normal working hours, from eight o'clock in the morning to four o'clock in the afternoon.[54]

The support of the British Government to the abolition of the elective franchise in 1867 was in keeping with its over-all policy of introducing Crown Colony Government wherever colonial legislatures would accept it.[55] The institution of Crown Colony Government in the Virgin Islands has to be seen against the general background of greater participation by the Crown in the affairs of the colonies. For example, in 1866, following the Morant Bay Uprising, Crown Colony Government was introduced in Jamaica. The autocracy of the Crown was seen as a necessary prerequisite to hold the balance between unstable and disorderly government by oligarchies and representative democracies based on an ignorant and inexperienced negro majority.[56] As far as the Virgin Islands were concerned, the British Government was convinced that the transfer of legislative power to the Crown was necessary to forestall possible prospective evils. So long as no considerable opposition to the measure could be anticipated, permission was given to institute the change.[57]

The Ordinance repealing all constitutional ordinances in force and reconstituting the legislature of the Virgin Islands was passed unanimously by the Legislative Council in April, 1867.[58] The existing Legislative Council was abrogated and replaced by six non-elected members, three ex-officio and three nominated, all of whom were to hold office during pleasure. The ex-officio members would be the Governor, the Colonial Secretary, and the Colonial Treasurer. The nominated members who were to be Virgin Islanders 'capable of acting in the discharge of their duties', were to be appointed by the President subject to the approval of the Crown. The Act abolished the principle of representation introduced in 1773 and ushered in the system of Crown Colony Government in the Virgin Islands.

After 1867, no constitutional changes occurred again in the Virgin Islands until 1902, when the Legislative Council was abolished. Several factors facilitated the change or made it necessary. The participation of the islands in the federation of the Leeward Islands, enabled the transfer of legislative power to the federal government and made the local legislature less necessary. The existence of federal officers to supervise certain common services, to some extent, made the re-organisation of the civil establishment possible while the poverty of the islands made it necessary. The failure of Crown Colony Government to fulfil the hopes for which it was created pointed to the advisability of removing the legislative function from the Virgin Islands altogether.

An important aspect of the creation of the federation of the Leeward Islands in 1871, relative to the constitutional history of the Virgin Islands, pertained to the special powers accorded to the federal legislature. Under the constitution, the subjects on which the federal government could legislate were specified, all other subjects remaining vested in the individual island legislatures.[59] Among the subjects on which the federal government could legislate included 'such other subjects in respect of each Presidency as the Island Legislature thereof may declare to be within the Competency of the General Legislature.'[60] In other words, an island legislature could delegate the responsibility of legislating on matters in which it was competent to legislate, to the federal legislature.

The Virgin Islands took ample advantage after 1872 of the provision enabling the transfer of legislative function. An ordinance was passed in May, 1878, authorising the federal legislature to pass laws relating to the super-annuation of public officers and for the creation of a fund for the relief of the widows and orphans of such officers.[61] Another ordinance in November, 1879 authorised the federal legislature to pass laws relating to aliens, friendly societies and commissions of enquiry.[62] Again, in April, 1882, the federal legislative council was empowered to make provision for the purchase and maintenance of a steam vessel for the service of the federation. A significant addendum to this legislation was the authorisation given to the federal legislature to charge the expenses on the revenue of the Virgin Islands.[63]

The above ordinances showed great caution in the transfer of power by the local legislature to an external body. Not so did two other ordinances passed in May, 1887 and February, 1890 respectively. The first authorised the federal legislature to impose stamp duties in the Virgin Islands, thus entrenching foreign control upon its financial supremacy.[64] The second declared all subjects, except the imposition and assessment of taxes and duties, to be within the competence of the federal legislative council.[65] Whatever jealousy of its own powers the Legislative Council of the Virgin Islands might have retained, however, was abandoned when in 1902 it declared the constitution of the Presidency a subject within the legislative competence of the federal legislature.[66] It paved the way for its own abolition.

The economic condition of the Virgin Islands made it necessary for administrative offices to be reorganised. It was not without justification that the Secretary of State for the Colonies expressed the general dilemma facing the colony when in April, 1869 he remarked that the civil establishment was 'out of proportion to the requirements of the Colony.'[67] With no less justification, but probably with greater misconstruction of the contemporary situation, did Governor Haynes Smith speak in July, 1888 of 'the absurdity . . . of a minute sub-division of offices with high-sounding titles.'[68] By that time considerable amalgamation of offices had already taken place, and his comment referred more specifically to the office of President of the Virgin Islands. But even so with regard to both his functions and his powers, the position of the President had become considerably altered since 1867.

The Presidency was attacked shortly after the introduction of full Crown Colony Government when the stress on more economical administration suggested that the President should be replaced by a President-Magistrate. The change promised to have two advantages: a large staff of subordinate officers would be unnecessary; and justice would be more efficiently administered.[69] The suggestion was rejected,[70] but on the appointment of a new President, Alexander Wilson Moir in August, 1869, he was warned to be prepared for modifications in his office to include executive and judicial duties in addition to those purely administrative.[71]

The opportunity to implement the decision of 1869 was provided by the creation of the federation of the Leeward Islands. The general supervision of the Virgin Islands administration offered by the federal officers not only permitted the abolition of certain offices but made it possible to amalgamate others and multiply administrative functions. And since federation increased the expenditure of the islands, it was necessary to secure compensatory economies. An Ordinance was passed in July, 1872 making the President an Assistant Judge of the General Court, a Justice in the several courts of Petty Sessions and of Summary Jurisdiction, and a general supervisor in and over the Treasury. His salary of £800 a year previously paid by the British Government was reduced to £500 to be paid by the local legislature.[72] During the following year his duties were revised and the President became ex-officio police magistrate and Treasurer. Also, his salary was further reduced to £300 a year.[73] In addition, the President was relieved in 1882 of his duties as Treasurer since these were found to be incompatible with his position as magistrate;[74] but in 1884, they were re-imposed upon him and he was furnished with a clerk to assist him in the Post Office.[75]

The final re-organisation of the President's (Commissioner's) functions was made in 1896 when in return for a saving of £150 a year in the fixed establishment, his office was combined with that of Medical Officer.[76] The change stemmed directly from the difficulty of securing suitable candidates who were prepared to work in a relatively out of the way and backward possession for a small salary. Only the hope of early promotion led some candidates to accept the appointment, and to undergo the 'temporary social banishment.'[77] By this amalgamation the Commissioner became Coroner and Crown Prosecutor also.

Federation altered the position of the President insofar as he ceased in effect to be a direct representative of the Crown and became instead the representative of the Governor of the Leeward Islands. Hence his administrative duties derived from the reorganisation of the Leeward Islands administration in the 1830's were redefined to cater for his new status as the mere 'organ of the Governor.' The local legislative sessions were no longer to be opened by a speech from the President but from the Governor.[78] On such occasions the Governor was to propose the local laws required; in his absence the President could only introduce legislation with his prior consent.[79]

In order to remove doubts concerning the actual position of the President vis-à-vis the Governor, it was decided that he should be appointed by Commission from the Governor rather than by Commission under the royal sign manual.[80] To emphasise the President's subordinate position he was required to conduct all correspondence with the Governor through the Colonial Secretary of the Leeward Islands. In addition, all local matters were to be managed by the President subject to the Governor's control.[81] As an external symbol of the President's decreased status his official designation was changed to that of 'Commissioner' in 1889.[82]

The addition of civil and judicial functions to the office of President and the decrease of its administrative responsibilities directly facilitated the abolition of the Legislative Council. The investment of the Governor with powers previously held by the President made a full transfer of legislative responsibility when desired, easier than it would otherwise have been. When to this was added a willingness by the Legislative Council to delegate its responsibilities to an external body, the way was well prepared for the abrogation of the legislature. The need to do this became increasingly evident after the introduction of Crown Colony Government in 1867.

The adoption of Crown Colony Government anticipated but could not prevent the difficulty of obtaining sufficient acceptable members to fill the Legislative Council. The result was recurrent crises between 1867 and 1902, albeit modified by the limited legislative activity of the Council, which served as a stimulus for its abolition. To be completely successful Crown Colony Government depended on the active co-operation of the nominated members especially in view of the constant changes among the administrative officials. In this regard it was important that persons should be appointed on whose support the President could at all times rely.

Crown Colony Government in the Virgin Islands was not the success it was expected to be because nominated members could not always be obtained prepared to give complete support to the President. Their position was regarded as unassailable; members though nominated by the Governor were actually appointed by the Crown, and retained office during pleasure. Being nominated they were not answerable to the people and so could not be removed at periodic elections. Assuming the position of more or less an unofficial opposition, they became in fact, the spokesmen of the people, expressing their discontent of measures with which they were dissatisfied. If it is accepted that Crown Colony Government satisfied one constitutional defect of the representative system by associating power with responsibility, it must be admitted that in the Virgin Islands, the executive could not dominate the legislature and eliminate opposition.

If opposition could not be eliminated, there was the need to keep it under control. Accordingly, a close check was kept on appointments to keep the number of nominated and ex-officio members in the Legislative Council equal.[83] The Constitution Ordinance of 1867 was amended in 1890 to authorise the Governor to fill all vacancies, ex-officio and nominated in the Legislative Council rather than only the nominated as specified in the earlier enactment.[84] To prevent a shortfall of ex-officio members in the Legislative Council, recruitment was made from the Executive Council, members of which were themselves officials. It was not always easy because the abolition and consolidation of offices made it increasingly difficult to secure candidates even for the Executive Council. As a result there was a progressive decrease in the membership of that body from four to three to two in an attempt to meet the difficulty.[85]

The problem of the Executive Council was also the problem of the Legislative Council. Under the Constitution Ordinance of 1867, the three ex-officio members of the Legislative Council were the Governor, the Colonial Secretary and the Colonial Treasurer of the Virgin Islands. The President could not be a member unless specially appointed as such. Following the re-organisation of the civil establishment after 1867, however, the office of Colonial Secretary was abolished, and those of Treasurer and President were merged. To overcome this problem any official whose support could be relied on was appointed to fill vacancies. When such individuals could not be found, the function of the Legislative Council remained in temporary abeyance.

A crisis occurred in the Legislative Council in January, 1896 with regard to the formation of a quorum of three members to transact business. On this occasion the only member of the Council was Joseph B. Romney, and the problem was overcome by the appointment of the Commissioner, Alexander Robert Mackay, and the Medical Officer, J. B. Davson, as members.[86] Another more serious crisis occurred in June, 1896 when the offices of Commissioner and Medical Officer were combined. To form a Legislative Council, Commissioner N. G. Cookman proposed the appointment of Frederick Augustus Pickering and William Dix whom he was certain would support all the measures introduced by him.[87] The proposal was rejected, however, because of the policy of not creating a majority of ex-officio members in the Legislative Council.

Joseph Chamberlain, the Secretary of State for the Colonies, was of the opinion that since there was no suitable person in the Virgin Islands besides the Commissioner who could be appointed as a member of the Legislative Council, it would be advisable to abolish that body altogether. The Governor, or in his absence, the Commissioner, could then make laws for the Presidency. In the meantime necessary laws could be passed by appointing either the Colonial Secretary, the Attorney General, or the Auditor General of the Leeward Islands to the Legislative Council of the Virgin Islands. Together with the

Commissioner and Mr. Romney, a quorum would be formed.[88]

The Secretary of State's suggestion was given in February, 1897, but it was not until 1902 that conclusive action was taken for the abrogation of the legislature. Action was deferred pending the report of the Royal Commission appointed in 1896 to enquire into the condition of the sugar industry in the British West Indies since recommendations relative to constitutional changes were expected from it.[89] The attention of the Colonial Office was also temporarily diverted by constitutional reform elsewhere in the Leeward Islands. Lastly, the appointment of F. A. Pickering as a nominated and Isaac Fonseca and Henry Smith, two recently appointed revenue officers, as ex-officio members of the Legislative Council, removed the urgency of immediate reform. By these appointments a Council consisting of two ex-officio members (the two revenue officers and excluding the President) and two nominated members (J. B. Romney and F. A. Pickering) was formed.[90]

Further exasperation with the Legislative Council developed in 1901 by the resignation of Joseph Romney from the Council as a result of differences with the Commissioner.[91] The occasion was used to put the 1897 decision into effect: in February, 1902, an Ordinance was passed by the Legislative Council enabling the federal legislature to make laws governing the constitution of the Virgin Islands.[92] In pursuance of this enactment the Virgin Islands Act was passed by the federal legislature bringing the Legislative Council to an end and vesting the power of legislating for the Presidency in the Governor of the Leeward Islands.

The Legislative Council held its last meeting on March 24, 1902,[93] but the Executive Council was allowed to continue. When in March, 1901, Governor Fleming suggested the implementation of the Secretary of State's proposal to abolish the Legislative Council, he contemplated the extinction of the Executive Council also. Drawing on the precedent of St. Helena, Chamberlain was willing to consider the possibility of retaining the Executive Council if suitable members could be obtained. The retention of the Commissioner as head of the local executive made it necessary to have such a Council to advise him. It was all the more essential considering the lack of telegraphic or even steam communication to facilitate speedy and regular contact with the Governor in Antigua.[94] The appointment of an Assistant Medical Officer to the Virgin Islands in 1901, and of an Instructor of Agriculture to the recently established Experiment Station, considerably lessened the difficuly of finding suitable members for the Council. Accordingly it was allowed to remain. In terms of the twentieth century politics of the Virgin Islands, the Executive Council wielded considerable modifying influence on legislation proposed by the Governor for the Virgin Islands.

The progressive reduction of the participation of Virgin Islanders generally in the political affairs of the islands constituted an attempt to muzzle their political rights. Prejudices were high against the 'working population' or the 'labouring class' whose calling it was to provide labour, and who were commonly and often quite unfittingly described as 'ignorant.' Equally untenable was the fallacy about the incapacity of Virgin Islanders to legislate. Under Crown Colony Government there was a marked decline in the number of sittings of the legislature, and the volume of legislative business transacted had noticeably decreased compared with, for example, the period of 'mixed' government between 1854 and 1867.

Crown Colony Government failed markedly in the proposal of effective measures to foster the economic development of the Virgin Islands. Instead, economies were sought for in modifications in the civil establishment through the amalgamation and abolition of offices, through the reduction of salaries, and through the participation of the colony in the Leeward Islands Federation. The resultant multiplication of the civil and judicial functions of the President and the vesting of his executive authority in the Governor, together with the transfer of the power of legislation for the Presidency to the federal legislature pointed to the abrogation of the Legislative Council. It had become superfluous though the reported difficuly in securing sufficient members stemmed from the long established prejudice against the inability of the vast majority of Virgin Islanders to legislate.

The abrogation of the Legislative Council deprived the inhabitants of even that measure of 'representation' by nominated members which had existed since the adoption of Crown Colony Government in 1867. Despite the transfer of legislative power to the Governor, the Virgin Islands remained a separate Presidency. Had any of the schemes for uniting the islands with one of the larger Presidencies been adopted, it is evident that they would have ceased to be an entity of government.[95] The continuation of even a severely modified form of government including the Executive Council, members of which seized every opportunity to express local sentiment, would provide the base for the development of the movement for the reinstitution of the representative system in 1950.

[1] C.O. 316/2. Minutes of Assembly, 20 Feb., 1786.
[2] C.O. 239/13. Maxwell to Bathurst, 26 May, 1826. No. 19, and 26 April, 1826. No. 17; C.O. 239/14. Maxwell to Bathurst, 8 Nov., 1826. No. 55.
[3] C.O. 239/39. MacGregor to Aberdeen, 15 April, 1835. No. 89, and enc.
[4] C.O. 239/45. Enc. in Light to Glenelg, 16 Feb., 1837. No. 100.
[5] C.O. 239/46. Enc. in Colebrooke to Glenelg, 6 June, 1837. No. 42.
[6] C.O. 884/1. West Indian. No. 111. Appendix No.3, p.9.
[7] C.O. 239/46. Enc. in Colebrooke to Glenelg, 25 June, 1838. No. 141.
[8] C.O. 239/85. Enc. in Higginson to Grey, 2 Nov., 1848. No. 55, and 3 Nov., 1848. No. 56.
[9] C.O. 239/85. Enc. in Higginson to Grey, 3 Nov., 1848. No. 56.
[10] C.O. 239/81. Cunningham to Grey, 27 Oct., 1846. No. 65; C.O. 239/85. Enc. in Higginson to Grey, 29 Nov., 1848. No. 66.
[11] C.O. 239/81. Enc. in Cunningham to Grey, 27 Oct., 1846. No. 65.
[12] C.O. 239/85. Higginson to Grey, 29 Nov., 1848. No. 66, and enc.
[13] C.O. 239/87. Higginson to Grey, 9 Oct., 1849. No. 62, and enc.; Trevelyan to Merivale, 26 Dec., 1849.
[14] C.O. 239/78. Fitz Roy to Stanley, 11 June, 1845. No. 30; Stanley to Fitz Roy, 14 July, 1845. No. 213.
[15] C.O. 239/88. Drummond Hay to Higginson, 21 Jan., 1850. No. 3.
[16] C.O. 239/89. Enc. in Mackintosh to Grey, 29 April, 1850. No. 33, and 29 Aug., 1850. No. 62; Grey to Mackintosh, 16 Aug., 1850. (Separate).
[17] C.O. 239/64. Enc. in Macphail to Russell, 26 Aug., 1841. No. 70; C.O. 239/65. Enc. in Macphail to Stanley, 6 Dec., 1841. No. 113; C.O. 239/78. Enc. in Fitz Roy to Stanley, 22 July, 1845. (Private); C.O. 239/81. Enc. in Cunningham to Grey, 10 Sept., 1846. No. 58.
[18] C.O. 239/88. Higginson to Grey, 9 March, 1850. No. 14, and 26 March, 1850. No.20; Grey to Higginson, 27 April, 1850. No. 217.
[19] C.O. 239/45. Enc. in Light to Glenelg, 14 March, 1837. No. 123.
[20] Anonymous: Letters from the Virgin Islands, illustrating life and manners in the West Indies. (London, 1843) p. 75.
[21] C.O. 239/13. Maxwell to Bathurst, 26 April, 1826. No. 17., 26 May, 1826. No. 19; C.O. 239/14. Maxwell to Bathurst, 8 Nov., 1826. No. 55; C.O. 407/1. Bathurst to Maxwell, 19 Aug., 1826. No. 33; Huskisson to Maxwell, 24 Dec., 1827; C.O. 239/18. Maxwell to Huskisson, 4 Jan., 1828. No. 1.
[22] C.O. 315/4. Acts Nos. 62-68.
[23] C.O. 239/16. Enc. in Maxwell to Goderich, 24 June, 1827. No. 32.
[24] C.O. 393/5. Goderich to MacGregor, 11 Feb., 1833. No. 1.
[25] C.O. 239/39. MacGregor to Aberdeen, 28 Feb., 1835, No. 64. and enc.; C.O. 239/42. Glenelg to MacGregor, 6 Dec., 1836. No. 104; C.O. 239/45. Light to Glenelg, 2 March, 1837. No. 118, and Light to Glenelg, 14 March, 1837. No. 123; C.O. 239/48. Grey to Spearman, 25 Nov., 1837; C.O. 239/45. Grey to Colebrooke, 30 Jan., 1838.
[26] C.O. 315/6. Act No. 102.
[27] P.P. 1840. Vol. XXXIV, p. 415.
[28] C.O. 239/88. Higginson to Grey, 20 May, 1850. (Private).
[29] C.O. 239/65. Minute by Stephen, on Macphail to Stanley, 6 Dec., 1841. No. 113.

[30] C.O. 239/48. Minute by Stephen, on Light to Glenelg, 16 Feb., 1837. No. 100; Light to Glenelg, 16 Feb., 1837. No. 102, and Light to Glenelg, 18 Feb., 1837. No. 103; C.O. 239/78. Minute by Stephen on Fitz Roy to Stanley, 22 July, 1845. (Private).

[31] C.O. 884/1. West Indian No. 111; Anthony De Vere Philips: Political and Constitutional Developments in the Leeward Islands: 1854-1871. (Unpublished M.A. Thesis, University of London, 1964) pp. 113-18.

[32] Sir Henry Taylor: The Autobiography of Henry Taylor. (Harper, New York, 1885. 2 Vols.) Vol. 1, p. 261.

[33] Anthony De Vere Philips: op.cit., p. 118.

[34] Morley Ayearst: The British West Indies: The Search for Self Government. (George Allen & Unwin Ltd., London, 1960). pp. 26-27.

[35] C.O. 239/96. Mackintosh to Newcastle, 26 Nov., 1853. No. 89.

[36] C.O. 239/95. Minute by Taylor, on Mackintosh to Newcastle, 10 Aug., 1853. No. 69.

[37] Ibid.

[38] C.O. 239/95. Newcastle to Mackintosh, 16 Sept., 1853. No. 58.

[39] C.O. 239/96. Mackintosh to Newcastle, 26 Nov., 1853. No. 89.

[40] C.O. 315/8. Act No. 214.

[41] C.O. 314/3. Mackintosh to Russell, 25 June, 1855. No. 52.

[42] C.O. 314/2. Grey to Mackintosh, 9 Nov., 1854. No. 31, and 16 Nov., 1854. No. 35.

[43] C.O. 314/3. Mackintosh to Grey, 5 Feb., 1855. No. 15, and enc.

[44] C.O. 314/2. Grey to Mackintosh, 26 Jan., 1855. No. 47; C.O. 314/3. Molesworth to Mackintosh, 14 Aug., 1855. No. 4.

[45] C.O. 314/6. Hamilton to Bulwer Lytton, 9 Nov., 1858. No. 18.

[46] C.O. 315/9. Ordinance No. 47.

[47] C.O. 314/11. Enc. in Hamilton to Newcastle, 11 Jan., 1862. No. 130; C.O. 314/15. Enc. in Hill to Cardwell, 22 June, 1865. No. 63

[48] C.O. 314/15. Hill to Cardwell, 6 Sept., 1865. No. 126; C.O. 314/16. Hill to Cardwell, 23 Feb., 1866. No. 36; enc. in Pine to Cardwell, 5 May, 1866, No. 84; Pine to Cardwell, 5 May, 1866. No. 77.

[49] C.O. 314/16. Enc. in Pine to Cardwell, 5 May, 1866. No. 84.

[50] C.O. 314/11. Enc. in Hamilton to Newcastle, 24 Feb., 1862. No. 115.

[51] C.O. 314/16. Enc. in Pine to Cardwell, 20 June, 1866. No. 113.

[52] C.O. 314/16. Enc. in Pine to Carnarvon, 29 Dec., 1866. No. 184.

[53] C.O. 317/32, 37 and 39. Blue Books for 1859, 1866 and 1867; C.O. 314/11. Enc. in Hamilton to Newcastle, 24 Feb., 1862. No. 155.

[54] C.O. 315/9. Ordinance No. 47. Clauses 16, 24 and 25.

[55] Morley Ayearst: op.cit. p. 30.

[56] Cf. H. Wrong: Government of the West Indies. (Oxford, 1923) p. 78.

[57] C.O. 315/17. Carnarvon to Pine, 7 March, 1867. No. 71.

[58] Virgin Islands Ordinances: 1866-1889. Ordinance No. 127. (No.5 of 1867).

[59] P.P. 1871. Vol. 111, pp. 47-52.

[60] Ibid., Clause 10, Sub-section 18.

[61] Virgin Islands Ordinances, 1866-1889. Ordinance No. 1. of 1878.

[62] Ibid., Ordinance No. 4 of 1879.

[63] Ibid., Ordinance No. 1 of 1882.

[64] Ibid., Ordinance No. 2 of 1887.

[65] C.O. 315/10. Ordinance No. 2 of 1890.

[66] Ordinance No. 1 of 1902.

[67] C.O. 314/21. Granville to Pine, 21 April, 1869. No. 62.

[68] C.O. 152/171. Haynes Smith to Knutsford, 30 July, 1888. No. 230.

[69] C.O. 314/21. Pine to Granville, 26 June, 1869. No. 122; Pine to Granville, 10 July, 1869. No. 128.

[70] C.O. 314/21. Granville to Pine, 16 Aug., 1869. No. 106.

[71] C.O. 314/21. Taylor to Moir, 12 Aug., 1869.

[72] C.O. 152/109. Baynes to Kimberley, 25 Sept., 1872. No. 153; Kimberley to Pine, 30 Dec., 1872. No. 197; Virgin Islands Ordinances, 1866-1889: Ordinance No. 2 of 1872.

[73] C.O. 152/109. Baynes to Kimberley, 25 Sept., 1872. No. 156; Kimberley to Pine, 30 Dec., 1872. No. 196; Virgin Islands Ordinances, 1866-1889: Ordinance No. 2 of 1873.

[74] C.O. 152/150. Glover to Kimberley, 26 Oct., 1882. No. 336; Kimberley to Glover, 24 Nov., 1882. No. 274; Virgin Islands Ordinances: 1866-1889: Ordinance No. 4 of 1881.

[75] C.O. 152/153. Neale Porter to Derby, 25 June, 1883. No. 187; Derby to Lees, 15 March, 1884. No. 63; C.O. 152/157. Lees to Derby, 26 May, 1884. No. 175, and enc.

[76] C.O. 152/203. Chamberlain to Fleming, 19 May, 1896. No. 128; C.O. 152/223. Fleming to Chamberlain, 12 Oct., 1897. No. 604.

[77] C.O. 152/171. Enc. in Haynes Smith to Knutsford, 30 July, 1888. No. 230.

[78] C.O. 152/126. Enc. in Berkeley to Carnarvon, 8 Aug., 1876. No. 193.

[79] C.O. 152/112. Enc. in Pine to Kimberley, 11 Jan., 1873. No. 14.

[80] C.O. 152/112. Kimberley to Pine, 6 Feb., 1873. No. 33.

[81] C.O. 152/114. Enc. in Irving to Kimberley, 28 July, 1873. No. 211, C.O. 152/112. Pine to Kimberley, 27 March, 1873. No. 66; C.O. 152/126. Enc. in Berkeley to Carnarvon, 8 Aug., 1876. No. 193.

[82] C.O. 152/176. Haynes Smith to Knutsford, 5 Dec., 1889. No. 333, and 16 Dec., 1889. No. 335; Knutsford to Haynes Smith, 6 Jan., 1890. No. 3.

[83] C.O. 152/168. Holland to Porter, 29 Oct., 1887. No. 192.

[84] C.O. 315/10. Ordinance No. 3 of 1890; C.O. 152/179. Haynes Smith to Knutsford, 7 Nov., 1890. No. 302.

[85] C.O. 314/19. Hill to Buckingham, 24 April, 1868. No. 87; Buckingham to Hill, 24 April, 1868. No. 87; C.O. 152/125. Berkeley to Carnarvon, 24 Jan., 1876. No. 15; Carnarvon to Berkeley, 25 May, 1876. No. 92; C.O. 152/191. Haynes Smith to Ripon, 23 Oct., 1894. No. 247; Ripon to Haynes Smith, 29 Nov., 1894. No. 214.

[86] C.O. 152/201. Fleming to Chamberlain, 8 Jan., 1896. No. 15; Chamberlain to Fleming, 25 Feb., 1896. No. 46.

[87] C.O. 152/215. Enc. in Fleming to Chamberlain, 19 Jan., 1897. No. 49.

[88] C.O. 152/215. Chamberlain to Fleming, 17 Feb., 1897. No. 75.

[89] C.O. 152/220. Chamberlain to Fleming, 22 Feb., 1898. No. 81.

[90] C.O. 152/229. Fleming to Chamberlain, 3 Feb., 1898. No. 91; Chamberlain

to Fleming, 17 March, 1898. No. 109.

[91] C.O. 152/261. Fleming to Chamberlain, 26 Feb., 1901. (Confidential), and enc.; Chamberlain to Fleming, 1 April, 1901.

[92] Ordinance No. 1 of 1902; C.O. 152/271. Melville to Chamberlain, 27 May, 1902. No. 233, and enc.

[93] C.O. 152/170. Enc. in Jackson to Chamberlain, 11 April, 1902. No. 155.

[94] C.O. 152/261. Fleming to Chamberlain, 9 March, 1901. No. 136; Chamberlain to Fleming, 8 May, 1901. No. 193.

[95] C.O. 152/152. Glover to Derby, 10 April, 1883. (Confidential); C.O. 152/153. Enc. in Glover to Derby, 6 June, 1883. No. 156; C.O. 152/168. Enc. in Porter to Holland, 27 Sept., 1887. No. 245.

Chapter 10

Twentieth Century Considerations

By the beginning of the twentieth century conditions in the British Virgin Islands had sunk to a very low level. As a result of poor planning or neglect, the islands possessed anything but a viable economy. The system of social services, such as it was, was in shambles and required complete remodelling. Moreover, the islands were devoid of legislative government, such laws as were made for them being passed by the Governor of the Leeward Islands and the federal legislature. Accordingly, the twentieth century was essentially a period of reconstruction.

A major occupation was experimentation to discover a suitable and effective formula for the economic development of the islands. The rate of political and social change was dependent upon the rate of economic progress and achievement. In turn, political development was considered essential to further and sustain economic and social planning and growth. Improvement in the social services was seen not as an end in itself but essentially as a means of giving impetus to further economic and political advancement.

Following the abrogation of the Legislative Council in 1902, the administration of the British Virgin Islands was the responsibility of the Commissioner assisted by the Executive Council which served primarily in a consultative and advisory capacity. The Council consisted of two officials and one non-official member until 1937, and thereafter by two officials and two non-officials. It was the Executive Council which formed the political nucleus for the eventual reconstitution of legislative government in the Virgin Islands.

Early meetings of the Executive Council were few and irregular, and members met primarily for ceremonial reasons. Initially, therefore, the

Council played an insignificant role in politics since the Commissioner sought to take the sole initiative in the formulation and implementation of policies. Accordingly, it became necessary for the Governor to advise him to have more frequent consultations with the Council. The adoption of this suggestion enabled the Council to play a more influential role in decision making — sometimes to a considerable extent. As a consultative body, it was a sounding board of public opinion, and it interpreted local attitudes which could then be translated into legislative action.

In keeping with their advisory capacity, the members of the Executive Council, either collectively or separately, rarely proposed measures for discussion and adoption. Nevertheless, since the Governor seldom introduced legislation pertaining to the Presidency, especially those of a controversial nature, without first consulting the Council, either directly or indirectly, the Council was allowed the opportunity of influencing the kind of legislation to be introduced. As far as taxation was concerned, the Council was sometimes able to block legislation. In process of time, the Council's ability in administration improved, and its skill was reflected in the firmness of decisions made, in the volume of business transacted (though this depended to a large extent on the Commissioner's initiative), and in the more frequent reversal of the Governor's decisions.

Because of the important functions performed by the Executive Council, schemes involving its abolition were rejected. Such was the case in 1916 when proposals were made for amalgamating the British Virgin Islands with St. Kitts-Nevis in order to simplify the Leeward Islands administration. The plan embraced the abolition of the Executive Council on the ground that it 'cannot be said to serve any useful purpose.' Had the proposal been adopted it would have meant the negation of a significant part of the existing political machinery of the British Virgin Islands. It was, however, rejected as being impracticable since the substitution of the administrator of St. Kitts-Nevis for the Governor of the Leeward Islands was no real improvement but merely the introduction of an additional step in the official hierarchy.

In purely administrative matters the Executive Council functioned well; its failings were more noticeable in the much more important field of economic development. It is true that in the disbursement of public funds, the Council was to some extent able to keep its finger on the financial pulse. But it could only ride on the crest of the wave of economic development, not control or guide it noticeably. No really constructive plan for the economic development of the Presidency emerged from the Council.

So long as the islands enjoyed a measure of well-being, public attention was not drawn to the manner in which the Executive Council operated. It was otherwise during periods of economic depression. At such times, demand was made for greater political power to be extended to the Presidency, based on the contention that economy and efficiency of administration would result. Besides, when an energetic and determined Governor was able to introduce additional taxation this was interpreted by the people as inability of the Executive Council to serve their better interests. Such beliefs undoubtedly influenced action to secure the repeal of seemingly unfavourable legislation and the introduction of a stronger political system based on popular representation.

The move to secure the restoration of legislative government in the British Virgin Islands resulted from economic depression in the 1930's. Unlike other British West Indian islands which were similarly affected, the Virgin Islands did not experience any outbreak of violence. However, constitutional reform was demanded to enable popular participation in government to accelerate the pace of social and economic reconstruction. Political consciousness was stimulated by the introduction of elected members in the legislatures of St. Kitts-Nevis, Antigua and Montserrat in 1936 as well as the passing of the first Organic Act for the United States Virgin Islands the same year. No trade unions or political parties were developed in the British Virgin Islands, but in 1938 the British Virgin Islands Civic League and the British Virgin Islands Pro-Legislative Committee of America were formed and these organisations demanded the reinstitution of an elected legislature in the Presidency.

The weak financial condition of the British Virgin Islands precluded the restoration of a Legislative Council in 1938,[1] and further action was postponed after the outbreak of the Second World War in 1939. Demands for reform were once more raised after the end of the war in 1945, based on the findings and recommendations of the Moyne Commission sent to investigate British West Indian conditions in 1938, and the further adoption of more advanced constitutions in several British West Indian colonies. Two petitions in 1949 from British Virgin Islanders for a partly elected legislative council and an executive council[2] climaxed resolutions adopted by the Closer Union Conference in Montego Bay, Jamaica, in 1947, calling for the extension of more legislative responsibility to West Indians.[3]

The growing economy of the British Virgin Islands both during and after the war made the British Government more accommodating to the idea of constitutional reform. Action here was in keeping with general British attitude elsewhere as it inclined in the direction of the political wind of change. Following recommendations of a Committee appointed for the purpose, a Legislative Council was restored to the British Virgin Islands by the Virgin Islands Constitution Act passed by the Leeward Islands federal legislature in July, 1950.[4]

The Legislative Council introduced in 1950 consisted of eight members of whom two were ex-officio, two nominated and four elected. The life of the Legislative Council was three years and the Commissioner was to serve as its president. For election purposes, the whole Presidency was treated as one constituency. Candidates for election had to satisfy income and property qualifications of £100 and £300 sterling respectively, but were unpaid if elected. Moreover, universal adult suffrage modified by a simple literacy test, and the secret ballot were introduced.

Under the new system, the Governor of the Leeward Islands could no longer legislate for the British Virgin Islands. Henceforth, this power would be exercised by the Legislative Council subject, however, to the Leeward Islands Act of 1871. The Executive Council was retained to serve in an advisory capacity without legislative functions. Of significance was the fact that two members of the Executive Council were to be two of the four elected members of the Legislative Council.

The Constitution of 1950 was envisaged as a temporary measure, not a final solution for the political aspirations of British Virgin Islanders. A significant step towards the recovery of legislative powers previously transferred to the federal legislature was taken in 1953 when the Revocation of Competency Ordinance was passed repealing the General Competency Ordinance of 1890 and the Constitution Ordinance of 1902. These Ordinances respectively had declared all subjects except the imposition and assessment of taxes and duties, but including the constitution of the Virgin Islands, to be within the legislative competence of the federal legislature.[5]

Elections under the Constitution of 1950 produced an imbalance in the legislature in favour of the urban population of Road Town. Also, the fewness of the elected members meant that the separate communities in the Presidency with their separate interests could not be adequately represented, especially those in the rural areas of Tortola and in the outlying islands. Besides, the special qualifications required of voters and candidates imposed restraints on the representative system. Equally important was that the Legislative Council could not exercise control over the Executive. The two ex-officio members automatically supported executive policies and the votes of the nominated members were uncertain as were those of the two elected members on the Executive Council. In case of deadlock, the President could use a casting vote in favour of the Executive. In short, the system could negate the benefits of representation.[6]

Reform in 1954 sought to repair the deficiencies of and correct the anomalies in the constitution. The Presidency was divided into five constituencies or 'districts' to return six elected members to the Legislative Council, two from the Road Harbour district and one from each other. A majority of the members of the Legislative Council was now elected since the number of official and nominated members remained unchanged. Even though candidates did not have to satisfy residence qualifications in order to represent a constituency, they would now have a moral obligation and re-election considerations to represent the interests of the constituents. The basis of representation was further strengthened by the abolition of the income and property qualifications for candidates seeking election and of the literacy test for voters.[7]

The main stimulus for constitutional reform until 1954 had come from within the British Virgin Islands. Subsequent political changes came primarily in response to external events, namely, the abolition of the Leeward Islands Federation in 1956, and the creation of the Federation of the West Indies two years later. Defederation enhanced the political status and legislative power of the British Virgin Islands by making them a colony in their own right and by transferring to the local legislature subjects previously reserved for specific treatment by the federal legislature. While the scope of legislation was widened, the legislature still lacked the power of initiation. This was left to the Commissioner (now called Administrator) acting in consultation with the Executive Council.[8]

The British Virgin Islands did not become a part of the Federation of the West Indies principally because the legislature was jealous of its newly acquired powers and it did not want to transfer these again to an external body.[9] The federation witnessed the abolition of the position of the Governor of the Leeward Islands with the result that the Administrator of the British Virgin Islands assumed the administrative and executive powers hitherto exercised by him.[10] In short, he became the direct royal representative in the colony. The increase in his powers, however, was not accompanied by any analogous increase in the powers of either the Legislative or Executive Councils.

A sense of uncertainty prevailed with regard to the direction which political and constitutional changes should take after 1958. Two alternative courses of action were considered, namely, amalgamation with the Virgin Islands of the United States, and continued development towards self-government in keeping with trends elsewhere in the British Caribbean.

Because of social and economic reasons, a considerable body of opinion in the British Virgin Islands favoured amalgamation with the United States Virgin Islands. Close relationship between the two groups of islands resulting from centuries of relatively unrestricted intercourse and family ties between their peoples had been strengthened by recent developments. Of importance were the periodic Inter-Virgin Islands Conferences of government officials begun in 1951 to undertake full and frank discussions on common problems. These conferences were more than an instrument of co-operation and expression of goodwill. They constituted one of the most powerful media whereby the relations between the two groups already so strong at the bottom could be consolidated at the top. The successes achieved by these conferences reinforced the strong arguments of those who stressed the economic and social benefits to be obtained from some form of political union.

Most of the public discussion on amalgamation was of an unofficial nature. Proponents voiced the opinion that if a referendum were conducted a majority of British Virgin Islanders would favour amalgamation.[11] According to one considered opinion, however, such hopes were 'a hang-over of many years — a sort of conditioned reflex handed down at a time when there was hardly any sign of internal development,'[12] a view that might very well have been correct. Amalgamation was seen essentially as a probable political solution to an apparent problem of economic backwardness. With the development of the economy within recent years and the possibility of still further prosperity in the future, the need for such a solution became less and less urgent. Besides, there has always existed a significant part of the population who for various moralistic and sentimental reasons — attachment to the land and to the British throne, the fear of losing their essentially British Virgin Islands identity and independence as well as their national spirit and distinction — and for hard-headed economic reasons — fear of higher taxation, competition and unemployment — opposed the idea of such a union.

Greater obstacles to amalgamation exist stemming from the fact that both groups of islands are dependencies. Amalgamation has not only to be approved locally but also in London and Washington. The British Government has already accepted in principle willingness to be guided by local popular opinion,[13] but it is not certain that the United States Administration would be similarly inclined. For that Administration, territories are an expensive asset; it is not enough that the British Virgin Islands possess high potential for tourism. The strategic benefits to be obtained from the advantageous geographic position of the colony may not prove sufficiently attractive for their acquisition even if majority opinion in the United States Virgin Islands favours it.

As time passed, the question of amalgamation appeared to be mere speculation somewhat in the moot class. As such, political development followed the line already laid down in other British West Indian colonies, that is, towards internal self-government and eventual political independence. For training towards that end, attention was focused on educating legislative members for responsibility in an essential aspect of parliamentary government — the ministerial system.

The 'Committee System' had been introduced as early as 1952[14] when two Committees, the 'Public Works and Communications Committee' and the 'Trade and Production Committee' had been formed to reflect the emphasis on economic development. Each Committee consisted of a chairman (who was an elected member on the Executive Council), as well as an official and unofficial member of the Legislative Council. By involving elected representatives in the decision-making process it was hoped to reduce criticism of the executive.[15] The Committee System, however, did not operate satisfactorily, its chief failing being 'responsibility without power.' While Committees were charged with certain responsibilities, policy-making was essentially the province of the Administrator, the Chairmen of Committees serving merely as advisers. They lacked even the authority to issue orders to government officers who were responsible directly to the Administrator in discharging their duties. Alternatively, they had to share with the administration the blame for failure.[16]

Following the constitutional reforms of 1954, the Committee System was modified to become the Membership System. Heads of Committees were no longer Chairmen but 'Members' who now had to support executive decisions in public or resign.[17] However, full ministerial responsibility was not accorded. Members occupied a middle position and their duties could be regarded 'as something more than completely advisory and something less than completely executive.' Members were fully entitled to advise heads of Departments, but 'matters of policy and the allocation of funds should always be referred to the Commissioner.'[18] It meant that Members had to support policies which they did not formulate.

It was not until 1960 that an attempt was made to define in writing the special responsibilities and the position of Members. The essential features of the Membership System as stated was that 'Members should be closely identified with the formulation and execution of policy in regard to the Departments and subjects falling within their purview.'[19] Nevertheless, Members' position vis-à-vis the heads of Departments and the Administrator was very vague since it was further stated that Members were not to be involved in the day to day administration of Departments or with the executive functions of government. Members became confused, and later attempts to clarify relationships only succeeded in compounding the confusion.[20] Effective control over the formulation of policy remained in the hands of the Administrator to the frustration of Members and elected representatives in general.

Political discussions after 1954 emphasised the need for a greater measure of executive control by local representatives. A third elected member to the Executive Council was sought in 1959,[21] while the demand in 1965 was for 'nothing less than the degree of control inherent in the ministerial system.'[22] These were positive evidences of greater political awareness and maturity of British Virgin Islanders acquired largely through the operation of the Legislative Council. Membership therein not only permitted the free expression of public opinion, but it forced upon the executive an awareness of the needs of the people. No longer was it possible for the executive to remain complacent over local problems.

The Legislative Council did not have the desired control over the executive, but its performance as a stern critic of executive action or inaction served as a compelling force demanding further action. As shown in its attitude towards the West Indian Federation, the Legislative Council demonstrated its ability to guide the future political destiny of the islands. The demand for a ministerial system showed an awareness of the need to strengthen the body politic to achieve economic development. At the same time, it expressed the legislature's earnest desire to be given that power.

Implicit in local political aspirations was the principle that any new constitutional arrangement should, at least in part, ensure the elected members more initiative in the direction of the colony's affairs so that a solid basis for self-government could be effectively laid. The principle was observed in the constitutional reforms of 1966 following the report of a constitutional commissioner, Dr. Mary Proudfoot, the previous year, which formed the basis of the new arrangements.[23] The elective element in both the Legislative and Executive Councils was increased: the former was now given seven elected members to three non-elected compared with six to four previously, while the latter was given three elected to two non-elected as against two to three hitherto. The life of the legislature was increased from three to four years.

In addition, the ministerial system was introduced catering for three Ministers, one of whom would be Chief Minister. The Administrator was to appoint as Chief Minister the elected member who in his opinion was best able to command the support of a majority of the elected members in the Legislative Council. In turn, the Chief Minister would advise the Administrator on the appointment and dismissal of the other two Ministers. The special responsibilities of the Administrator (or Governor since 1970) were defence and internal security, external affairs, the public service, the courts and, for a time, finance. Other matters were left to the control of the Ministers, and the Administrator had to seek and act on the advice of the Executive Council.[24] The new system was an advancement over the old, but full internal self-government is not yet a reality.

Political and constitutional changes in the British Virgin Islands in the present century were largely dependent upon the state of their economy. Attempts made prior to 1950 to restore the Legislative Council failed essentially because of the poverty of the islands. Constitutional advancement from 1950 stemmed largely from an awareness of the value of political action in the solution of economic problems but also because of the enhanced economy.

As suggested by the political changes, economic recovery in the British Virgin Islands can be divided into two phases with the Second World War (1939-1945) separating them. The first phase was marked by severe fluctuations in planning and achievement with efforts made by a somewhat ineffective administration to instil in an agricultural community, conditions of organised labour. With the strengthening of the political and administrative machinery after

The Agricultural Experiment Station, Road Town, Tortola

the war, development was more rapid and continuous.

By the beginning of the twentieth century, the economic organisation of the British Virgin Islands possessed two basic features. Firstly, although the islands were predominantly agricultural, there was an absence of large-scale plantation-type cultivation, agriculture being undertaken on small peasant holdings; and secondly, emphasis was placed on live-stock production for export.[25] Economic planning during the ensuing decades sought to build upon these bases. An Agricultural Department centering on an Experiment Station established in September, 1900, and located on the outskirts of Road Town, Tortola, was made the focal point for economic development. The Station was intended to demonstrate to farmers the best methods of soil management and cultivation, and by experimentation under local conditions to improve the overall quality of plants and animals. Periodic agricultural shows and lectures also would serve to awaken interest in scientific agriculture. An essential part of its functions was the introduction and encouragement of new economic crops.

The major effort of the Station was directed towards encouragement of cotton, sugar and tobacco production. Cotton had never completely disappeared from the British Virgin Islands and in 1901 its cultivation was revived. Progress was steady, encouraged by loans under a Cotton Industry Aids Act. All cotton produced was purchased by the administration on a ready-cash basis and a ready market was provided by the Fine Cotton Spinners' and Doublers' Association Limited in Britain at guaranteed prices.[26] Industrial incentive was provided by the installation of an oil-engine in 1910 to facilitate ginning and by the introduction of a bonus or deferred payment system in 1916.[27] Under this system, uncertainty over payment was eliminated since payment was made to farmers in accordance with the market outlook and later, when all accounts had been received, they were allocated 75 percent of the credit balance.

From about 1908 cotton proved of considerable benefit to the British Virgin Islands, being second only to livestock among exports. Table 11 shows the quantity of cotton exported from 1904 when shipment started to 1920 when the boom ended.[28] Production collapsed after a post-war boom as a result of a combination of circumstances: unfavourable marketing conditions, farmers' notion that they were not receiving fair returns especially after abolition of the bonus system in 1919, and more so, infestation by the pink-boll worm and cotton stainer.[29] No effective measures were adopted to deal with these pests; for example, the only action taken to control the pink-boll worm was the ill-understood close season, that is, the clearing and temporary abandonment of cotton plots. Only 1,802 pounds of

Table 11

Cotton Exports of the British Virgin Islands, 1904-1920

Year	Weight (lb)	Year	Weight (lb)	Year	Weight (lb)
1904-5	4,100	1910-11	50,337	1916-17	14,083
1905-6	7,775	1911-12	43,003	1917-18	10,403
1906-7	10,033	1912-13	31,775	1918-19	23,332
1907-8	32,520	1913-14	28,035	1919-20	23,425
1908-9	42,044	1914-15	31,361	1920-21	49,682
1909-10	23,139	1915-16	22,750		

cotton lint were exported in 1923 compared with 49,682 in 1920, and production in subsequent years was negligible.[30]

Extensive cotton cultivation was revived in 1935, and the adoption of remedial measures to off-set the initial outbreak of disease produced good results; between 1937 and 1939 production rose from 19,185 to 57,238 pounds.[31] However, the outbreak of the Second World War curtailed production, and by 1943 the industry had not only ceased to be a factor of economic significance, but the crop, to all intents and purposes, had passed out of existence.[32]

Along with cotton, an attempt was made to re-awaken interest in sugar production through experiments with better varieties and the maintenance of a small Station works to manufacture muscovado sugar at a moderate rate to growers.[33] These methods were fruitless; sugar so made was of poor quality and suffered from severe competition from imports from other Leeward Islands. Consequently sugar production ceased in the 1920's, all canes grown being used solely for the manufacture of rum, encouraged by the United States Prohibition.

With the failure of cotton and sugar production in the 1920's attempts were made to salvage the economy through tobacco cultivation. Experiments had been started in 1920; in April, 1923 a cigar factory was opened, and in 1924 and 1925, as many as 32,489 and 87,857 cigars respectively were manufactured. By 1927 a total of 118,467 cigars were being produced, and development was climaxed by the establishment of a private cigar factory.[34] Thereafter, however, the tobacco industry declined rapidly due to attack by the tobacco beetle and unfavourable marketing opportunities aggravated by the world depression of 1929-1932.

In view of the importance of livestock to the economy of the British Virgin Islands, especially since there was a ready if fluctuating market in neighbouring islands, it is surprising that more attention was not shown towards improving strains and otherwise creating conditions necessary for expansion. Interest was limited to an occasional importation of breed animals but any real improvement was meagre before 1939.[35]

The Second World War marked a turning point for the livestock industry and for the economy of the islands in general. The establishment of military installations in the United States Virgin Islands resulted in an increased demand simultaneously for livestock and labourers from the British Virgin Islands.[36] Since there were fewer men in the Presidency to work, cotton cultivation was neglected and emphasis was placed on livestock production. The swing from agriculture to stock-rearing continued after the war when immigration restrictions in the American Virgins forced many British Virgin Islanders to return home. The general shortage of meat throughout the Caribbean enhanced the possibility of other markets.[37]

The main objective of economic planning after the war was the promotion of the livestock industry as the basis of the agricultural economy of the British Virgin Islands. Efforts were made to improve breeds and to promote grassland management and soil and water conservation. Specialised opinion from overseas was sought and obtained. The major obstacle was farmers' lack of capital, and beginning in 1951, it was the administration's main concern to provide it. Substantial financial contributions were obtained from the British Government compared with the dribble of the pre-World War II period.

Three schemes in operation in the Presidency by 1954 for agricultural development were all concerned with the live-stock industry. In the absence of banking and loan facilities, an agricultural credit scheme was introduced to provide farmers with loans from a revolving fund for the improvement and extension of pastures with the farms as collateral. Loans bore an interest rate of three percent and were to be repaid in instalments over a period of four years.[38] The other two schemes were necessary to enable maximum benefit to be derived from the first: one was for the purchase of improved breeds by the Agricultural Department; and, the other was to secure additional pastures for livestock to promote breeding and the perennial availability of stock to potential buyers. Free grants totalling $26,600 (U.S.) were obtained from Colonial Development and Welfare funds to finance these projects. The result was improved methods of grassland management including the use of fertilisers and the introduction of the pangola grass, the development of the Nellthrop breed of cattle, and the acquisition by government in the Paraquita Bay area of 120 acres of land to be used as a holding ground.[39]

Appreciable success was achieved from the government's policy as illustrated by Table 12 giving official statistics of livestock production at three different periods.[40] Production in 1954 was 23.8 percent higher than that of 1946; in 1962 it was more than double that of 1954 thereby justifying the measures adopted for improvement. Since farmers tended to conceal the actual numbers of their livestock, to an estimated 20 percent, it is evident that the islands had more livestock than recorded.

Table 12

Livestock Census, British Virgin Islands

LIVESTOCK	1946	1954	1962
Cattle	4,560	4,519	6,000
Pigs	668	1,160	5,000
Sheep	710	1,130	2,500
Goats	3,034	4,443	10,000
Equines	725	762	1,100

By the early 1960's the economic goal was not merely the development of production but the achievement of economic self-sufficiency in the shortest possible time. Reliance on livestock alone was unlikely to achieve this end especially since export values were beginning to decline. The result was a progressive swing towards tourism.

Official interest in tourism was shown as early as 1953 when a Hotels Aid Ordinance was passed to encourage hotel construction, though the measure suffered from later changes in policy.[41] Before the end of the decade, however, the prospects for tourism were better. A tourist boom in the United States Virgin Islands provided the opportunity for a parallel development in the British Virgin Islands. Since the American territory was attracting away British Virgin Islanders it was necessary to develop an equivalent economy if these people were to be retained. Agriculture was unlikely to improve the local standard of living; tourism could; and besides, its development was likely to promote agriculture.[42] Consequently, in 1961 the administration accepted as a 'firm policy' the promotion of tourism as the mainspring of development.[43] Since then there has been a steady increase in this 'industry'.

Meanwhile the relatively increased prosperity after the Second World War allowed increasing attention to be given to the problem of taxation. Except for minor amendments in customs duties in 1902, 1905 and 1919, the system of taxation existing at the end of the nineteenth century remained virtually unchanged until around the middle of the twentieth century.[44] Lack of adequate administrative personnel to assess and collect revenues was the principal condition discouraging increases in taxation in view of the popular tendency at evasion. The first tentative beginning was made in 1946 with the introduction of an income tax, and the gradual stengthening of the executive and administrative machinery after 1950 allowed further

The Beef Island Runway

The Wickham's Cay Development Project

additions to be made. Thus in 1956 the land tax was made a fixed charge on each acre instead of being based on the assessed value. In addition, the existing graduated assessment on the notional value of houses was replaced by a regular charge of one percent. The export tax on livestock was raised in 1960, and the import tax on motor spirit, fuel oil and alcohol was increased in 1963. In each case the increase was due to the growth of the livestock industry and of tourism, but tax proposals had to be modified to encourage investment in order to facilitate these industries.[45]

The tempo of economic activity generated by private and public spending was assisted by substantial grants-in-aid from the British Government, which were awarded regularly from 1946.[46] These grants constituted a sizable portion of budgetary expenditures reaching as much as 68 percent in 1956 and 71 percent in 1961.[47] Since then increasing local revenues permitted a reduction; by 1963 grants had already fallen to as low as 52.5 percent and further reductions were experienced in later years.[48]

As a result of increased prosperity expressed in increases in government revenues from $5,179 in 1901, to $261,928 in 1961, and to $613,262 in 1964, significant advances could be achieved in the field of social services. As late as 1949 it was reported that 'few projects have been executed in the past and it cannot be said that the Development problems . . . have been tackled yet.'[49] Since then essential services such as education and housing have been undertaken or developed — for example, primary education was expanded while secondary education, begun since 1943, was stabilised and strengthened after a weak and uncertain start;[50] and, housing projects, such as those at Huntums Ghut and Macnamara, were completed. Besides, many other private dwellings were constructed.[51]

The area most beneficially affected by the economic resurgence was communication since developments here could in turn give further impetus to economic growth. Until 1958 there were only twelve miles of motorable roads in the British Virgin Islands together with over sixty miles of unsurfaced earth roads.[52] Within the next twelve years the road system was vastly improved and extended with the construction of Drake's Highway linking West End and East End of Tortola, the Queen Elizabeth's Bridge joining Tortola and Beef Island, and the Waterfront Highway, part of the Wickham's Cay development project. In addition, airstrips were constructed on Beef Island and Virgin Gorda to cater to the tourist traffic. The increased tempo of business activities necessitated the installation and development of telephone and telecommunication services in the 1960's. At the same time, desire for additional amenities of the sophisticated modern society was reflected in the introduction of radio broadcasting.[53]

Increase in local revenues together with the relative decrease in external aid point to the conclusion that the British Virgin Islands seem well on the way towards achieving their primary objective, namely, the attainment of economic self-sufficiency. Nevertheless, the colony still suffers from capital deficiency. Apart from agriculture and tourism capital generating enterprises are practically absent. There is a lack of any large-scale manufactures, and the only mineral, salt, is not obtainable in commercial quantities.

Lack of adequate opportunities for full employment has resulted in the continuous emigration, both temporary and permanent, of British Virgin Islanders. Emigration has saved the colony from acute population pressures, but at the same time, by draining the islands of essential skills, it has served to retard development. The loss has not been replaced by the immigrants from the Commonwealth Caribbean who have entered within recent years. Consequently, there has been almost complete reliance on the initiative of political leaders for planning and direction for economic development.

The history of the British Virgin Islands in the twentieth century has demonstrated the importance of legislative government in achieving progress. When the islands were more or less under external control before 1950, economic growth was negligible; thereafter, the restoration of a legislature enabling greater local participation in directing local affairs has been followed by rapid economic expansion. As such, therefore, the strengthening of the political machinery by permitting more self-government seems imperative if greater prosperity and eventually complete economic self-sufficiency are to be achieved.

[1] Governor, Leeward Islands to the Commissioner, British Virgin Islands, 24 Oct., 1938. No. 2397; Governor, Leeward Islands to the Secretary of State for the Colonies, 29 Oct., 1938. No. 57; Secretary of State to the Governor, 21 Dec., 1938. No. 31.
[2] The Petitions, dated October, 1949 and December, 1949 respectively, were worded similarly.
[3] Cmd. 7291. Conference on the Closer Association of the British West Indian Colonies, Montego Bay, Jamaica, 11-19 Sept., 1947. Part I. Report. (London, H.M.S.O., 1948) p. 7.
[4] Virgin Islands Constitution Act. Leeward Islands No. 1. of 1950.

[5] Virgin Islands Ordinance No. 7 of 1953.

[6] Ref. No. Adm. 15/48. Cruikshank to Macdonald, 26 May, 1953.

[7] Virgin Islands Constitution and Elections. Virgin Islands No. 7 of 1954.

[8] Leeward Islands. No. 13/0031. Blackburne to Wallace, 27 Jan., 1956.

[9] Cf. Extracts from the Minutes of a Meeting of the Legislative Council of the Virgin Islands held on 14 Sept., 1951. (Mimeo.) p. 4; 25 Feb., (Mimeo.) p. 12, Paragraph 118; and 9 July, 1957.

[10] Letters Patent passed under the Great Seal of the Realm constituting the Office of Administrator of the Virgin Islands and making provision for the Government thereof, 22 December, 1959.

[11] British Virgin Islands Newspaper 'Island Sun', 22 June, 1963, p. 4. Article by Mr. Douglas Williams.

[12] Editorial, 'Island Sun', 18 January, 1964, p. 5.

[13] 'Islands Sun', 11 January, 1964, p. 1; Address of His Honour the Administrator at the opening of the Second Session of the Fifth Legislative Council, 17 Nov., 1964. (Mimeo.) p. 5.

[14] Extract from Governor's speech to Members of the Legislative Council of the British Virgin Islands, 11 Jan., 1952; Governor to the Secretary of State for the Colonies, 14 Jan., 1952. No. 57.

[15] Extract from the Minutes of a Joint Meeting of the Executive Council and the Finance Committee of the Legislative Council held at Government House, Tortola, 9 January, 1952.

[16] Address by His Excellency the Governor at the Opening of the Second Legislative Council of the British Virgin Islands, 16 Oct., 1954 (Mimeo) p. 5.

[17] Address by His Excellency the Governor at the opening of the Legislative Council of the British Virgin Islands, 16 Oct., 1954. (Mimeo.) p. 6.

[18] Memorandum of His Honour, the Commissioner (Col. H. A. C. Howard) on the Organization of Duties — Members Offices, 25 October, 1954. (Mimeo).

[19] Memorandum on the Membership System as in existence in January, 1960.

[20] Circular No. 17/62. Operation of the Membership System, 6 Nov., 1962; Circular No. 18/62. Operation of the Membership System, 23 Nov., 1962.

[21] Brief on the Constitution of the Virgin Islands with particular reference to the Executive Council. (Mimeo., 1959).

[22] Debates of the Legislative Council of the British Virgin Islands. Hansard of the Meeting of 12 October, 1965.

[23] Colonial No. 36. British Virgin Islands. Report of the Constitutional Commissioner — 1965. (London, H.M.S.O., 1965).

[24] Cmnd. 3129. Report of the British Virgin Islands Constitutional Conference 1966. (London, H.M.S.O., 1966).

[25] J. L. Illingworth, Report on the Present Agricultural situation in the British Virgin Islands. (Mimeo., 1930); A. V. Hall, Data on Land Tenure in the British Virgin Islands. (Mimeo., 1943); West Indian Census of Agriculture in Barbados, the Leeward Islands, the Windward Islands and Trinidad and Tobago. (The Government Printery, Jamaica, 1950), pp. 8-9.

[26] C. O. Wynne to the Colonial Secretary, 24 July, 1906 and 5 Oct., 1906. No. 137; Robert Earl to the Colonial Secretary, 27 June, 1908; T. L. E. Clarke to the Commissioner of Agriculture, 10 May, 1915.

[27] Leslie Jarvis to the Secretary, British Cotton Growing Association, 15 March, 1910; Peebles to the Secretary, B.C.G.A., 6 Nov., 1919. No. 320/263.

[28] Report on the Agricultural Department, Tortola, 1921-22 and 1922-23. (Barbados, 1924) p. 25.

[29] Ibid., p. 24; J. L. Illingworth, op. cit., pp. 4-5.

[30] Report on the Agricultural Department, Tortola, 1923-24 to 1927-28. (Barbados, 1929) p. 2.

[31] W. Campbell Roy, Report on the Botanic Station, Tortola, during the period September 1, 1932 to August 31, 1937. (Mimeo.); C. C. Skeete, Report on a Visit to the British Virgin Islands and St. Thomas, June 18-30, 1938. (Mimeo.); W. Campbell Roy, Report on the Agricultural Department, Tortola, during the period 1 September, 1937 to 31 December, 1940.

[32] Annual Report of the Agricultural Department, 1942, p. 2.; Memorandum from A. V. Hall to the Commissioner, 19 November, 1943, in which he refers to the 'apparent finality of this year's cotton crop'; J. V. Lockrie, 'Cotton Industry, British Virgin Islands.' Memorandum dated 3 Dec., 1947; H. R. Hutson to the Commissioner, 8 Dec., 1947.

[33] Reports on the Experiment Station, Tortola, Virgin Islands, 1905-1906 and 1909-1910, p. 6 and p. 11 respectively.

[34] Reports on the Agricultural Department, Tortola, for 1921-22 and 1922; 1923-24 to 1927-28.

[35] Report on the Experiment Station . . . 1905-1906, p. 6; Report on the Botanic and Experiment Station . . . 1913-1914, p. 23; W. Campbell Roy, Report on the Botanic Station . . . 1932-1937, pp. 10-11.

[36] W. Campbell Roy, Report on the Agricultural Department . . . 1937-1940., pp. 2-6; Annual Report of the Agricultural Department of the British Virgin Islands, 1942 (Mimeo.) p. 2.

[37] Governor, Leeward Islands, to the Secretary of State for the Colonies, 11 Sept., 1951. No. 136.

[38] Public Notice, 18 Jan., 1952. No. 9/52.

[39] Biennial Reports on the British Virgin Islands for 1957-1958, 1959-1960 and 1961-1962.

[40] G. L. Bellot and G. E. V. Dawson, Report on the Livestock Census, 1954. (Mimeo., 1954); D. E. Faulkner, Report on Livestock Development in the British Virgin Islands. (Mimeo., April, 1962) p. 13.

[41] A. de K. Frampton and H. C. Biggs, Report and Development Programme. (Mimeo., 1957).

[42] Carleen O'Loughlin, A Survey of Economic Potential, Fiscal Structure and Capital Requirements of the British Virgin Islands. (Supplement to Vol.11, No.3, Social and Economic Studies, U.W.I., 1962) pp. 6-9.

[43] Statement of Government policy on the application of the Aliens Land Holding Regulation Act, 27 October, 1961.

[44] Memorandum on Taxation, 1950 by the Commissioner of the British Virgin Islands.

[45] Report of the Fiscal Committee. (Mimeo., 1960); Carleen O'Loughlin, A Survey of Economic Potential . . . of the British Virgin Islands. (1962).

[46] Address by the President on the opening of the British Virgin Islands

Legislative Council, 16 Oct., 1954. (Mimeo.) p. 4.

[47] Address by His Honour the Administrator at the Opening of the Third Session of the Fourth Legislative Council at Road Town on the 10 Jan., 1963. (Mimeo.) p. 6.

[48] Address delivered by His Honour, the Administrator over Radio ZBVI on 13 Sept., 1965. (Mimeo.); Address by the Administrator to the Legislative Council, Dec., 1965. (Mimeo.)

[49] Report of the Development and Planning Committee, Dec., 1949. (Mimeo.)

[50] Report of a Committee to review the Education System of the Virgin Islands. (Mimeo., 1957?)

[51] Biennial Reports on the British Virgin Islands for 1959-1960 and 1961-1962.

[52] Ibid.

[53] West Indies Chronicle. Special Issue. British Virgin Islands. (Published by the West India Committee, November, 1969).

Index

Abolition Act (1807) 72, 97, 103
absentee-landlordism 72, 74, 77, 85,
    131, 191
Act of Emancipation 93, 121
administration
    introduced 22
    decadence 23
    strengthened 24, 25-26, 31, 33
    reorganised 207, 208-209, 211,
        213
    developed 231-233
administration of justice (see judicial
    system)
Administrator
    replaced Commissioner 222
    executive powers
        increased 222-223, 224, 225
    appointed Chief Minister 226
    replaced by Governor 226
aged 110, 114, 147, 169, 171
agricultural credit scheme 230
American Civil War 138
Amsterdam 50
Anegada
    part of the Virgin Islands 2
    remained British 13
    settlement 47
    cotton cultivation in 47
    vessels stranded on 64
    land transfer 135-136

    sub-treasurer for 150
    doctor's visit to 177
    school built in 179-180, 183
    shipwrecks on 199
Anglicans 90-91, 180
Anguilla 11, 48, 59, 104, 160
Antigua
    firm British footing in 22
    free port in 52
    convoys from 57
    trade with 59
    British troops despatched
        from 157
    reinforcements from 158
    seat of government 200
    communication with 212
    constitutional reform in 220
Anti-Slavery Society 93
apprenticeship (of slaves)
    introduced 93
    unnecessary period 120
    regulations governing 120-121
    resistance to 121
    working arrangements 122-123
    employment 124
    end of 124-125
    (of liberated Africans) 97-103,
        116
    (of children of paupers) 173
arson 83

articled servants 123-124
Assembly
  initial attempt to create 26
  instituted 30-31
  composition 32
  unsettled state 34-37
  friction with Council 44, 165,
    196-198, 200
  response to emancipation plan 93
  changes in 148
  control over taxation 151-154
  rejects petition for education
    grant 155-156
  reform 1854 158
  attitude to debt payment 162-163
  selection of candidates for public
    relief 169-170
  avoided expenditure on social
    services 169-170, 178
  replica of House of Commons 194
  functions 195
  attitude to taxation 154, 158,
    162, 164, 196-198
  replaced by Legislative
    Council 203
artisans 73, 78, 81
asylum (lunatic) 187, 188
attorneys 73
Atrevido 98

Bahamas 52
banking facilities (absence of) 230
Barbados
  Leeward Islands separated
    from 21, 22
  4½% levy on 31
  trade with 59
  packet station transferred to 141
Batterie, Captain Peter 20
batteries 27, 30
Baugher's Bay 107
Beef Island
  population 22, 23
  free from cholera 176
  airstrip on 233
Bell, Sir Peter van 5

benefit societies (see friendly
  societies)
Berkeley, Leeward Islands
  governor 178
Bermuda 52
bills of exchange 179
Bishop
  of Barbados 91
  of Antigua 155, 179, 180
Bisse, Thomas 20
Blackstock, William 48
Board of Education 181
Board of Health 175, 176
Board of (Poor Law) Guardians 114,
  172-173, 174
Board of Trade 37
Board of Visitors 179
book-keepers 73
Bott, Rev. Alexander 179
Brandenburgers 5, 6
Brazil 61
Bredal, Erik
  settles St. John 8
  disputes British claims 9
British navy 44
British North America 28, 64
British Virgin Islands Civic
  League 220
British Virgin Islands Pro-Legislative
  Committee of America 220
Bristol 59
budgetary deficits 161, 164
Burn, W. L. 71
Burt, Governor William 36, 50

Cadwallader, John 88
Caicos Islands 52
Candelaria 98
Candler, Captain 23
Carlisle, Earl of 6, 9
carpenters 78
Catholic faith 27
cattle
  in Barbuda 19
  slave property 84
  emphasis on 136

reared for export 138, 231
fall in prices 142
tax on 153, 156, 157
removal of tax 158
(see also, livestock)
cattle-mills 79
Chads, President J. C. 156-157
Chalkley, Thomas 88
Chalwill, Abraham 48
Chamberlain, Joseph
plan for education 183
suggested abolition of Legislative
Council 211
retained Executive Council 212
Chance 11
Chapman, Walter 11
charcoal 138, 139
Charles I 6
Chateau Bellair 156
Chief Justice
appointed 33, 35
salary withheld 36
authorised to grant trade
licences 54
paid by British Government 159,
170
office reorganised 160
paid by Virgin Islands 164
position abolished 185
Chief Minister 226
Chipman, Doctor 178
cholera 142, 176, 177
Christianity 29
(see religious teaching also)
Church of England 179
(see Anglicans and clergyman
also)
Churchill, President 174
cigar factory 229
cigars 229
circuit court 26, 29, 185-186
Citters, Arnout van 3
civil establishment
(see administration)
Claxton, Robert 105, 107, 108
clergyman (Anglican)
first appointed 88

financial provision for 90
provided education 91, 170,
178-179
failed to establish friendly
societies 171
withdrawal to St. Thomas 189
rivalry with Methodists 189, 191
clerks 73
Closer Union Conference (Montego
Bay, 1947) 220
close season 228
coaling station 133
cochineal 48
Codrington, Governor
Christopher 5, 6, 19
coffee 53-54, 55, 60-61
Colbert, Jean-Baptiste 10
Colebrooke, Sir William 201
Collector of Customs
appointed 33
gave falsified clearances 54
identified foreign produce
exported 55
disposed of liberated
Africans 97-99, 105
reported on treatment of
Africans 100
established Kingstown 107-109
inadequate to prevent
smuggling 149
remained after 1853 riot 157
Colon 141
Colonel of the Military Regiment 33
colonial agent 33
Colonial Development and
Welfare 230
Colonial Land and Emigration
Commissioners 135
Colonial Office
disliked open ports 64
opposed metairie system 111
unable to improve Virgin Islands
agriculture 159
favoured constitutional
reform 197, 201
recommended abolition of
Assembly 202

reform in the Leeward
Islands 212
Colonial Secretary (of Virgin Islands)
appointed 24, 33
duties 25
member of Executive
Council 206, 211
office abolished 160, 211
(of the Leeward Islands) 211
coloureds (see free negroes and
coloureds)
Colquhoun, Patrick 75-77
Columbus, Christopher 1, 6
commercial crisis 126, 142
Commissioner (of Education) 181
Commissioner (of the Virgin Islands)
replaced President 209
medical and legal duties 178,
185, 208-209
administrative control 218-219
president of the Legislative
Council 221
replaced by Administrator 222
Committee on Public Buildings 172
committee system 196, 224
Commonwealth Caribbean 234
communications 122, 175, 189,
212, 233-234
Company of America 10
compensation (slave) 93, 173, 196
consolidated debt
accumulated 64-65, 147-148
difficulties in paying 161-163
liquidated 163
constabulary
absence during slavery 170
appointed for Kingstown 109
quelled 1848 disturbances 155
beaten in 1853 riots 156
involved in 1856
disturbances 151
maintained order 184
constituencies
(1734) 26
(1776) 32
(1837) 201
(1950) 221

(1954) 222
constitutional reforms
Constitution Act (1776) 32-33,
75
Constitution Act (1837) 201
Constitutional Amendment Act
(1854) 158, 203, 204
Constitution Ordinance
(1859) 158, 204-206
Constitution Ordinance
(1867) 206, 210, 211
Constitution Ordinance
(1902) 212
Virgin Islands Constitution Act
(1950) 221
Continental System 62
contracts (written and verbal) 128,
129, 131
convoy system
instituted 43, 57
diluted defence 44
Virgin Islands a rendezvous 56
value 57, 59
lapsed 62
Cookman, N. G. 183, 211
Cooper Island 47
coopers 78
copper mining 27, 112, 139
cotton
small quantities produced 24
expanded cultivation 27, 29, 38,
47
prices 46, 61
exports 46, 47, 60
seized by privateers 49
decline in production 61, 93,
138, 148, 152, 229
produced by slaves 84
cultivation revived 138, 142,
228-229
Cotton Industry Aids Act 228
Council
first created 26, 30-31
dismantled 31
functions 26, 195
composition 32, 73
unsettled state 34-37

replica of House of Lords 194
friction with Assembly 44,
    196-198, 200
opinion of Assembly 199
abolished 199
(see Executive Council also)
Council of Trade and Plantations 3,
    13, 22, 25
Court Bill 34-37, 38
Court of Chancery 65, 134, 135
Court of Justice 25, 34, 185-186
    (see judicial system also)
Crab Island (see Vieques)
Criminal Code 131
Crown Colony Government
    introduced 143, 158-159, 202,
        206, 213
    reasons for 205-206
    essential features 205
    value 188, 213
    failure to fulfil hopes 159, 207,
        213
    weaknesses 210-213
Cuba 61
Curacao 53
currency, shortage of 123, 128
curricula 91, 182
customs duties 149, 153, 158
HMS Cygnet 85

Danes
    settled St. Thomas and St.
        John 6-7, 8-9
    purchased St. Croix 12
    disputed right of sovereignty 6-13
    trade with Tortola 24
    vessels taken by privateers 49-50
    sugar exports through Virgin
        Islands 54
    slave trade 71-72
Danish West India Company 6, 8, 12
Danish West Indies
    acquired 6-13
    taken by Britain 13-14, 52, 57,
        62

Virgin Islands trade with 59, 175
recognition given the United
    States 50
emigration to 132-133
abolished slavery 133, 154
purchased by United States 14
(see Danes, St. Thomas, St. Croix,
    and St. John also)
Dartmouth, Lord 32
Davson, J. B. 211
Dawson, Dr. James 35
deep-wells 188
defences 23, 44
deferred payment (bonus)
    system 228
Demerara 123-124, 132
Denmark 8, 53
Department of Agriculture 159,
    227, 230
deputy-governor
    appointed 20, 23
    functions 21, 24
    difficulties 22
    abolished (for Virgin Gorda) 31
diarrhoea 176
Dinwiddy, Robert 28
diseases 72, 174, 175
disturbances (see riots)
Dix, William 211
dockworkers 133, 141
doctors 157, 172, 174, 177, 178,
    187
domestics 78, 81, 100, 101, 124,
    128
Dominica 52, 177
Dougan, John 98-99
Drake's Highway 233
drought 11, 23, 126
Drummond Hay, E. H. 149, 179,
    198
Druyer, Baron 50
Dunkirk 50
Dutch
    settled in Tortola 3, 18
    disputed right to Tortola 4
    departed Tortola 5
    settled on St. Croix 10

recovered Saba and St.
Eustatius 20
built fort on Tortola 23
trade with Virgin Islands 24
introduced slaves 71
Dwarris, Fortunatus 83
Dyett, Isidore 136, 154

East End Meeting (of Quakers) 88
Eastern Division 32
East Indies 61
economic conditions
backward state 18-19
rapid development after 1735 27
productivity 30-31
era of prosperity 43-61
decline 61-66, 125-127, 136-141,
163-164, 218
revival 226-233
economic self-sufficiency (a
goal) 231, 234
education
undertaken by religious
denominations 83, 86, 169,
170, 189
schools established 89-91
for liberated Africans 109, 110,
113, 116
petition for education grant
refused 155-156
legislative provisions for 178-183
supervision (local and
federal) 182
low standards of 91, 182-183,
188
expansion 233
secondary education started 233
effective occupation 1, 9
electorate 32, 199, 206, 221-222
ejection (from plantations), 130,
131, 132
Elliot, Governor Hugh 85
emancipation
proposed 91-92
planters' response to 92
alternative proposal 92
introduced 92-93

effects 147
emigration
of whites 61, 65, 74, 93, 99, 199
of slaves 72, 86
of liberated Africans 100-101,
105, 116
of apprentice 123-124
of ex-slaves 125, 132-133, 141,
142, 229
value 234
endowed grammar school 179
Esmit, Adolph 5, 7
Established Church 89, 155, 161,
170, 178
Estaugh, John 88
exceptional aid (for
education) 182-183
Executive Committee 202
Executive Council
functions 195
disagreement with
Assembly 196-197, 199-200
remodelled 203
support given to the
President 205
difficulty in getting members 211
retained in 1902 212
expressed local sentiment 213
directed local affairs 218-219
failings 219-220
advisory role after 1950 221, 223
elected members in 224-226
policy making functions 226
expenditures 147-148, 151, 162,
164, 175
Experiment Station 159, 212, 227
exports
to St. Thomas 19, 24, 63, 72,
139-142, 148
to North America 28, 59
to Britain 28, 46-47, 55, 58-59,
60, 62-63, 127, 139, 228-229
to United States 59, 60, 63, 141
to West Indies 24, 59, 141, 229

Fahie, John 47

Fat Hog Bay 88
Fat Hog Bay Division 26
Fat Hog Bay Meeting (of
	Quakers) 88
Federation of the Leeward Islands
	(see Leeward Islands Federation)
Federation of the West Indies 222,
	225
fertilisers 230
Fielding, Joshua 88
financial problems 147-165, 194
Fine Cotton Spinners' and Doublers'
	Association Limited 228
fishing 19, 28, 110, 138, 139
Fleming, Gilbert (Lieutenant
	General) 48
Fleming, Governor Alexander 183,
	212
floating debt 162, 163
Fonseca, Isaac 212
foodstuff 49, 51, 60, 80-81, 121
fort 23, 30
fortifications
	absence of 22
	built 44
	constructed by slaves 80
four and a half percent duty
	levied in the Leeward Islands 20
	introduced into the Virgin
		Islands 31-32, 34, 38
	suspension sought 65
	abolition 65
franchise 32, 201, 203
free negroes and coloureds
	origin 73
	size of group 72
	disabilities 75
	upward mobility 77-78
	economic enterprise 75-77
	trade, agriculture, and
		property 77
	militia service 75
	political privileges 74, 78
	dichotomous position in
		society 78
	removal of civil disabilities 78, 86
	pursuit of education 89, 90

	relation with liberated
		Africans 102
	taxation of 151-152
	social services 169-170
free port
	requested and denied 29-30
	introduced 43, 52-54
	anticipated benefits 53, 56
	privileges 53-54
	goods entered 55, 60-61
	decline 62
	unlimited privileges sought 65-66
Free Port Acts 53-54, 55
freeholders 32, 75
French West Indies 46, 55, 141
friendly societies 114, 116, 171-172,
	188, 207
fustic 49

Gawthrop, Thomas 89
General Competency
		Ordinance 208, 221
Georges, William Payne 85
Germain, Lord 37
Germans 14
Glasgow 59
goats 84, 138, 231
Gordon, William 122
Goveia, Professor Elsa 79
Government
	by deputy-governors 20-21
	by deputy-governors and
		Councils 24
	by representative
		legislature 30-37, 194-203,
		221-226
	by Crown Colony
		Government 203-213
	by Commissioner and Executive
		Council 218-221
Grand Master of the Order of
	Malta 10
grants-in-aid
	for education 181-182
	from British Government 180,
		233

grassland management 230
Grenada 52
ground provisions 27, 71, 80, 108,
    110, 138
Guadeloupe 10, 49, 141
guinea grass 138
Gumbs, Deputy-Governor 48

Haiti 55-56, 86, 141
    (see St. Domingue also)
Halifax 59
Hall, Captain 23
Hall, Professor Douglas 79
Hamilton, Governor Walter 8, 22, 23
harrows 79
Hart, Governor John 9, 24, 25
Havana 48
hawking 77, 152
Hawkins, Robert 155
health officer 175, 190
Henselm, Captain John 20
Hetherington, Richard 49
hides 48
Hill, Abraham Chalwill 78
Hodge, Arthur 84-85
Hodgskins, Thomas 11
hoeing 79
horses 19, 84, 138
hospital 110, 175
Hotels Aid Ordinance 231
houses 81, 111, 121, 128, 152
housing projects 233
hucksters 77
Hume, Captain 8
Hunt, John 88
Hunthum, William 3
Huntums Ghut 233
hurricane
    (1819) 57, 64, 196
    (1837) 110-112
    (1867) 126, 141, 186
    (1871) 126

Illegal trade 2, 5, 22, 23, 29, 54, 55,
    88-89
    (see smuggling also)

Import Duties Act 149
imports 19, 54-55, 59-60, 63-64, 71,
    139-141, 229
income tax 109, 153, 158, 231
independence 224
indigent 114, 172, 173
indigo 48
industrial education 179-180
Industrial Revolution 46
infirm 110, 113, 114, 115, 147,
    169, 171
infirmary 172-174, 187, 188
Inspector General of Schools 182
Inspector of Police 184
Instructor of Agriculture 212
inter-colonial trade 19, 24, 59,
    60-61, 63-64, 139-142
internal self-government 224
international law 11
Inter-Virgin Islands Conferences 223
Irish settlers 18
Isaacs, Rogers 86, 197
itemised clearances 150

Jail
    for liberated Africans 105, 109,
        110
    as extra punishment 131
    maintenance of 147, 170,
        184
    condition of 186
    inadequacy 187-188
jailer 157, 160, 161
Jamaica
    invited Virgin Islands settlers 24
    free port created in 52
    packets en route for 56
    trade with 59
    size of peasant holdings 136
    doctor left for 178
    Executive Committee for 202
    Crown Colony Government
        introduced in 206
Johnson, Sir Nathaniel 4, 7
Jordan, Joshua 155
Josiah Bay Estate 85

Jost Van Dyke
    sovereignty not questioned 2, 13
    beginning of cultivation 27
    political representation 32
    vessels stranded on 64
    Quakers in 88
    illegal occupation of land in 134
    sub-treasurer for 150
    outbreak of smallpox in 177
    size of the electorate 199
Judicial system
    introduced 24
    need for better system 25-26, 27,
        34-35
    strengthened 35-36, 170
    negation 184-186
    burdens on 18
    President as magistrate 208-209
jury system 185-186
Justices of the Peace
    appointed 24, 37
    duties 25, 134
    remuneration 170
    extinction 185

King of Spain 1
Kingstown
    school in 91
    created 107-110, 171
    led to slave revolt 86
    destruction by hurricane 110-112
    abandoned 116

labour-saving devices 79, 126
La Dorothea 50
laissez-faire 188
Landing Waiter and Searcher 149,
    160
land-ownership 112-113, 127,
    134-135
land-rent 107, 131, 136
land-tax 134, 148, 151, 152-153,
    158, 233
Latham, John 88
Lawes, Sir N. 24

Leeward Islands
    legislature of 18
    settlers and woodcutters from 19
    separated from Barbados 21-22
    justice administered in 25
    4½% duty imposed on 31
    Virgin Islands a colony in 33
    privateers in 52
    communication with 56, 212
    inefficiency of agriculture in 79
    slave provision in 82
    common stamp issue for 161
    administration reorganised 200,
        209
    general legislature proposed
        for 201
    constitutional retrogression
        in 202
    amalgamation of Virgin Islands
        with 201, 213, 219
    local competition with imports
        from 229
Leeward Islands Act (1871) 207,
    221
Leeward Islands Federation
    imports from 138
    union of Virgin Islands with 148,
        159, 207, 213
    financial contributions
        to 159-160, 178
    federal debt 160
    supervision of education
        centralised in 182
    creation of circuit court in 185
    central lunatic asylum in 188
    special powers of federal
        legislature 207
    transfer of powers to 207-208
    affects Virgin Islands
        administration 208-209
    leads to abrogation of
        legislature 210
    defederated 222
Legislative Council
    introduced (1854) 203
    composition 203
    destructive element in 158

reformed (1859) 204;
   (1867) 206; (1890) 210
inability to find members
   for 210-213
crises in 211, 212
abolished 212, 213, 218
restored (1950) 221
composition 221
weaknesses 221-222
reformed (1954) 222
lack of executive control 224-225
ability to guide political
   destiny 225
elected members increased 226
importance 234
L'Elizabeth Christine 50
letters of marque 49, 51, 52
Lettsome Estates 85
Lettsome, John Coakley 89
liberated Africans
   origin 97
   support from British
      Government 97, 99-100, 104,
      107, 109, 110, 112, 113, 114
   apprenticeship 97-103, 116
   religious instruction 98, 107
   numbers 98-99
   disposal 99-100
   treatment 99-101
   occupation 100, 112, 113
   emigration to St.
      Thomas 100-101, 105
   limited opportunities 101,
      105-107
   relation with other social
      groups 102, 108, 113, 116
   mating patterns 102
   attempted transfer to
      Trinidad 103-104
   freedom 104-105, 107
   treatment of indigent, aged and
      infirm 105, 114-115
   establishment of
      Kingstown 107-109
   failure of integration
      attempt 108-109, 114
   education 91, 109

taxation 109-110
hurricane disasters
   (1837) 110-111
landownership 112-113
abandonment of Kingstown 116
formation of friendly
   societies 116
impact on the Virgin
   Islands 116-117
licensed trade 54, 62
Lieutenant Governor 21, 29, 30, 31,
   194, 195
lime (building) 110, 112, 113, 138,
   139
Liverpool 59
livestock
   rearing of started 19
   importation of 53
   destruction of 64
   slave property in 84
   destruction of crops 107
   improved breeds needed 138
   exports 141, 142, 228
   export duties on 153, 157
   increased emphasis on 227,
      229-230
   census 231
Lloyd, Owen 48
loans 65, 230
London 59, 181, 224
Londonderry, Governor (Lord) 11
London Yearly Meeting (of
   Quakers) 88
Longden, President J. R. 163
Longue 13
Lords of Trade 6, 24, 26, 29, 36, 66
lumber 49, 51, 60, 110
lunatics 147, 184, 187-188

Mackay, Alexander Robert 211
McCleverty, Thomas 113
Mackintosh, Governor R. 202
Macnamara 233
MacQueen, James 85
malingering 82

Manuella 98, 99
manufactures (lack of) 234
manumission 82, 89, 123-124, 132, 230
markets 46, 60-64, 141-142, 228, 229, 230
Martinique 10, 49, 141
masons 78
Master in Chancery 32
Mathew, Governor William 25-26
Maxwell, Governor, 85, 107, 200
medical care
    for slaves 82, 121, 169
    for liberated Africans 101, 105, 113, 116
    for paupers 173, 174
    for free population 132, 175, 177-178
membership system 224-225
mercantile Ordinance 157
Messa, Juan de 13
metairie
    proposed for liberated Africans 111, 116-117
    introduced on plantations 128-129
    failure 129-130
    dissatisfaction with 131, 142
Methodist missionaries
    undertook conversion of slaves 89-90
    assisted liberated Africans 107, 108, 116
    provided education 90, 170, 178-183, 188
    prevented violence 151
    requested non-taxation 155
    provoked 1853 riots 155-156
    and friendly societies 171-172, 188
Methodist Society 90, 156, 171, 172, 180, 181
Middleton, Earl of 4
Milan, Gabriel 7
Military Regiment 33
militia 24, 31, 74, 75, 102, 148, 155, 170, 195

Militia Acts 44
milling operations 79
mill-timber 53
minerals (lack of) 234
    (see copper also)
ministerial system 226
Moir, Alexander Wilson 208
molasses 24
monarchical succession (1688) 4
money-bills 44, 196
Monthly Meetings (of Quakers) 88
Montserrat 22, 220
Moody, Thomas 98-99
Morant Bay Uprising 206
Moth, Frederik 12
Moyne Commission (1938) 220
Murray, Sir George 104
muscovado sugar 27, 229

National School (in Road Town) 91
Navigation Laws 46, 52
Negro Education Grant 180
Nellthrop (breed of cattle) 230
Nevis 22, 104, 219, 220
Newcastle, Duke of 9
Newfoundland 59
New York 59
non-praedials 125
Norman Island 48
North America 47, 59
North and South Sound Division 26
North Carolina 48
North Sound 64
Norton, Dr. Herbert 178
Nottingham, Mary 89
Nottingham, Samuel 89
Nuestra Senora de Guadeloupe 48, 49
Nugent, Lieutenant Governor John 36

Ogilvie, Doctor 178
oil-engine 228
ordinances 25
Organic Act (1936) 220

out-door poor relief 114, 173-174
overseers 73

packet station
    introduced 43-44, 56-57
    lapsed 62
    removal 65, 141
    restoration sought 66
pangola grass 230
Paraquita Bay 230
Park, Governor Daniel 19, 21
parliamentary grant 161, 164, 188
pastures 79
patrols 149, 150
patrons 75
Payne, Sir Ralph 30, 31, 33, 34
Peace of Amiens 60
peasant farming
    conditions promoting 124-133
    made easier 127
    development 133-136, 142, 147,
        227-230
    result 136-141, 230
Pedder, Robert G. 163
periaguas 28
Peter Island 47
petty-trading 77, 141-142, 152
Phillip, John 8
Pickering, Frederick Augustus 211,
    212
Pickering, Isaac 83
Pickering, John 88, 89
pigs 138
pink-boll worm 228
pirates 7, 8, 13, 14, 22, 48
ploughs 79
Poincy, Philippe de Louvilliers de 10
police force 103, 109, 147, 155,
        170, 184
poll (capitation) tax 75, 148, 151,
        152, 164
population
    inadequacy of 18-20, 37
    increase of 20, 22-23, 24, 28-29
    decrease of 99, 129, 141

poor-house 114, 173-174
poor relief 169-174, 184
Powder Acts 44
Powell, Dorcas 88
praedials 125
President (of Virgin Islands)
    superseded Lieutenant
        Governor 195
    functions 189, 194-195
    salary 159, 164, 178, 209
    as doctor 178
    as magistrate 185, 208-209
    inability to develop Virgin
        Islands 159
    treatment of liberated
        Africans 100
    advised by Council 196
    differences with Assembly 198
    powers increased 200, 205
    appointed from outside 201
    lacked legislative support 205
    powers reduced 208-210
    designation changed to
        Commissioner 209
Price, President J. 135
prior discovery 1
prisoners 147, 170, 184, 186-187,
        188
privateering
    in the West Indies 2
    base in St. Thomas 8, 13-14, 50
    facilities for 23, 56
    slaves employed in 28
    in the Virgin Islands 43, 48-49
    depredations 47
    expansion of policy 49-50
    against neutral vessels 50
    against United States vessels 51
    prospects 52, 55, 62
    protection against 57
Privy Council (see Executive
        Council)
Probyn, Governor Thomas 200
proprietary rights 1
proprietorship 10, 21-22
Prosper 84
Proudfoot, Dr. Mary 226

provision grounds 81, 109, 123,
128, 130
Provost Marshal 24-25, 33, 160,
187, 200, 203
public debt (see consolidated debt)
public health measures 174-178, 188
public works 163
Purcell, James
appointed Lieutenant
Governor 29
reported on production of Virgin
Islands 27
sought freeport facilities 29,
52-53
requested civil government 29-30
death 31
Puerto Rico
attacks from 5, 13
backed piratical raids 13
slaves escaped to 27-28, 82
privateering from 28
emigration to 141

Quakers
beginning in Virgin Islands 88
and slavery 88-89
decline of Quakerism 88-89
impact on society 89
quarantine 142, 176, 177, 188
Queen Elizabeth's Bridge 233
Quieting Bill 34-37, 38

radio broadcasting 234
Rector 91, 171, 172, 197
(see clergyman also)
referendum 223
Register of Voters 203
Registry Office 134
Reid, Irving and Company 126, 128,
133
religious teaching 83, 86-91, 98,
169-170, 172
representative government
introduced 30-34
discredited 34-37, 195-206
withdrawn 206-213, 218-221

restored 221-226
retail trade 77
revenue protection force 149, 150
revenues 56, 148, 149, 151,
161-163, 164, 231, 233, 234
Revocation of Competency
Ordinance 221
revolving fund 230
rice 50
right of sovereignty
principles governing 1-2
islands affected 2-3
to Tortola 3-6
to St. Thomas and St. John 6-9
to St. Croix 9-13
effects on islands 13-14, 18
riots
(1790) 83
(1823) 85
(1830) 85-86
(1831) 86, 148, 170
(1848) 154-155, 198
(1853) 155-157, 181, 189, 203
(1856) 150-151, 204
(1887) 158
(1890) 158
Road Division 26, 32
Road Harbour 54, 56, 64
Road Harbour District 222
Road Meeting (of Quakers) 88
Road Ordinance 157
roads 80, 122, 175, 189, 233
Road Town
political representation for 32
schools in 91
emigration of liberated Africans
to 105
distance from Kingstown 107
sub-treasurers for 150
disturbances in 154, 204
public meeting in 156
health regulations for 175, 188,
189
vaccinations given in 177
higher standard of education
in 181, 182, 183
police activities confined to 184

voting in 206
political imbalance in favour
   of 221
Experiment Station near 227
Romney, Joseph B. 211, 212
Royal Commissions
   (1896) 212
   (1938) 220
Royal Mail Steam Packet
      Company 133, 139-141, 142
rum 49, 50, 229
rural constables (see constabulary)

Saba 4, 20
St. Bartholomew 47, 141
St. Christopher
   settlers from in St. Croix 10
   French quarter acquired 11
   relative prices in 19
   firm British footing in 22
   removal of settlers to
      suggested 23
   administration of justice in 25,
      186, 188
   convoy from 57
   liberated Africans in 104
   union of Virgin Islands with
      proposed 36, 219
   administrative reform 200
   elected legislature
      reintroduced 220
St. Croix
   possession disputed 2
   early settlement and
      abandonment 10-11
   attacked by Spaniards 10
   right of sovereignty 11-13
   purchased by Danes 12
   captured by British 13-14, 46
   attracted away settlers 28
   trade attacked by privateers 49
   American factories in 50
   attracts Virgin Islanders 133
   slave revolt (1848) 154
St. Domingue

received French from St.
   Croix 10-11
slave revolution in 46, 47, 60
trade with 49, 54, 62
(see Haiti also)
St. Eustatius 4, 13, 20, 24, 48, 49,
   141
St. George Parish 90
St. Helena 212
St. John
   settled 8-9
   right of sovereignty to 6-9
   taken by British 13-14
   received liberated
      Africans 100-101
   quarantine against 177
St. Kitts (see St. Christopher)
St. Lucia 178
St. Martin 141
St. Thomas
   possession disputed 2
   settled 6-7
   sugarcane introduced 7
   base for pirates and privateers 8,
      44-45
   right of sovereignty 6-9
   ill-effects on Tortola 5, 19
   taken by British 13-14, 46, 53,
      62
   trade with the Virgin Islands 19,
      24, 59, 63, 64
   trade attacked by privateers 47, 49
   free port in 53, 62
   slave trade entrepot 72
   military aid to suppress revolt 86,
      157, 158
   received liberated
      Africans 100-101
   emigration to 132-133, 205
   market 139-142, 152
   source of employment 141
   promoted smuggling 141-142,
      148-150
   quarantine against 177
Saka Bay Division 26
salaries 147
salt 162, 234

Salt Island 47, 162
HMS Scarborough 8
schools
    denominational 90-91, 178-179,
      180-182
    at Kingstown 108, 109, 110
    government 179-180
    grant-in-aid 181-183
    endowed grammar school 179
school-leaving age 181-182
Sea Cow Bay 111
Sea Cow Bay Estate 84
sea-island cotton 46
secession 36
Second World War (1939-1945) 220,
    226, 229, 230, 231
secret ballot 221
self-mutilation 83
sergeant-at-arms 200
shallow-wells 188
sheep 19, 138, 152
Shepheard, Sir Joseph 5
Shew, Robert V. 111, 116
Shirley, Governor Thomas 37, 51,
    55
Sierra Leone 104
slaves
    fugitives 8, 27-28, 29
    purchased at St. Thomas 19
    provision grounds 47, 80
    limited economic
      opportunities 47, 81-82
    employed as seamen 59
    introduced into Virgin Islands 71
    sources 71-72
    occupational differences 78
    field labour 79-80
    treatment 80-81, 91-92, 170
    food and clothing 80, 81, 169
    evidence in law courts 81
    medical care 169
    housing 81, 169
    inferior social status 72-73, 81
    slave laws 81-82
    manumission 82, 89
    compulsory allowances 82
    resistance 82-83

    amelioration 83, 84, 91-92
    slave property 84
    disturbances and revolts 84-86
    marriage and family life 86
    religious instruction and
      education 86-91, 169
    emancipation 91-93
    relation with liberated
      Africans 102
slave compensation 93, 173, 197
slave revolts (see riots and slaves)
slave trade 19, 71-72
small-pox 175, 177
Smith, Governor Haynes 208
Smith, Henry 212
smuggling
    facilities for 5, 138
    recommendations to prevent 28
    indulgence of colonists in 43
    of sugar and cotton 46-47
    supported by officials 54
    effectiveness after 1815 62
    large-scale operations 64
    weakened revenues 141-142
    of consumption and export
      goods 148
    unsuccessful attempts to
      suppress 149-151
    led to violence 151, 154-155, 158
    dissatisfaction expressed in 164
social amenities 147
social services
    during slavery 169
    for free people 169-170
    poor relief 170-178
    education 178-183
    police protection and
      justice 184-186
    prison 186-187
    lunatic asylum 187-188
    fundamental weaknesses
      of 188-190
    improper system 188, 194, 218
    improvements 233-234
social stratification 71
soil 61
soil conservation 230

South American Republics 64
South Division 32
special constables (see constabulary)
Spain 48
Spaniards
    attacked St. Thomas 5
    attacked St. Croix 10
    attacked Tortola 13, 19
    seized slaves 71
    settled Vieques 133
Spanish Town 2
squatters 134, 136
Stamp Duty Act 162
stamps 161
Stanley, John 51
Stapleton, Colonel William
    captured Tortola 3, 18
    instructions to 7, 9
    appointed deputy-governor 20
    death 4
Stephen, James 111
stipendiary magistrate
    appointed and duties 121
    inadequate number and
        handicaps 122
    encouraged apprentices to expect
        freedom 125
    jurisdiction over squatting 136
    appointed constables to arrest
        smugglers 151
    secured repeal of land-tax 153
    popularity of 154-155
    supervised by President 200
    position abolished 160, 185
street warden 175, 190
sub-treasurers 150, 151, 153
Suckling, George 36
sugar
    revealed West Indian wealth 2
    introduced into St. Thomas 7
    expanded production into Virgin
        Islands 24, 27, 29, 38
    prices 46, 61
    exports 46, 47, 60, 127
    seized by privateers 49
    free port imports 53-54, 55
    marketing opportunities 46, 61

decline in industry 61, 93,
    125-126, 138-139, 142, 148,
    152, 164, 165
cultivation revived 228, 229
imported 138, 229
Sugar Duties Act (1846) 126
suicide 83
Sunday schools 90, 179
Supreme Court 185-186

task-work 123
Taylor, Henry 111, 197, 202
taxation
    early provision for collection 25
    a function of Councils 26
    occasional levy 27
    public participation in
        recommended 29
    cause of legislative friction 44
    suspended 65, 147-148
    attempts to exempt liberated
        Africans from 109, 110, 115
    principles applied to 151
    extended to free negroes and
        coloureds 151-152
    extended to ex-slaves 141,
        152-153
    modifications in system 148, 165
    addition opposed 149-158
    unpopularity of 38, 151-154,
        157-158
    taxable items 151
    more efficient collection 153-154
    led to violence 150-151, 154-157
    special levy for poor
        relief 169-170
    evasion 171, 231
    attitude of Assembly
        towards 158, 162, 164,
        196-198
    improvements in 231-233
telecommunication 234
Telegrapho 160
telephone 234
tenant-at-will 130
terracing 79
Thatch Island 151, 204

Third Dutch War 3
Thomas, Governor George 30
timber 8, 53
tobacco 2, 48, 50, 53, 228, 229
Tobago 52
Todman, T. P. 179
Tortola Monthly Meeting (of
    Quakers) 88
tourism 224, 231, 233
trade
    entrepot 5, 14
    illegal 2, 5, 22, 23, 28, 29, 54,
        55, 88-89
    North American 28, 47, 59
    West Indian (see inter-colonial
        trade and West Indies)
    Spanish colonial 54-55, 62
Treasurer 149, 153, 170, 171, 206,
    209, 210
Treasury 29, 161, 162, 177
Treaties
    Alliance and Commerce (1670) 6
    Amiens (1802) 14, 46
    Copenhagen (1733) 12
    Neutrality (1686) 11, 13
    Nymwegen (1679) 3
    Paris (1815) 14
    Westminster (1674) 3
Trinidad 52, 85, 103, 132, 136
Turner, Jonathan 19

United States of America
    purchased Danish West Indies 14
    War of Independence 49
    trading factories in the Danish
        Islands 51
    trade attacked by British
        privateers 51
    trade with Virgin Islands 59, 60,
        63, 141
    War of 1812 with Britain 62
United States Prohibition 229
United States Virgin Islands 220,
    223, 229-230, 231
    (see Danish West Indies, St.
        Thomas, St. Croix, St. John)

universal adult suffrage 221

vaccinations 175, 177, 188
Valley Division 26, 32
Valley Town 32
verbal contracts (see contracts)
vestry 170
Venus 98, 99
Vice-Admiralty Court
    established 33, 43, 49
    functions 54, 57
    suspended and restored 51
    limited scope 62
Vieques 7, 23, 132-133
Virgin Gorda
    sovereignty not challenged 2
    inhabitants petitioned to
        remove 11
    attacked by Spaniards 13
    settled 19
    population increase 19, 22-23,
        24, 28-29
    administration 24-25, 26-27, 31
    militia 24
    agricultural production 27
    political representation 32
    cotton cultivation 47
    school in 91, 181
    copper-mining in 112, 139, 141
    squatting 134
    doctor's visits 177
    size of electorate 199
    airstrip on 233
Virgin Islands Act (1902) 212
Virgin Islands Constitution Act
    (1950) 221
Virgin Islands Mining Company of
    Liverpool 112
voters 199, 206

wages
    bargaining 122-123
    planters' ability to offer 111,
        126, 127-128
    operation of system 130, 131

wage-rent disputes 124, 131
  failure 125, 133, 142
  workers' dependence on 131
Walton, Captain John
  appointed Lieutenant
    Governor 21
  sought proprietorship 21-22
  failure 23-24, 37
Wars
  American Independence
    (1775-1783) 43, 47, 49, 50,
    51, 55
  French Revolutionary and
    Napoleonic
    (1793-1815) 13-14, 43, 46,
    47, 49, 51-52, 57, 60, 75
  Seven Years' (1756-1763) 30, 43,
    49
  Spanish Succession
    (1702-1713) 8, 23
  Third Dutch (1672-1678) 3
  War of 1812 (1812-1814) 62
ware-housing port 66
Washington 224
water-conservation 230
Waterfront Highway 233
water-supply 188
Welsh settlers 18
Wentworth, Trelawney 83, 185
Westergaard, Waldemar 6-7
Western Division 32
West Indies 28, 49, 52, 63, 64, 65,
    66, 71, 124, 161, 194, 202,
    212, 224
West Indies Encumbered Estates
    Act 135
Westlake, J. 1
Weymouth, W. T. 180
White Bay Meeting (of Quakers) 88
White, William 25
whites
  population 18-20, 22-23, 24,
    28-29, 99, 129
  conspicuous consumption 59
  cohesiveness 73
  emigration 61, 99, 129
  size of class 72-73, 74, 90
  landownership 73
  privileges 73-74
  economic decline 61-66, 74,
    125-127, 129
  customary and legal
    obligations 74
  subordination of other classes 75
  property 77
  religious pursuit 86, 89
  fled Tortola 157
Wickham's Cay 233
Wilhamet 199
HMS Winchelsea 23
Windward Islands 56
Women's Monthly Meeting (of
    Quakers) 88
wood-cutting 11, 13, 19
Woodley, Governor William 30
Woolrich, Thomas 80-81
workhouse 172-174
world depression 229
wrecked goods 163
written contracts (see contracts)

yellow-fever 177
Young, Vice-Admiral 57